12-2-74

Britain in the Common Market:
a new business opportunity

Britain in the Common Market:
a new business opportunity

Edited by
M. E. Beesley and D. C. Hague

Longman

LONGMAN GROUP LIMITED
London

*Associated companies, branches and representatives
throughout the world*

© Manchester Business School 1974

First published 1974

ISBN 0 582 44308 3

Library of Congress Catalog Card Number 73-86106

and printed in England
by
Richmond Press Limited, Wilmslow, Cheshire, England.

Contents

Contents (continued)

Preface

This book contains the record of a Conference held jointly by the London Graduate School of Business Studies and the Manchester Business School. It was the first joint venture of the two institutions and we chose as its theme the current condition of the British economy and the ways in which joining the EEC was likely to change it.

Originally, it had been hoped to hold the Conference in Switzerland in November 1972. This proved impossible, but we were fortunate that Economic Models Ltd. and the Peterlee Development Corporation were both enthusiastic when we suggested holding the Conference, under their auspices, in the Conference Centre of the Peterlee Development Corporation, in March 1973.

We intended to provide each participant with a printed set of the ten papers to be presented at the Conference, to be held in late 1972. These papers, which make up the first part of this volume, were in final draft by May 1972, and printed and bound by the time Norway decided not to join the EEC. This explains why the papers refer to 'The Ten' (including Norway) and not 'The Nine'. The papers were sent in advance to those who attended the Conference and taken as read. At the Conference, each speaker first brought his own paper up to date. There was then a general discussion. A detailed record of what was said at the Conference itself is therefore given at the end of the volume.

The book gives an up-to-date assessment, by leading authorities from the two Business Schools, of the position of the British economy. It also discusses the impact that joining the EEC is likely to have on the economy in general, and on British business in particular.

M. E. BEESLEY
D. C. HAGUE
11th June 1973

Introduction

As was explained in the Preface, the Conference upon which this book is based was held in Peterlee, Co. Durham. Peterlee, a new town with some 25,000 inhabitants, is a new business opportunity in itself. It offers to businesses cash grants and tax allowances for investment, rent-free or low-rent factories, a plentiful and flexible labour force and a growing tradition of work on research and development in highly technological fields. It is well placed to serve the markets of the North-East, the Midlands and Europe, and to work on behalf of the North Sea Oil Industry. Apart from its own interest, Peterlee therefore provided an excellent setting for our discussions of the way that joining the EEC is likely to affect the British economy.

The need for a 'United Europe' became a common theme for statesmen after the end of World War II. However, even with the passage of nearly two decades, it is only in the economic field that significant progress towards European integration has so far been made. The first concrete step was the integration of the steel industries of The Six: West Germany, France, Italy, Belgium, The Netherlands and Luxembourg. Immediately after the Second World War, Allied controls had been imposed on the coal, iron and steel industries of the Ruhr. These controls could not be permanent, and the French answer to the question of how they could safely be removed was the Schumann Plan. This sought to make war between France and Germany both 'unthinkable' and 'materially impossible' by linking Germany firmly into an integrated West European coal and steel industry. The Schumann Plan provided the basis for the Treaty of Paris, signed by The Six in April 1951, which set up the European Coal and Steel Community. The UK was invited to join the ECSC, but she refused.

The ECSC continues to thrive, but later attempts to set up a European Defence Community, and even a European Political Community, foundered, mainly because of French opposition. However, these failures merely increased the enthusiasm of 'Europeans' for extending economic integration. Plans for the establishment of a general common market within The Six, and for cooperation in the fields of energy and transport, were adopted, as the basis for further discussions, by the foreign ministers of The Six at Messina in 1955. Again, the UK was invited to participate and, this time, the British representatives played an active part in the early discussions. However, the UK wanted to see the creation of a free trade area, not a customs union. This view was opposed by those in Europe who sought the creation of a supra-national Union which would go beyond mere economic integration. Britain therefore withdrew from the negotiations, and the remaining six countries signed two treaties in Rome in March 1957. One established Euratom; the other the EEC. Both institutions came into being on 1 January 1958. The later treaty, now usually referred to as the 'Rome Treaty', led to a customs union, with a common external tariff, within which there was industrial free trade, a common agricultural policy and moves towards the establishment of other communities.

Britain remained aloof until the early 1960s and, pursuing the idea of a free trade area rather than a customs union, played a leading role in the establishment of EFTA in 1960. Then, in 1961, Britain finally decided to apply for membership of the EEC. After two unsuccessful attempts, Britain joined the EEC on 1 January 1973, along with Denmark and Ireland, to convert with The Six into The Nine. After a referendum, in late 1972, Norway decided not to join.

The Peterlee Conference was concerned with the condition of the British economy soon after The Six had become The Nine. As can be seen from the papers and from the record of the discussion, three major themes dominated the Conference.

First, and in a sense least important, there was the relatively short-term problem of the way that activity and employment in the UK was likely to alter during 1973 and 1974. When the Conference was held, in March 1973, it was less clear than it is now (May 1973) just how fast the GNP was rising and just how quickly unemployment was falling. Even so, Terry Burns rightly brought forward the date at which he predicted that growth would have to be slowed because unemployment would be approaching the minimum tolerable level.

This faced the Conference with a much more fundamental problem. No matter what view one takes of the precise timing one advocates for the UK to slow the rate of growth of GNP, it is clearly the Government's intention to run the economy close to (or even above) the limits of capacity during 1973 and 1974. I should myself argue the case for taking the risk of allowing GNP to grow at 4 per cent, or even a little more, for a year or two. As Terry Burns pointed out in his session of the Conference, the trend rate of growth of productivity (output per man) in the UK appears to be around $3\frac{1}{2}$ per cent. Attempting to run the economy beyond this limit for a year or two may not lead to the increased optimism, changed attitudes and improved efficiency needed from both management and labour if the long-run rate of growth of productivity is to be increased. But it just might do so. With a degree of protection from a floating pound, this is a rare opportunity to take the risk. However, as Terry Burns and I both pointed out in the Conference, serious consequences would follow from attempts to make the economy grow substantially more quickly than productivity is increasing. While there is just a chance that it might be possible to raise the trend rate of growth of productivity to 4 per cent in the fairly near future, there is no hope whatever of quickly raising it to 5 or 6 per cent. We were both accused of pessimism by some businessmen at the Peterlee Conference, because we cannot see Britain quickly (if ever) reaching the West German rate of growth of productivity, without there first being a long and traumatic period of change in British economic and social arrangements.

The second, and perhaps the most important, theme of the Conference dealt with a number of interrelated long-run issues. As I said in my own paper, I am confident that joining the EEC will not be the kind of non-event for the UK that decimalisation of the currency was. The consequences of joining the EEC will show themselves progressively, but are likely to be very significant. We are already beginning to see the effect on agricultural prices. From July 1973 we shall begin to see the effect of EEC membership on tariffs, exports, economies of scale and learning, technological change, and so on, in British industry. At the same time, increasing numbers of firms within The Nine are likely to be taken into the ownership of firms or institutions in other parts of The Nine. The Conference displayed considerable interest in the possible effect of EEC membership on industrial location, with a consensus that British industry was likely to be even more strongly attracted to the South and East of the UK, unless unexpectedly strong regional policies were developed. Other influences, considered especially by Professors Rose and Beesley, were the effects on Britain's financial system and its competition policy. Professor Rose suggested that, on balance, adopting EEC policies would be likely to make the British financial system less rather than more efficient. However, the discussion of Professor Beesley's paper left one feeling that competition policy was more likely to be strengthened than weakened by joining the EEC. Professor Morris wondered whether joining the EEC would provide the kind of stimulus to the British nation that the Second World War had. Professor McClelland pointed out that British business would now have to deal with two governments – one in Whitehall and one in Brussels.

The third theme of the Conference was the changes in the UK which were taking place largely independently of the EEC. Professor Simmonds looked at changes in marketing and in retailing, not least the development of hypermarkets. Professor McClelland and Lupton dealt with the emphasis towards greater Government intervention in the economy, not least the attempt to devise an effective prices and incomes policy. This may well turn out to be one of the most important developments of all, with both Labour and Conservative Governments keen, at least for a time, to intervene in the economy in a detailed way. Finally, as I explained in my paper, I believe that there will be a continuing tendency for an increasing proportion of Britain's GDP to be exported and imported, though this may be partly a result of the fall in tariffs resulting from EEC membership. However, the parallel trend towards an increasing proportion of economic activity taking place in the service sector is one which owes little or nothing to our joining the EEC.

Given that the greater proportion of those attending the Peterlee Conference were senior British businessmen, it is not surprising that the issue which generated most emotion among those present was that of redundancy. There was a clear feeling in the Conference that, in the recent past, British business had not been sufficiently humane in the way that it had treated its employees. When difficult economic conditions, or takeovers, had led businesses to ask whether they should be reducing the numbers of their senior managers, the response had been harsher than most of those who came to Peterlee would accept.

These, then, were the main themes of the Conference. The detailed arguments are set out in the remainder of the book. To this, the reader is now invited to turn.

D. C. HAGUE
11th June 1973

Conference papers

Developing a successful company in the United Kingdom

Arthur F. Earle

In this opening paper of our conference I think I have some obligation to begin by reminding you of some of the elementary facts about the United Kingdom which will underlie what I and my colleagues will be developing in greater detail during our time together.

The United Kingdom

Firstly, the 'United Kingdom' of what? The expression covers England, Wales, Scotland and Northern Ireland. I will not go into the history of these individual nations or of their union, not because it is without interest and significance in present-day affairs but because it is much too long and tortuous a story of war, intrigue, religious dispute of which echoes still rumble in Northern Ireland and in the nationalist movements in Scotland and Wales. The wonder is that a nation emerged at all, but emerge it did and in a power and strength which at the height of the British Empire dazzled the world.

In the United Kingdom as it now stands with a population of 56 millions, England is by far the dominant country with 83 per cent of the people; Scotland contributes 9 per cent, Wales 5 per cent and Northern Ireland 3 per cent. A simple political map of the United Kingdom conceals, therefore, considerable variations in population density. The tendency is for the English percentage of the population to increase, and within England itself for the density in the south-east to increase. These demographic facts are, of course, matters for consideration in much greater detail by those interested in studying the location of manufacturing operations, distribution systems, marketing plans, etc.

By far the largest urban concentration is, of course, London – more than seven times as large as its nearest rival, Birmingham, but the dominance of London in the life of the United Kingdom is – with due apologies to my Manchester colleagues – far greater than the population figures suggest. Indeed it is probably fair to say that London represents a concentration of government, finance, culture, communications media, and industrial top management to a degree unequalled in Europe except by Paris. Numerous Government policies are directed towards reducing this concentration but it is difficult to detect much diminution in the centripetal attraction of the metropolis. One of the consequences is that central London office rents are the highest in the world.

At the other end of the spectrum are Northern Ireland, most of Scotland and Wales, the south-west and north-east of England, where the population tends to decline, unemployment is high, the traditional local industries are in decline. These are, not unnaturally, the areas to which Government seeks to direct new investment as the prospective foreign investor considering the establishment of a new plant will quickly discover.

For particular industries there are, of course, other patterns of concentration usually explained by historical circumstance – the location of coal or mineral deposits, the existence of waterways and ports, the hinterland of particular kinds of agricultural production. Very often these patterns persist long after the original justification has ended because of the concentration of labour possessing the related skills which has developed.

These reflections remind one also of another aspect of British history which is important in understanding the present industrial environment. England was the cradle of the industrial revolution and the triumphs and evils of what was for Britain for the most part a glorious nineteenth century, have left deep scars on the twentieth-century landscape and labour relations.

Here then is a first glance at the little group of islands sitting on the north-western shoulder of Europe – a shade smaller than West Germany in size and a close second to her in the populations of the countries of the enlarged community.

I now focus more closely on the topic of this paper – developing a successful company in the United Kingdom. In approaching such a broad topic I will be dealing briefly with many of the matters which my colleagues will be considering in greater detail. This, too, will be part of my introductory function.

Business in different countries

My title implies, of course, that there is something different to be said about developing successful companies in the United Kingdom from what could be said about successful development elsewhere. I think this to be true and that indeed part of the recipe for success in any country will be the adoption of management practices peculiar to that country. But part of the recipe for success will also be the adoption of management practices beneficial in any country. One can of these talk only of the application of the general principles of good management in a particular setting.

There is an interesting debate of some standing in the management education world about the teaching of international business. Some hold that it is best taught as part of existing courses on the grounds that, for example, the general principles of marketing apply to international marketing with minor adjustment. Others take the opposite view in thinking that it is essential to pull all international aspects into a new course or courses looking at marketing, finance, production as aspects of international business. Closer to the first are those who think the best approach is to study countries as environments for business. It is this latter approach which I shall follow in this paper both because I believe it to be the right one, and because such a method serves a better introductory purpose.

The particular character of the UK

The economic environment of the United Kingdom is that of a mixed social and free enterprise kind. A substantial proportion of the Gross National Product is produced by Government or Government-owned enterprise – 27 per cent in 1970 up from 24 per cent a decade earlier. State-owned activities include the postal and telephone services, railroads, much road transport, gas, electricity, steel, the major airlines, most of the health services, all university and most of further education. Twenty-five per cent of total employment in 1970 was provided by the State or State-owned enterprise. As a proportion of total investment the impact of the state is significantly higher. In 1970 fixed capital formation by the State sector represented 45 per cent of the national total as compared with 40 per cent a decade earlier.

Control of this vast expenditure and of its great potential as an influence on the level of economic activity is highly centralized in London – in the last analysis in the Treasury Department. The scale of government spending has, however, proved difficult to manipulate in the short run and other fiscal weaponry has tended to predominate, although occasional forays into restricting State corporation purchasing, e.g., electricity and airlines, have in the recent past had dramatic effects on the fortunes of the heavy electrical engineering and aircraft industries.

As for the fiscal practices of the British Government, I would note the unusually heavy reliance which has been placed on regulation of the terms of hire purchase (instalment) selling and on purchase taxes affecting the kinds of goods bought on hire purchase. Since hire-purchase selling is of particular importance in automobiles, household appliances and other high priced consumer durables, and since these goods have also been subject to high rates of purchase tax, these industries have suffered repeatedly since the war the major initial impacts of shifts in fiscal policy.

Purchase taxes and hire-purchase regulations may both soon disappear. The former are to be replaced by a uniform rate Value Added Tax and a powerful Committee of Enquiry under the chairmanship of the late Lord Crowther recommended that Government should cease employing the latter, though Government has not yet indicated acceptance of the recommendation. When and if realized these are big and important changes which will radically shift historic patterns of consumer expenditure.

One further point must always be kept in mind in considering the United Kingdom economy. It is an extraordinarily 'open' economy. Exports and imports of goods and services each year total to figures which each are equivalent to approximately 30 per cent of the GNP. This makes market analysis for a prospective investor a tricky business. He must decide to what extent he is aiming at domestic and export sales, and even in respect of the former he must evaluate the extent to which his domestic customers will depend directly or indirectly on the course of exports.

These are, of course, difficult judgments at the best of times. In the face of the changes which entry into the Community will make in both domestic and export markets their complexity becomes frightening. Part of the outcome will, of course, depend on the pace of inflation in the United Kingdom compared with the rest of the Community and the rest of the world. I personally find it difficult to be optimistic about this. Part will depend on the freedom with which exchange rates will be adapted to the realities of the situation. The United Kingdom has not been very good at this in the past though the Chancellor in last March's budget indicated a new flexibility of thinking had become fashionable. Whether this is so or not we know enough now to be confident that changing or floating exchange rates will not be choices which a single country will make unilaterally without trouble.

Is the manufacturer of a consumer product aiming solely at a United Kingdom market, and not reliant to a high degree on import costs, free from such considerations? Not really, because in such an open economy the Government must quite quickly respond to its balance of payments situation by influencing the level of domestic demand. The United Kingdom Treasury has acquired great skill and experience at depressing demand. Its abilities in the other direction have been less tested and inspire less confidence.

The manufacturer of consumer products has some additional problems to ponder. Retail distribution in the United Kingdom is highly concentrated. There is nothing like the Robinson Patman Act of the United States which – however imperfect – exerts pressure on big and powerful buyers not to try to use their bargaining power to the hilt.

If one takes the top fifty British companies and leave out the two international oil giants, Shell and B.P. and their subsidiary Shell Mex, and the four pure retailing companies, the remaining forty-three companies averaged a return before taxes on their capital employed of 12·6 per cent in 1970. The retailing companies averaged 24·8 per cent.[1] One lesson from this, in my topic of developing a successful company in the United Kingdom, is to get into the retailing business in a big way. For reasons that I will come to, that is more difficult than one might think, but there are in fact other useful lessons to be drawn to which I will revert as well.

Developing a business in the UK

Location

The first problem facing the prospective businessman in the United Kingdom is whether to acquire a going concern or the land and buildings of one on the one hand, or to start a new operation. In the former case his location, at least to begin with, is determined by his purchase. In the latter he can locate where he wishes, subject to securing the relevant planning permissions.

I have already referred to the existence of numerous Government policies directed towards influencing the location of industry and in particular towards influencing the location of new investment in the various kinds of development areas, generically called 'assisted areas'.

[1] *The Times 1,000 Leading Companies in Britain and Overseas*, Times Newspapers Limited, London, 1972.

These influences are in part of a negative kind. An Industrial Development Certificate (IDC) must be obtained from the Department of Trade and Industry for any building for factory use not in an assisted area and of over 929 sq. m (10,000 sq. ft) in the South-East or 1,393 sq. m (15,000 sq. ft) elsewhere whether this be a new building or an extension, or conversion of an existing building.[2] After an IDC is received permission must still be sought and obtained from the relevant local planning authority. IDCs are often refused in the more prosperous and congested areas and apart from refusals there are probably far more applications withdrawn after discussion, or simply not made, when a refusal seems likely.

Other factors than employment distribution may influence the grant of an IDC in an unassisted area. A strong case that the proposed plant is part of a pattern that will involve the development areas, or that the output is important from an export or import-substitution point of view will be helpful. Considerations of a special unemployment problem in an unassisted area – e.g., a local shortage of jobs for women – may be taken into account. Generally speaking, however, any prospective investment in new factory building in the more prosperous industrial areas will be difficult to promote. At the very least it has to be demonstrated that the possibilities and incentives to invest in the development areas have been carefully considered.

The pattern of these incentives has varied over the years. Government factories in development areas are built to general and particular designs and rented or sold on deferred terms at attractive and stable rates fixed over substantial terms. Investment in new industrial buildings everywhere now gets 40 per cent depreciation in the first year and plant and machinery, new or secondhand, is allowed 100 per cent depreciation in the first year. In the development areas, in addition, however, rates of 20 to 22 per cent cash grants are made against the cost of buildings, new plant and machinery, and these are not taken into account for depreciation write-offs for tax purposes. It is intended that these grants should be maintained at least until 1979. The cash grants are, of course, immediately useful to every investing company which receives them. The depreciation allowances are only of benefit if there is a taxable profit against which to offset them but there is a three-year carry-back provision so that an

---

[2]   These figures announced by the Secretary of State for Trade and Industry (*Hansard*, 22 March 1972, Col. 1544) represent a very substantial loosening. The previous limit was 1,000 sq. ft anywhere, including the development areas where no limit now applies.

existing company which has been paying taxes can get its benefits quickly.[3]

There is one further point which should be mentioned in connection with foreign investment in the United Kingdom which represents an important change in policy introduced in the budget of last March. I refer to new liberalization of access to sterling financing for foreign companies. Subsidiaries of foreign companies making new direct investments in the assisted areas may draw finance without restriction from sterling sources. Subsidiaries of EEC companies now enjoy freedom from such restrictions on direct investment anywhere in the United Kingdom.

Taking the location decision

The evaluation of these governmental influences on plant location is therefore a complex problem and one requiring close study by any prospective investor. It is, of course, far from being the only set of considerations important in the location and method of investment decision but the amounts of money involved are large and they will play an important part in determining the size and ease of financing the capital commitments required. At the same time these influences are for the most part short-run and the differences in the attractions to go into an assisted area as compared with an unassisted area are probably less in Britain than in most other EEC countries.[4] It is the longer-run differentials, transportation costs, environment, supply and militancy of labour, wage costs, which evaluated rightly or wrongly by investors determine the need for special inducements to go to the development areas. It is difficult to offer any general counsel on these matters since so much depends on the nature and markets of the particular product and on the investor involved. I can point to highly successful investments in all of the combinations of existing company take-overs, green field site operations, development areas and congested areas – and to just as wide a range of failures.

There is one great advantage in starting from scratch, which is true everywhere but has always seemed to me especially true in the United Kingdom. That is the opportunity to develop your own

---

[3] Two publications available from the Department of Trade and Industry give full details of the areas and incentives available: *Room to Expand – The Assisted Areas* and *Incentives for Industry in the Assisted Areas*.

[4] Mr Thorpe, Leader of the Liberal Party, made this point in commenting on the March budget. *Hansard*, 22 March 1972, Col. 1559.

company culture – if that is not too sociological a word – rather than having to try to live with an inherited one. Let me give you a simple illustration of what I mean. Most British manufacturing plants have a number of eating halls to which employees are allocated according to rank. There is a lot to be said for having only one. To try to get away from segregated facilities once they are established, however, is a very difficult matter for you are taking away something which is a privilege and it will be bitterly resisted, and resented. Strangely enough there seems to be little problem if you start a new operation with only one facility and stick with it. One could cite many examples of this kind. It is much easier to have 'open' offices than to change to them from a system of private offices for all and sundry if that is what you have inherited. These, and many others, may seem, no doubt, superficial details but they can have an important bearing on long-run efficiency. The foreigner who seeks to change an established way of doing things seems to be much more offensive than the foreigner who invites new people to do things his way from the beginning.

Recruiting and developing management

How many non-British?

That is an apt point at which to switch to another topic: that of recruiting and developing management. The United Kingdom is liberal in its traditional willingness to admit foreigners to work. Many foreigners, particularly Americans and Canadians but also Europeans, find the British environment attractive. There is therefore little bar on how widely the investor can cast his net for managerial talent.

There are, of course, limitations of other kinds on how high a proportion of foreign management it is wise to use. They tend to be more expensive, they take time to learn local conditions, they may not get on with their British colleagues. A high proportion of foreign senior management may easily discourage efforts to recruit good Britishers who fear being permanently restricted to subordinate roles. On the whole I think experience indicates the proportion should be kept small, and limited to men who quite obviously have something special to offer.

The recruitment consultant

Recruitment of management in the United Kingdom has been

undergoing a quiet revolution over the last decade moving from reliance on a company's advertising, or word of mouth, through the consultant who advertises for a named or anonymous client and does the initial screening, to the full American type executive search of 'head hunting' consultants. Most of the major American search firms and a few similar firms of British origin now operate offices in London, often of substantial size. While American companies were the principal clients for the executive search firms in the beginning, more and more British firms are using them and, from what I hear, with satisfaction. Some years ahead the spread of the method may make it less advantageous as compared with the more traditional methods but for the present there are considerable management resources under-utilized in British companies who will not respond to advertising and who have to be approached if some much needed mobility is to be achieved. I think most new foreign companies would be well advised to work with one of the search consultants for their more senior appointments. It is likely to be more expensive than other methods both in terms of fee and in terms of the salary required to attract a man whom the employer is approaching rather than the other way round. But it is also in my experience likely to yield a better and more precisely suitable man in a shorter time.

The financial-comptroller

There are two types of men that I think the company which hopes to be successful will want to take special care in selecting, and will probably have unusual difficulties in finding. The first is the good financial-comptroller type. There are lots of accountants but the great majority have a public accounting training and are likely to be short in the funds management and cost control areas. It is easy, in other words, to get good record keeping, but much more difficult to get a finance man who will make a strong management and profit contribution. Part of this problem lies in the training of accountants and the absence of other methods of preparing financial men and both the professional accounting institutes and the development of high level management education will help in these respects. Part of the explanation derives from the high demand and good returns for able financial men in the very rapidly expanding financial institutions of London.

The production executive

The other kind of man the would-be successful manufacturing

company specially needs is the engineer/production executive. Here again there is no shortage of engineers in the United Kingdom. Only a small proportion, however, are university trained and most have derived their professional qualifications after an apprenticeship and part-time study to pass the professional institute's examinations. These are good practical men but their experience tends to be limited and few emerge into general management. Conversely the graduate engineer seldom gets much experience in shop-floor production. It is, I think, largely due to this that the record of the United Kingdom in exploiting and applying engineering technology is poor, even though many breakthroughs originate in her drafting offices and laboratories. It is also I think the long existing shortage of the kind of men I am talking about which explains the persistence of high indirect labour ratios and low productivity which appear regularly in comparative productivity studies.

Many other explanations are offered for these results, and for the even more interesting phenomenon of studies which show a persistent pattern of superior performance in American companies as compared with their British competitors in the same line of business. My own observations lead me to believe that more than anything it is due to different standards of quality in the financial/cost control and the engineering/production functions and I would urge any new investor to look at these most carefully when he is building a management cadre.

Management development

To turn from management recruitment to management development, the facilities now available offer much greater assistance to managements than was the case a few years ago. This conference is being presented to you by two post-graduate business studies schools which did not exist seven years ago. They are now producing a substantial flow of MBAs of a quality I think equal to any in the world and it is possible for a businessman to recruit such men who couple with their Master's degree almost any type of first degree or professional qualification, with two or three years' experience in industry between the two. Apart from the major schools at London and Manchester there are many other institutions now offering management education and training at all levels. Our two schools and many other bodies offer a wide range of executive programmes so that any company willing to make the investment need experience no difficulty in finding means to up-date and refresh an existing management structure.

International companies ought to think seriously of using such facilities as part of their general management development efforts. The content and aims of the British programmes are as highly developed as any in the world. The differences in them from similar work in the United States or elsewhere lies primarily in the extent of exposure to the British environment, international cases and a substantial cross-section of rising British and international executives in business and government. It is difficult to think of a better way of developing one of your non-British employees for work in Britain or for work with British companies, wherever he is based, than this. Professor Morris will be speaking about the characteristics of British management in much greater detail.

Finance

Equally Professor Rose will talk in detail about finance in the United Kingdom and the rapidly changing scene in the London money markets – unquestionably one of the most sophisticated and adaptable set of institutions in the world today. I would like only to repeat my reference to the substantial lessening of exchange control represented by the changes in the rules governing access by foreign firms to sterling financing. Since the war the United Kingdom Government has maintained exchange controls which have required both foreign and domestic companies to secure Bank of England permission for transactions of many types. It is fair to say that the very considerable powers of the Bank have been applied even in the periods of greatest balance of payments strain with an absolute minimum of inconvenience to business. Over the years I have heard very few complaints about exchange controls inhibiting or preventing any reasonable transaction except the outward movement of capital by British corporations or residents. It has been true, however, that a foreign investor coming into the United Kingdom was expected to bring his capital with him rather than raise it on the local markets. This has meant the assumption of exchange risks as well as normal business risks and while that is probably not too unusual for a long-term capital commitment there is much to be said for raising a substantial proportion of funds in the currency and area where one is going to do business. It makes one much more interesting and much better known in the City and in the financial Press – a local coloration is much more quickly acquired. This may be as much of a nuisance as a blessing at times but on the whole is probably a good thing for most companies, and particularly so if you foresee the possibility of wanting to raise money locally in the future, even if it may be optional now.

Local knowledge

Because of the restrictions which have existed, at least in part, comparatively few foreign-owned investments in Britain have had local shareholders or locally held long-term debt. Many have, however, appointed British non-executive directors to their boards to secure local knowledge and connections. The need for such external help varies, of course, according to the nature of the industry. If one is going to have much to do with Government the availability of a colleague who knows his way around Whitehall can be very helpful. Lawyers and accountants are not so common on boards as in the United States since their services and advice are easily available through ordinary professional channels. Merchant bankers are often included in boards and offer a wide range of connections though many companies are reluctant to form too close a connection with a financial house.

Trade association

Another source of help and advice is the network of trade, employer and professional associations which in the United Kingdom is broad and comprehensive. Not everyone can afford to have an ex-Permanent Secretary[1] as a non-executive director but everyone can belong to one or more of the ubiquitous associations which coordinate and represent the views of their members. These associations ultimately come together in the Confederation of British Industry. The CBI, and for particular purposes the individual associations, have a unique function in the relationships between industry and Government. Government for its part wants a body to which it can look for industry opinion and while it can talk to a few large companies individually it needs to have a source of consensus views representing all sizes and kinds of companies. From the point of view of companies the associations provide sources of knowledge of industry statistics, of Government thinking and means of bringing pressure if a sufficient consensus among members exists.

On the other hand participation in association affairs can be time consuming and boring. It can also be inhibiting to competition

---

[1]   A Permanent Secretary is the chief civil servant of a Ministry.

which presumably the would-be successful company welcomes. I do not mean by this that associations engage in restrictive practices, which would be illegal, but they do provide more contact with competitors than some would consider healthy. Some foreign and domestic companies encourage their executives to become heavily involved, others discourage it. I lean to the latter view but am bound to say that given the place of trade associations in the consultative and influence network it would not be wise to opt out entirely.

Directors

Assuming that, as one can for most purposes, a United Kingdom operation will take the form of a United Kingdom company one will have executive directors as well as non-executive directors to consider. The status in the British scene of the title of Director is much more important than any other executive title. It is an appointment which should be made with great care and a clear understanding on both sides of the relationship which is intended and of the management philosophy of the company and the man. This seems an excessively elementary caution but there are more than a few horror stories arising from clashes between the philosophy of strong line chains of command with the philosophy which regards all directors as equal outside of the board room as well as in it.

Terms of employment

These considerations bring one naturally to the question of salaries and other terms of employment.

Salaries

Salaries of executives are notoriously difficult to discuss in general terms. Not only are there wide variations relative to turnover, number of employees, capital employed, but often substantial and inexplicable variations where these factors appear to be comparable. What follows must therefore be taken as a rough guide to what is known from various surveys over recent years. British executives receive, apart from the Dutch, the lowest gross compensation among the West European countries and all of these are substantially below United States levels. They pay income tax at higher levels than in Europe, again with the exception of the Dutch. A survey of some 4,000 executives in 850 companies carried out by

Management Centre Europe in 1971 showed that in *net* salaries chief executives in various countries received[5]

	000 D.M.
France	95·1
Switzerland	93·8
W. Germany	77·2
Italy	71·5
Belgium	67·3
United Kingdom	57·7
Netherlands	54·2

Similar patterns appeared for functional executives, the British being at the bottom of the table in production, research, purchasing and personnel.

This relative inferiority appears to be worsening. The same survey indicated that as against nominal increases in all countries of between 10 and 13 per cent in 1970 the net benefit after allowing for taxes and inflation was:

	per cent
Italy	8·4
W. Germany	7·8
Switzerland	6·7
France	6·5
Netherlands	6·2
Belgium	5·4
United Kingdom	4·0

In one respect British managers seem to do better than average in that many are provided with a company automobile – nearly 65 per cent in one broadly based United Kingdom survey in 1970.[6]

Taxation

The incidence of tax has, of course, been an important factor in limiting British salaries. There simply has seemed little point to salary increases to be taxed away at high marginal rates. Nor has it been easy to devise incentive schemes such as share option or share purchase plans making the benefits exempt from income tax.

---

(5) *The Times*, London, 12 July 1971

(6) *Survey of Executive Salaries and Fringe Benefits in the United Kingdom.* AIC Salary Unit, London.

Great efforts and ingenuity have been applied to this problem and the laws have changed frequently to stop successful loopholes as they have been devised. Share options were virtually killed in the 1966 budget but this year's budget has made them possible again and no doubt many new plans will appear during coming months. This is, however, of little value to the foreign-owned business unless the shares concerned are quoted on the London market.

The British themselves are, of course, used to, and resigned to, the levels of tax now prevailing. It is more surprising that there has been a tendency in the last year or two for foreign executives – Americans in particular – to seek employment in the United Kingdom with the object of establishing a permanent shift of residence. This is undoubtedly in part temporarily due to the recession and lack of job opportunities in the US though the job market has not been good in the United Kingdom either. A large factor seems to be an affection for the comparative peace and stability coupled with largely familiar institutions, language and practice which the Americans at least find. This argues that there are compensating virtues in British life which offset for some international executives the taxes and salary levels prevailing.

Where the right conditions can be fulfilled it is often possible for a foreign company to place some staff in the United Kingdom with a significant measure of income protection from taxes. Where the individual concerned is not domiciled – i.e., can establish that he regards his permanent home as being elsewhere and where his salary can be paid abroad pursuant to an employment contract negotiated and concluded abroad, he may be taxed on a 'remittance' basis, that is only on the money he brings into the country. This is subject to various restrictions but it can relieve a man who qualifies of British tax on his savings at his highest marginal rate. His total global position will of course depend on the tax treatment accorded in his own country and the country where his payments are received.

All of these matters must be studied carefully by the company which wants to establish a good compensation pattern and plan. They must not only be fair as between foreign and British executives employed in the operation, but must be seen and accepted as being fair.

Other terms of employment

Similar efforts ought to be made to avoid any sense of discrimination between foreign and domestic employees in terms of promotion possibilities. Here I refer not only to possibilities within the United Kingdom but in other operations abroad and above all in the parent headquarters. The best British executives will not be attracted to joining or remaining with an international company which takes a view that their potential is limited to opportunities arising only in the United Kingdom operations.

Such questions arise frequently in terms of organization and control of the United Kingdom business. To what extent should a foreign parent treat the United Kingdom operation as autonomous and self-regulating, participating from the outside only by shareholder representatives at the Board level? Or, at the other extreme, should one seek through detailed reporting and visitations by functional executives from outside, by internal auditing, etc. to monitor day-to-day progress? There are no easy answers to these questions and much will depend on the people, the philosophy, and the circumstances of both the United Kingdom operation and the parent.

Wider influences

But I would say this: the United Kingdom does subject the local manager to a wide variety of pressures to conform to interests other than those of the shareholder. Some of these are very subtle as, for example, the honours system which is so powerful an incentive to many men who have achieved high office. The pursuit of a knighthood may well lead such a man to take views of outside activities, of export efforts, of benefactions, of investments in the development areas which he might not do otherwise. Other influences may be more direct in the form of difficulties with ministries or an industrial association or criticism in a powerful national Press. The United Kingdom is a well developed and integrated society in which all of these influences have a proper and useful part to play in making the society work. It is important, therefore, for an external shareholder to recognise their existence.

There is a great tendency in the United Kingdom to rely on 'voluntary' guidelines on prices, wages and other matters. There are those in the United Kingdom and elsewhere who believe that it is quite wrong for businessmen or unions to comply with such policies and that if such directives are required they should be legislated. Others think that voluntary schemes are preferable to a steadily increasing volume of legalized intervention. I would argue only that where restrictions on freedom are to be accepted voluntarily one should evaluate carefully why it is desirable to volunteer.

Marketing

I shall touch only briefly on marketing which Professor Simmonds will be covering in detail in the next talk. The basic market research for an industrial product is not, I think, materially different from what it is anywhere else. For consumer products, however, one must take into account the degree of concentration which exists in retail distribution and which I mentioned in my introductory review. Even if some variation of Robinson Patman legislation appears in Britain – and I would rate this as a real possibility in the next year or two – I do not think it will do much to diminish retail concentration. The influence of the rigorous control of land development has been to make urban shopping centres highly concentrated and the possession of sites on the High Streets is an unassailable advantage of the big retailing groups. This is why I said earlier that it is not easy to get into the highly profitable business of large-scale retailing.

The situation leaves a manufacturer with three options:
1. To plan on the assumption that a substantial volume of business will have to be done at substantial discounts in price whether in his own brand or on a private label basis.
2. To create a brand image and demand by heavy advertising expenditure aimed at improving bargaining position *vis-à-vis* the big retailing chains.
3. By-passing the big retailers by using selected dealers, a direct-selling or mail order sales plan.

The first option may be attractive to the firm with large volume low-cost production which may be achieved by higher investment per man or better technology, design and production control than the competition.

The manufacturer with an internationally known brand supported by a good volume of advertising, particularly in English language magazines, is well placed to follow the second plan. Many of the household names of the US market have done well using such a method.

The third plan is probably the most lengthy process and the most expensive in terms of marketing costs since it depends not only on the development of a brand image and demand but also on the creation of selling forces and services. The record of direct selling,

B

other than that of the largest comprehensive mail order retailers, is not encouraging.

Three case studies

I intend now to apply these reflections on the UK environment to a consideration of three successful foreign owned companies, Heinz, Gillette and Hoover, which earned on their capital employed before taxes in 1970 18·5 per cent, 26·0 per cent and 21·1 per cent respectively as compared with the 12·6 per cent I have already mentioned for the forty-three largest non-oil manufacturing companies. All are American, long established, much above average in return on capital employed and engaged in the manufacture of consumer products. I have chosen long-established companies because short-run success does not necessarily mean much and there is indeed some evidence to suggest that American companies in Britain, which have been best researched, tend to begin with above average profits and then decline towards the average of British companies. It is the companies which over a substantial length of time have built a major market position and maintained high profitability that one must look for the methods of success. Virtually all such companies are, until now at least, American, and are in consumer products, or in such fields of specialized technology – e.g., IBM, MMM or Texas Instruments, that the technological advantage may so overwhelm other considerations as to make study of their operations unrewarding for general purposes.

Heinz

Let us take Heinz first, a company which began business in the United States in 1869 and now produces well over a thousand varieties of packaged food – far beyond its famous '57 varieties' trademark. Heinz began its UK business by exporting to the market in 1886 and bought its first small factory in London in 1905. This was the first overseas investment and has been followed by many more, including some in the EEC. In the UK and elsewhere the policy of the company in respect of overseas investments up to 1958 was consistent – to start from scratch rather than by an acquisition. Administration and research are in the west and north of the London area as also is one main manufacturing plant, the other two being in Lancashire and the North-West.

Heinz adopts a policy of leaving a subsidiary company to develop its products, with the single exception of tomato ketchup, to suit the local market and only overall quality of product and package are required to meet parent company supervisory standards. The varieties of product so developed are the response to sophisticated United Kingdom market research and are heavily supported by advertising. Increasing competition is being met and is to be expected from private label brands and advertising is being relied upon to maintain consumer loyalty to the Heinz label.

There are about 150,000 grocery stores in the United Kingdom and since 1960 Heinz have been cutting back on the number they have tried to cover by direct call. Faced with the concentration of retailing we have noted earlier, they have sought to reflect this in more concentrated selling force activity and distribution networks using the best automation and data processing networks available.

The equity capital is owned by the parent company to the extent of 91 per cent with the remaining 9 per cent in the hands of United Kingdom institutional investors. The common stock is not quoted in the United Kingdom but a small amount of preference shares in foreign currency and small amounts of debentures in sterling denominations are quoted on the London Stock Exchange. The Managing Director and management of the United Kingdom company have been British for the last twenty-five years. The Managing Director reports to the Senior Vice-President – Europe who is one of three Senior Vice-Presidents responsible for broad divisions of the world operations. A serious effort is made to demonstrate that international careers are open to British executives, and UK executives have served as Presidents of the Canadian company, as Area Vice-President for North America and as Senior Vice-President–Europe. This kind of career pattern reflects the fact that management development is taken very seriously. The company retains a full-time executive to supervise its management development plans and the world corporation recognizes it as a prime responsibility of each company manager.

Gillette

Gillette is not quite so old in the United States where the company was formed in 1901, but its first sales office was opened in London in 1905, the same year as Heinz bought its first factory in the same city. Gillette established factories in Leicester in 1909 and Slough in 1920. Now manufacturing is concentrated in factories to the west of London. In 1931 following a merger in the United States of Gillette and Auto Strop, the UK subsidiaries were merged and became Gillette Industries Limited.

Until the Second World War the business of the company was wholly razor blades but subsequently diversification acquisitions by the parent corporation have been reflected in a corresponding spread of the United Kingdom company's product range.

From the beginning Gillette used the United Kingdom company as a base for exports and these have expanded as dramatically as the domestic sales. In this Gillette has been quite different from Heinz. In 1971, 58 per cent of Gillette's total sales were exports as compared with a Heinz figure of under 4 per cent.

In its marketing activities Gillette operates brand management and sales management line activities reporting to and being coordinated by a Marketing Manager. These activities are heavily supported by market research and advertising. Gillette has had a marked success in publicizing its name by sponsoring the leading competition in that most English of sports, cricket.

In its highly successful export sales marketing operates through area line management with staff brand groups. They have shown remarkable flexibility in these activities of which perhaps the most striking example is that they succeed in marketing to all the East European countries and have been quite prepared to engage in complex barter transactions to enable them to do so over and beyond the normal State trading plans.

Gillette in a world sense is fairly tightly controlled by the parent corporation. Research and development activities in the United Kingdom are directly under control and all other activities operate within budgets and disciplined financial procedures.

Executive development is viewed as a top priority in Gillette and the company's personnel is truly international so that planned mixing and movement of various nationalities takes place as a matter of course.

Gillette Industries Limited is not quoted on the London Stock Exchange but the shares of the parent company are quoted as a foreign currency security.

Hoover

Hoover is the biggest of the three companies in the number of employees and profit. The first sales office was established in London in 1919 and its success led to the establishment of the first manufacturing plant in West London in 1932. Vacuum cleaner manufacture remains concentrated there. With the company's entry into the washing machine business after the war, and subsequently as additional manufacturing space became necessary, it has been added on green field sites in the assisted areas of Wales and Scotland. The Welsh buildings have all been erected by the company while the Scottish buildings have been built on the company's land and rented on long lease from the Government. Both arrangements have worked well and have received assistance from and contributed greatly to the Government's development area plans. The company now has a total of over 200,000 sq. metres of manufacturing space.

Selling in the United Kingdom was until 1964 carried out on a resale plan, i.e., the company's large force of sales and service men sold the goods initially to retailers and then played a major role in selling them on to the consumer by house calls. This sales plan had important advantages at a time when few British housewives were familiar with vacuum cleaners and later with washing machines. In such circumstances home demonstration was essential and the ubiquitous Hoover salesman made the company's name a part of the English language. As market saturation increases, however, such a sales plan becomes unnecessarily expensive and the company turned over its home selling and servicing activities to dealers with great advantage to all concerned in 1963–4.

In the export markets, where Hoover has consistently done by far the largest share of the export business in the product fields it covers, the pattern has been for the most part an initial use of distributors, followed by the establishment of directly-owned selling companies, followed by – when warranted – the establishment of manufacturing facilities. Exports account for 23 per cent of the company's total volume.

Marketing research and advertising support what are now much reduced sales forces who spend a major part of their time in training dealer personnel in reselling activities.

Unlike Gillette or Heinz, Hoover has a substantial public share ownership existing in the United Kingdom – about 45 per cent of the combined 'A' and 'B' shares being so held. There is, therefore, a great deal more interest in the company in the financial world and Press than in the other two cases. This has the advantage of giving a 'home company' image to the company, but also necessitates that recognition must be given to accountability towards the interests of the minority shareholders. Perhaps its most important advantage is in offering the possibility of share related incentive schemes to the British employees. One major scheme was established in the postwar period and it is hoped that another can be designed in the light of the new attitudes to such schemes indicated in the budget of last March.

Until 1960 the United Kingdom company was almost wholly British managed and was substantially autonomous with some liaison with the parent company on engineering and design. At that time a strenuous effort was made to take better advantage of the global knowledge and experience of the group and Hoover Worldwide Inc. was formed in New York to coordinate many aspects of the world activities. This has unquestionably served the British company well and through the sharing of the chairman and chief executive of both the parent and the British company, a high degree of coordination is achieved with the retention of a high degree of autonomy and initiative. Significantly, since these changes, the opportunities for British executives have been enlarged. The joint managing directors of the British company – one for UK operations and one for export – have become senior executives of Hoover Worldwide Inc. and another of the British sales executives has become President of Hoover in Canada.

The United Kingdom company has always been a leader in the field of management development and general training activities, both internal and external. It was one of the first companies in Britain to introduce a graduate training scheme, supports many management schools and training colleges, and operates a large apprentice-training scheme for young engineers.

Some lessons

Those, then, are three thumbnail sketches of successful foreign-owned companies which established themselves in the United Kingdom and grew to be outstanding in their fields in terms of market recognition and profitability. What can we draw from their experience relative to the United Kingdom environment in the terms in which I have described it?

It is noteworthy that all three companies began as sales offices selling imported products. They knew their markets and had at least partially developed them before commencing manufacturing operations. All three have invested heavily in building and main-taining a brand image. The energetic pursuit of a well based marketing policy is clearly a common factor.

The manufacturing is predominantly in the south-east in the case of Heinz and Gillette. Only Hoover has taken substantial advantage of the facilities offered for investment in the assisted areas. The only rule that emerges is the one I suggested earlier in considering Government influences on location – the balancing of advantages and disadvantages is a complex decision which can only be made by careful study of the circumstances of the particular investor. If made with reasonable care, it is unlikely to be an important determinant of ultimate success or failure.

The decision about having local shareholders does not seem an important determinant of success, nor does the decision about exporting. The three companies demonstrate patterns of success achieved with wide variations in the degree of external control exercised.

One factor is common, however, and I think of great importance. All three companies have made great efforts to develop their people and to make them feel full citizens of the world group. All three companies, and others I could name who follow the same policies and who are equally successful, obtain in exchange for their efforts an ability to attract good executives and to keep them in a high state of morale. Anyone who wants to develop a successful company is half-way to his goal if he can do that.

Marketing in the United Kingdom

2

Kenneth Simmonds and Philip Law

Introduction

This paper provides a picture of markets, marketing institutions and marketing practice in the United Kingdom[1]; it shows how these have been changing over the last decade; and projects the major changes expected by 1980.

There are significant changes in what consumers buy, where they buy it, and an increasing sophistication among those who market to them. As buying habits change there will always be declining institutions, failures and unsuccessful innovations, but also opportunity. In 1972 there is opportunity in the United Kingdom for the aggressive innovator.

The British consumer

Demographic factors

The United Kingdom's population was 56 m. in 1971 and is expected to be 59 m. by 1981. This increase, at 7 per cent, is significantly lower than the 11 per cent expected for the rest of Europe. As a result of the postwar baby boom and longer life expectancy, the number of people below 35 and above 75 will grow at over twice the average rate. Forty-six million people live in England, 5 m. in Scotland, under 3 m. in Wales and 1½ m. in Northern Ireland. Eighty per cent of the population live in urban districts and, for example, 8 m. live in Greater London. Of all the EEC countries only the Netherlands has a higher proportion of urban dwellers. Greater London has a density of 12,600 persons per square mile;

[1] Sources of statistics quoted throughout this paper have not been quoted in detail. The reader wishing to go into more depth is referred to *The IPC Marketing Manual of the United Kingdom*, International Publishing Corporation 1971. A wide range of basic sources are covered in this comprehensive collection of statistics.

the average is 900 for England and for the entire United Kingdom (230 per square kilometre). Much of Scotland has under 50.

Of roughly 40 m. adults, 27 m. are married, and 13 m. single, widowed or divorced. There are 18 m. households in Great Britain with an average number of persons per household of 2·94. In Northern Ireland, households have an average of 3·61 persons. It is notable that 61 per cent of all households have no children under 15 years old.

Of the adult population, 83 per cent of the men and 42 per cent of the women work. The overall percentage is increasing slightly (59 per cent in 1961 to 61 per cent in 1969) caused mainly by the increasing numbers of housewives holding jobs. The percentage of housewives employed is significantly higher than the average figure for the whole of Europe.

The student population among those over 15 years of age is rising and will rise even further when the school leaving age is 16 and the university system expands. In 1969 only 3 per cent of the total population were in full-time education beyond 15; three-quarters of the adult population had left school by 15.

In Britain only half the working population is engaged on production; the other half provides services. In June 1970 the working population of 25·6 m. was distributed as in Table 2.1. The very small proportion of the population engaged in agriculture, about 3 per cent, contrasts strongly with Italy at 23 per cent, France at 20 per cent and Germany and the Netherlands at 10 per cent.

TABLE 2.1   *Distribution of working population (June 1970)*

	millions
Production industries	11·0
Agriculture, fishing, etc.	0·4
Transport, distribution	4·3
Insurance, banking, etc.	1·0
Professional and scientific	2·9
Catering, miscellaneous services	1·8
National and local government	1·4
Armed forces	0·4
Employers, self-employed	1·8
Wholly unemployed	0·6
	25·6

Incomes and standard of living in the United Kingdom

The United Kingdom Gross National Product grew at an average annual rate of only 2·9 per cent between 1960 and 1969 and measured in $ per head in 1969 was below France, Germany, Belgium and the Netherlands. One reason for this was that the mass migration from the farms to industry in so many countries in recent years had already happened in Britain. Also Commonwealth resources and preferential access to Commonwealth markets were lost; devaluing sterling was delayed; and associated economic controls depressed demand.

Incomes have been rising faster than prices for the last twenty years and this trend is likely to continue in the short run. At the same time the standard working week in manufacturing has shortened from forty-four hours in 1959 to forty hours in 1969. The number of married women working has rapidly increased.

In 1970 male administrative, technical and clerical employees earned an average of £36 per week and manual workers about £28. There is a wide dispersion about these. In Table 2.2 married couples are treated as one unit.

TABLE 2.2   *Distribution of personal incomes 1969/70 tax year*

Range of annual income (£)	Before tax No. of incomes (millions)	%	After tax No. of incomes (millions)	%
less than 500	2·0	9	2·5	12
500– 999	6·7	31	8·2	38
1,000–1,499	6·2	28	6·9	31
1,500–1,999	4·2	19	2·9	13
2,000–3,000	1·9	9	0·9	4
more than 3,000	0·8	4	0·4	2
	21·8	100	21·8	100

In terms of wealth there is a far greater disparity between rich and poor, 1 per cent of the population owning nearly a quarter of the private wealth in the UK.

TABLE 2.3   *Pattern of family expenditure (1969)*

% of income spent on:	West Germany		Italy		France		Netherlands		Belgium		Luxembourg		United Kingdom	
	m	c	m	c	m	c	m	c	m	c	m	c	m	c
Food, beverages and tobacco	35·6	29·1	45·4	35·4	43·0	31·6	31·0	22·1	35·3	26·0	34·7	28·6	32·3	25·9
Clothing and footwear	9·1	8·9	9·2	8·8	9·2	9·8	11·5	9·8	11·5	10·9	12·6	13·7	7·3	7·6
Housing, fuel and light	12·5	13·5	14·9	15·1	12·7	12·8	11·9	10·8	16·5	17·1	15·8	18·3	17·4	20·8
Appliances and furnishings	7·9	8·3	5·3	7·1	7·4	8·7	8·7	8·7	7·4	8·7	7·4	7·6	5·8	6·9
Medicines and toiletries	2·3	2·6	1·9	2·4	4·3	4·6	2·1	2·9	2·9	3·5	2·3	2·6	1·8	2·2
Transport and communications	5·9	8·2	5·9	10·4	9·6	14·0	6·2	9·8	7·2	10·5	7·5	9·2	10·9	10·0
Education and entertainment	5·3	6·3	5·3	6·6	5·4	7·5	7·0	8·0	4·8	5·8	5·4	6·2	3·8	4·3
Other goods and services	5·1	9·3	4·5	5·7	3·1	4·4	4·8	7·3	4·5	5·9	3·0	3·5	7·5	8·4
Taxes and social security	16·5	13·7	7·5	8·5	5·3	6·5	16·7	20·7	9·9	11·6	11·4	10·4	13·1	13·9

m = Manual workers' households.   c = Clerical workers' households.

Consumer spending patterns

Table 2.3 compares the spending patterns of manual and clerical workers in the Six and the United Kingdom. The most noticeable difference is the greater proportion of income spent by the French and Italians on food and by the British on housing, fuel and light. Housing is the second largest category of expenditure in the United Kingdom and is continuing to grow. Each year the proportion of occupier ownership of houses increases and has now passed 50 per cent of all dwellings.

Food accounted for 26 per cent of total consumers' expenditure in 1970 but is declining in importance. Real spending increase by only 5 per cent between 1963 and 1969 compared with 13 per cent for total consumers' expenditure. Within the food category there is a continuing trend towards more convenience foods. This trend is caused partly by technological advance, partly by the improvements packaged foods make possible in distribution and marketing, and partly by the increased proportion of working wives. These influences will continue in the future. Only 2 per cent of food spending went for frozen foods. This percentage should grow significantly.

TABLE 2.4 *Family expenditure in 1970*

Average number of people per household		2·95
Persons working		1·40
Average weekly household expenditure:	(£)	(%)
Housing – rent, rates, repairs	3·59	12·6
Fuel, light and power	1·79	6·3
Food	7·35	25·7
Alcoholic drink	1·27	4·5
Tobacco	1·37	4·8
Clothing and footwear	2·64	9·2
Durable household goods	1·85	6·5
Other goods	2·12	7·4
Transport and vehicles	3·91	13·7
Services	2·58	9·0
Miscellaneous	0·10	0·3
	28·57	100·0
Other payments recorded:	(£)	
Income tax and surtax	4·60	
National insurance	1·26	
Purchase or alteration of dwellings	1·57	
Life assurance, etc.	1·21	
Other	1·04	

The fastest growing categories of spending in real terms over the period 1963 to 1969 were:

	per cent
Motor vehicle running costs	66
Communication services	34
Recreational goods	25
Housing	21
Fuel and light	21

Spending on consumer durables on the other hand increased only 7 per cent.

For many consumer durables the market has reached the stage where the major demand is for replacement purposes. The market will increasingly be looking for new models. The United Kingdom has a particularly high ownership of television sets, radios and record players, but lower ownership rate than most EEC countries for dryers, refrigerators and deep freezes. See Table 2.5.

The ownership of cars is widespread and there are some 10 million cars on the road but there is still a great potential. Road building has fallen behind most European countries though and traffic densities are increasing.

The British worker has fewer statutory holidays than his European counterpart. His leisure increased little in the 1960s. Expenditure on entertainment and recreational goods, however, has been growing rapidly, to £1,110 m. in 1969. Holidays abroad are now common-place, and over £400 m. was spent on them in 1969.

TABLE 2.5 *Pattern of ownership of durables in Europe*

	UK	West Germany	France	Belgium	Netherlands	Italy
Durables per '000 population – 1967						
Vehicles	261	202	247	206	166	149
Telephones	218	180	140	179	216	132
Wireless	462	325	139	310	220	74
T.V.	273	185	143	239	200	145
Ownership of durables (% households) – 1969						
Vacuum cleaner	83	87	59	61	98	17
Washing machine	56	66	60	62	80	47
Refrigerator	61	87	80	53	76	71
Iron	95	96	95	90	97	89
At least 1 car (% households) – 1969						
	50	48	56	45	48	42

National characteristics of the consumer

How are British consumers different from those of other cultures? Most of them live in towns or cities and the Englishman's house is still his castle, but within the four nations there is a wide diversity of languages, customs and habits, arising from differences in race, geography and history.

The British culture is predominantly an indoor one, or at least introvert. Climate affects this, but also two-fifths of the population list home decoration and improvement as one of their major interests. A fifth of the population are 'very interested' in gardening. People do not eat out much (family expenditure averaged £1 per week in 1970) and this figure shows little sign of increasing. This may, of course, reflect the average Briton's traditional disdain for the pleasures of eating. If he entertains, it is usually at home, but not often, as he finds time for sixteen hours of television viewing a week.

Britain is a class conscious country. Movement between classes is relatively uncommon, although improved education and communications make it easier for the clever youth to get on. The working-class man, with a close-knit family and a history of poverty and insecurity, suspects innovation and the high flier. The petrol pump attendant dreams of winning the football pools, not of being manager of a chain of service stations. This may help to explain the poor standard of service to which the British have become accustomed, and organized labour's resistance to innovation. The middle classes, in spite of their more adventurous tastes, closely watch the *status quo* and are experts at detecting the social climber.

Six social grades are conveniently used to classify the adult population of the United Kingdom, producing the distribution of Table 2.6, page 32.

Purchase decision making within the household varies according to the product and the amount of money being spent. The decision on large, long-term items, such as furniture and household appliances, is shared, but on the short-term items is assigned to a particular family member. Food is mainly the wife's responsibility and women buy almost all the detergents. Men at extreme ends of the social scale buy their own clothes, as do women, but middle class women buy basic clothes for their husbands. A much higher proportion than usual of decisions among young married couples are shared, while in wealthy families the various members tend to specialize. Two recent surveys have revealed the growing influence

TABLE 2.6   *Social stratification of the United Kingdom market*

Social Grade	% of all adults	Social status	Occupations of head of household
A	3	Upper middle class	Higher managerial, administrative or professional
B	11	Middle class	Intermediate managerial, administrative or professional
C1	22	Lower middle class	Supervisory or clerical and junior managerial, administrative or professional
C2	31	Skilled working class	Skilled manual workers
D	25	Working class	Semi and unskilled manual workers
E	8	Those at lowest level of subsistence	State pensioners or widows (no other earner). Casual or lowest grade workers

of women over purchase of alcoholic drink and petrol. As more supermarkets stock liquor, so it becomes part of the weekly food purchase.

Housewives make between two and four shopping trips a week and one-stop shopping is uncommon, the average being $2\frac{1}{2}$ stops. The frequency of trips will fall, but storage space in most British homes limits this. Kitchens and refrigerators are small and only 1 per cent of households currently own a deep freeze. But both the mobility and the sophistication of consumers are increasing and they are willing to travel further and less frequently on their shopping trips.

The intermediate buyer

What are the characteristics in the United Kingdom of retail and wholesale buyers for the consumer goods firm and the industrial buyer for the industrial firm?

The growth of multiple and voluntary retail groups has meant that the manufacturer deals with fewer and more sophisticated customers. Buying is becoming more centralized and done by specialists who, with higher sales volumes to service, have an increasing bargaining position. Stories proliferate among brand managers in consumer goods firms about the buying characteristics and personal idiosyncrasies of some dominant buyers. Manufacturers seek more and more to retain control over their output through spending on brand image. This way they help to get their products onto the supermarket shelves and to keep it there. Advertising for items sold in the supermarket already takes over three-quarters of commercial television spots and with further growth anticipated it can be expected to remain very high. The large retailers' strength also shows in their adopting 'own label' lines. Nielsens estimated in 1969 that for sales of eighteen supermarket lines ranging from baked beans to household bleaches, over 30 per cent were accounted for by 'own labels'.

Industrial buyers traditionally have dominated suppliers more than retail buyers. Except for motor vehicles and electrical appliances, however, the general impression is that purchasing is rather low-key. In Hugh Buckner's recent study, *How British Industry Buys*, price was considered one of the most important factors in purchasing. But even here one half of the respondents indicated that they would not change suppliers unless there was a price reduction of at least 5%. There are few signs of any major rejuvenation in purchasing. Procedures are fairly lax with many organizational positions influencing a decision. Examples of aggressive purchasing strategy are rare; many successful suppliers have never been forced to survive by developing a carefully balanced mix of product features, price, delivery and sales effort.

Marketing channels in the United Kingdom

Retail outlets

Types of shop

In Britain a large number of small independent retail outlets have always existed alongside some big chains. In the last ten years, however, the supermarket has made major inroads into the number of small stores. Real growth in retail turnover has been small so that the development of larger stores has been at the expense of the smaller units, particularly in grocery stores, which represent the largest grouping. But there have also been proportionately greater reductions in specialist food stores such as fishmongers and greengrocers as consumers have switched to the supermarkets for items stocked by these outlets.

The decline will continue; there are likely to be 450,000 shops by 1975 as against 500,000 in 1966 and 570,000 in 1961.

Supermarkets

The abolition of resale price maintenance in 1963 considerably increased the advantages of larger volume supermarkets. Self-service outlets accounted for about one-fifth of total grocery turnover in 1961 but about two-thirds by 1971. Only about a quarter of all outlets, however, are self-service and under 5 per cent supermarkets. Nielsen estimated that 3,500 supermarkets of over 371 sq. m (4,000 sq. ft) sold 28 per cent of all food in 1969.

The first supermarkets opened in the early 'fifties were conversions of existing self-service stores. The initial reaction was unfavourable because food rationing was still in existence and there was no prepackaging. However, ten years after the first supermarket, there were 600 in Britain and 500 more were opened in 1970 alone, bringing the total to 4,400. The early stores had sales areas of around 185 sq. m (2,000 sq. ft), but the average size has increased continuously since then; new supermarkets opened in 1971 averaged 1,254 sq. m (13,500 sq. ft) in area.

In comparison with EEC countries, the United Kingdom is behind Germany and the Netherlands in the self-service share of grocers' shops and grocery turnover. Germany, however, has almost 50 per cent more grocers' shops for each 10,000 people – reflecting its higher rural population.

By the middle 'seventies supermarkets could be handling 18 to 20 per cent of retail turnover, because first, there are the out-of-town super-stores, giant shops with more than 9,290 sq. m (100,000 sq. ft) of selling space and a very much wider range of merchandise than now. Complementary to these will be large city centre stores with a much smaller range of goods. Sizes here will be 929 to 1,858 sq. m (10,000 to 20,000 sq. ft). Finally, voluntary groups are planning 'neighbourhood' supermarkets, smaller than the city centre stores, **but** offering products to meet most of the daily needs of local people.

Recently, so-called discount stores have appeared, mainly in the North of England, growing out of supermarkets as supermarkets grew out of self-service stores. They chiefly comprise the large superstores referred to above and smaller, specialist shops usually located in back streets. Frills in both, and therefore overheads, are minimized so that prices can also be kept down. The superstores offer a wide range of foods and non-foods at prices substantially below recommended selling prices. The specialist shops usually deal in durables, such as carpets or motor accessories, which have little or no service content. They are essentially wholesalers selling directly to the public. There are no total figures for this kind of operation, but the signs are that it is growing.

Shopping centres

All the shopping centres so far and most of those planned will be inside urban areas. By 1975 Britain will have some form of shopping centre in nearly every major city. These vary widely in size and scope, depending on how much land is available, but share certain features. Shopping is done on foot, and car parking is provided on, or adjacent to, the site.

Their success varies. The Elephant and Castle Centre in London and the Bull Ring in Birmingham have been much criticized and many sites remain unlet. Seven years after opening the Bull Ring complex is not fully occupied.

The out-of-town shopping sites characterized by the Woolco development and including Asda (Associated Dairies), Morrison and Quicksave have been slower to take off than continental hyper-markets but now look likely to have high growth as motor-car usage develops. The scheme gaining most attention is Brent Cross in North London. Many schemes, however, flounder because local authorities are very reluctant to grant planning permission.

Retail organizations

Retail sales are broken down by type of organization in Table 2.7. It reveals a considerable change in their relative importance, from independents and co-operatives towards multiples, department stores and mail order.

TABLE 2.7 *Retail sales in the United Kingdom in 1970 by type of organization*

	Sales (£ million)	*Index at current prices* 1966 = 100
Independents	6,480	116
Multiples	5,130	135
Co-operatives	1,060	107
Department stores	680	125
Mail order	570	132
Total	13,920	122

Independent traders

Four-fifths of the retail establishments, run by independents, have nearly 65 per cent of the workers. Yet they do under half of all business. Their market share has declined from 54 per cent in 1961 to 47 per cent in 1970. They are having a hard time. They are often unable or unwilling to modernize and their role as arbiter of taste and guarantor of quality is increasingly being lost.

The attack by the multiples has been fiercest in the grocery business. The independents have produced the most sophisticated response. By banding together into voluntary groups they gain the advantages of cheaper prices through bulk buying, joint promotional activities, of raising extra finance for modernization and can in general behave like multiples. There are now over twenty groups, involving some 150 wholesalers and 36,000 retail outlets. The voluntary group idea has been spreading into areas other than grocery. The total given above includes 5,500 outlets in fields like food, liquor, clothing and electrical goods.

In hardware and consumer durables, independents have improved their share of the business recently. Independent grocers have lost market share, from 53 per cent in 1961 to 43 per cent in 1970, but concurrently voluntary groups or symbol independents, in increasing their share from 13 to 23 per cent have been star performers in the last three years.

Current forecasts are that weeding out of independents will continue and that their market share will be 40 per cent by the mid-'seventies. Their survival will depend on flexibility and adaptability, not attributes for which they have been noted in the past. The independent shopkeeper will survive if he offers the customer something different: late opening, after sales service, or proximity for the last minute purchase.

The advent of cash and carry wholesaling has been a help. The development sprang from difficulties encountered by small units in obtaining small and regular deliveries from manufacturers and traditional wholesalers, but has proved to be profitable itself.

Multiples

This is the most successful form of retail trading of recent years. (In the UK a multiple firm consists of ten or more shops under the same ownership, with central management.) The multiples originally concentrated on a narrow range of merchandise, particularly on convenience goods. Now, however, multiple grocers such as Tesco and Fine Fare are branching out into non-food items to bolster margins. Increasing numbers of them are selling liquor. Nielsen reported that over 2,600 multiple grocers had off-licences in 1970 – 40 per cent more than the previous year. Marks & Spencer now derives only 70 per cent of its £400 m. turnover from clothing, and has become the UK's largest retailer of some food lines. Woolworths have had some success with their Woolco Stores.

Multiples started at the end of the nineteenth century. There are now about 1,300 organizations employing over 600,000 people. Their market share continually increases and it is forecast that they will have more than 40 per cent in the mid-'seventies. Their performance in the grocery trade has been spectacular. Four chains, Allied Suppliers, Fine Fare, Sainsburys and Tesco, now control a quarter of the country's grocery business, and the multiples together have over 40 per cent of this trade. Food manufacturers cannot ignore their enormous purchasing power.

Multiples have also been growing faster than their competitors in most other product fields. They are well-equipped for shopping demands in the 'seventies, but as they have already cut out the middle-man's margins and have the advantages of bulk buying they will have to increase efficiency by improving their own operating methods.

Co-operative societies

The Rochdale Pioneers of 1844 were not the first people to found a consumer co-operative, but by charging market prices and sharing the profits among the members they succeeded where others before them failed. The number of societies grew rapidly, reaching a peak of over 1,400 in 1900; but a continuous process of merger and rationalization has reduced these to about 300. The membership has grown from under 2 m. in 1900 to over 13 m. – nearly half the adult population – now. Turnover grew with the membership, reaching a peak in the mid-'fifties.

In 1942 the Co-operative movement pioneered self-service and supermarket trading in Britain, and by 1957 they had 2,000 self-service grocery branches, 60 per cent of the national total. They were the first retail group to integrate backwards into wholesaling. And yet they were very slow to respond to the challenge presented by the multiples in the 'fifties. In 1970 co-operative societies had $7\frac{1}{2}$ per cent of the retail market, a fall from the 9 per cent share they had in 1966. Nearly 80 per cent of their trade is in food and yet they lost market share in food from 18 per cent in 1961 to 14 per cent in 1970. Clothing and footwear account for 10 per cent of their business and here turnover has actually declined by 6 per cent in spite of the rise in prices.

These bad figures goaded the movement into action. More than 80 of the 200 factories have been closed and the own label product range has been rationalized under a single Co-op logo. Mergers increased: so has advertising expenditure. Millions of pounds (£10 m. in 1968 alone) was spent on store modernization. The Dividend Stamp scheme, whereby the dividend takes the form of trading stamps, has been a great success. The decline in the Co-op's share of retail trade now seems to have halted. The Co-ops themselves forecast a share of retail trade rise to 12 per cent by the mid-'seventies. Others say that it will stay the same, as many of their stores are in bad locations.

Department stores

Department stores have increased their turnover from £540 m. in 1966 to £680 m. in 1970, in line with the growth in other sectors. Their market share has remained at about 5 per cent since 1961. Over half of the 1966 turnover came from independents, but most of the advances in operating techniques have come from the national groups such as Debenhams and the House of Frazer.

The distinguishing features of department store trading, a high degree of personal service and a wide variety of merchandise, have been whittled away in recent years. The sector has been slow to choose whether to meet the multiples head on by cutting overheads and reducing the number of lines or to trade up and abandon most of the popular trade. This sector has many prime city centre sites, occupied in the boom times at the beginning of this century. While these may be cheap to service financially, many of them are in need of extensive modernization and they may also find that their customers have drifted away to the suburbs. By opening suburban branches and setting up 'shops within shops' to cater for particular customer groups the stores have held their share and they are expected to do as well, if not better, in the future.

Mail order firms

Mail order sales have grown from £230 m. in 1961 to £570 m. in 1970, a business done by about 500 organizations, of which the largest are GUS, Littlewoods, Grattan and Freeman's. If all the specialist mail order firms are included there are more like 2,000 active companies, and total turnover is about £620 m.

The general companies, typified by the four mentioned above, accounted for the spectacular growth in the 'sixties and now have 80 per cent of the business. They sell through two million agents who each have an illustrated catalogue advertising upwards of 5,000 different items. Their traditional market has been in the C and D social classes (see Table 2.6). In the last two or three years their business has been hit by increased postal charges, growing competition and problems of finding and retaining good agents.

Attempts to trade up into the A/B social classes have usually been disastrous. However, the specialist companies have been very successful in this area with women's clothing, furniture and toys, and it is here that the future growth will take place. Their main problem is to contact the appropriate customers, whether through the media or by purchasing mailing lists.

Direct selling operations

Direct selling in the home is the oldest form of marketing but has also had an unsavoury reputation. To counteract this, the Direct Sales & Service Association was formed in 1965. It guarantees merchandise, prohibits misleading advertising and switch selling and insists on selection and training schemes for salesmen. It claims membership representing 70 per cent of direct sales in the UK. Turnover has grown from £80 m. in 1961 to about £450 m. in 1970, and the current 15 per cent growth rate is forecast to continue.

The trade mainly consists of household stores, cosmetic and costume jewelry and clothing, although many washing machines were sold in this way in the early 'sixties. For cosmetics in particular the customer is attracted by the personal service and the wide range of products. The DSSA calculates that over 200,000 representatives are at work, mainly women working part time. As they usually operate close to home they often perform a useful social role, drawing neighbours together for 'buying parties' and calling on lonely housewives.

Wholesale organizations

There is a wide variety of sizes and types of firm in wholesaling and their turnover was £15 m. in 1965. The distinction between wholesaling, retailing, and manufacturing is now much less sharp. Cash and carry warehouses deal with the public, wholesalers and retailers are banding together into chains to combat the multiples, and manufacturers are integrating forward into distribution.

Wholesalers have been under pressure since the War. Not only have their low margins been reduced by their inability to pass on rising costs but also their role in the distribution chain is decreasing in importance. The industry has been slow to respond. A recent NEDC booklet[2], *A Look At Wholesaling*, based on 1968 fieldwork, said about the (admittedly small) sample of firms visited:

> '... the quality of management in the firms visited varied immensely.... The structure of the wholesale trade is relatively unsatisfactory; ... Far too few firms have carried out operational research studies .... The working party was struck by relatively depressed level of remuneration ....'

But these strictures do not apply to every wholesaler. Many firms have mechanized their ordering, packing and loading operations and shrink-wrapped palletized loads are replacing brown paper and string.

The initiative for voluntary group or symbol chains of independents has often come from the wholesalers. Cash and carry wholesaling turnover has grown from £100 m. in 1963 to £500 m. today. General wholesalers have been setting up for themselves or buying into manufacturing and retail operations. Selective distribution, whereby the wholesaler distributes to chosen retailers only and often develops his own brand as well, helps to ensure more aggressive retail selling.

Marketing functions

Advertising

Britain's population is more immediately accessible to the advertiser than elsewhere in Europe. Newspaper circulation was 477 per 1,000 of population in 1967 as against 328 in Germany and 248 in France. About 90 per cent of households have television receivers, almost all with access to the commercial channel, a much larger penetration than in Germany and France and about the same as the Netherlands. Spending on advertising is about 1·4 per cent of the GNP and has stayed about this level since 1960.

For 1970 the £546 m. spent on advertising was allocated over the media as in Table 2·8. Of the total, 70 per cent went to display advertising, 20 per cent to classified advertising and 10 per cent to

[2]   N.E.D.C. for the Distributive Trades, *A Look at Wholesaling*, 1970.

trade, technical and financial advertising. There has been a drift away from magazines and periodicals towards television, but television still claims only 35 per cent of the display budget.

TABLE 2.8 *United Kingdom advertising classified by media (1970)*

	£ millions
National newspapers	108
Regional newspapers	118
Magazines and periodicals	51
Trade and technical journals	53
Other publications	11
Press production costs	34
Total press	375
Television	125
Poster and transport	22
Outdoor signs	17
Cinema	6
Radio	1
	546

The British national newspapers have attained very large circulations for a combination of reasons – an emphasis on literacy in schooling, geographically compact populations, and a smaller number of newspapers than other western nations. Britain also has a high readership of magazines, although the levels for magazines and newspapers are gradually falling. The most remarkable thing about the United Kingdom magazine readership, though, is the large number of general and special interest magazines published weekly or monthly and their high circulation rates.

This wide readership has meant that advertising cost per 1,000 is lower in the United Kingdom than in any EEC country. The newspaper rates per 1,000 readers are about one-third of those in Germany and one-sixth of those in Italy.

Television viewing is a growing national pastime. Average household viewing is around $4\frac{1}{2}$ hours per day. The advent of colour television, and reductions in purchase tax on receivers will further boost viewing. In 1971, colour sets took off with about 1 m. purchased to give a total stock of $1\frac{1}{2}$ m. It has been forecast that by 1980, 50 per cent of homes will have a colour set. Those viewers with colour sets seem to view more than those with black and white, notice colour commercials more, and find them more compelling.

British television has three channels – BBC1, BBC2 and ITV. The BBC channels carry no paid advertising whatsoever and claim around 45 per cent of the viewing. The commercial television channel is controlled by the Independent Television Authority (ITA) which has divided the country into thirteen television areas, and allocated contracts to television companies in each. Hours of operation are roughly from 14.00 until 24.00 hrs. on weekdays and 12.00 to 24.00 hrs at weekends. These times are to be extended. Advertising conditions are set by the ITA and limit the amount of advertising to seven minutes each hour. In total, then, about one hour of commercials is transmitted each day. Advertisements must conform to ITA's strict code of standards. It is hard to compare costs but for network coverage for a given spot length they appear to be slightly cheaper than France and more expensive than Germany before allowing for differences in expected viewing.

There is as yet no commercial radio in Britain, though legislation has been passed permitting a chain of sixty local stations covering about 70 per cent of the population. Commercial radio broadcasts are beamed into Britain from Europe and, briefly in the late 'sixties, from pirate stations moored outside territorial waters.

Cinema-going, which was very high by European standards, has been steadily falling. Average weekly admissions fell from 5·6 m. in 1966 to 3·9 m. in 1970. Advertising in cinemas is thus of decreasing importance but still reaches a significant number of potentially less-distracted viewers.

Costs of advertising for all media are contained in a quarterly publication, British Rate and Data (BRAD), and details of actual spending in a monthly publication by Market Expenditure and Analysis Ltd. (MEAL), *The Monthly Digest*. So it is possible to be reasonably scientific about allocating an advertising budget and to get fairly reliable figures on competitor spending.

Sales promotion

'Below-the-line' promotions have grown into a £500 m. a year business, but this growth is slowing. In the 'fifties and early 'sixties promotions took the form of self-liquidating offers and cheap competitions. Current emphasis is on gift and coupon schemes and is more subdued. There is now more cooperation between manufacturers and retailers and pooling of information between manufacturers. Advertising agencies, having let this business slip, have made a come-back. Consumers are getting tired of promotions, which averaged 1,000 a month in groceries alone in 1970, and the redemption rates are dropping. A recent self-liquidator attracted 150 redemptions, but sold an additional 200,000 packs during its run. Self-liquidators are also getting more costly. £400 off a £1,200 emerald ring is a recent, extreme example. Banks, bookstores and petrol companies are increasing their expenditure on promotions to give their brands a competitive edge. Free samples and coupon trading have become very popular recently. Nielsen figures suggest that 1972 coupon redemptions will be some 250 m. as against about 23 m. in 1960. Twenty manufacturers account for 80 per cent of the coupons used, having an average redemption value of 3·4p.

Trading stamps now comprise a £30 m. per year market, dominated by Green Shield, with roughly a 60 per cent share, and Sperry & Hutchinson, with 10 per cent. The Co-operative Societies make up most of the other 30 per cent. Twenty-four million adults drawn from all socio-economic groups are claimed to collect Green Shield Stamps, and half the housewives in the country have had at least one gift. There is not much room for expansion of franchises as Green Shield and Sperry & Hutchinson now have some 35,000 outlets between them.

Transportation and storage

Though in a small country, British industry's total distribution cost is about 15 per cent of the ultimate selling price of its products. Marketers are becoming increasingly aware of transport costs and the scope for reducing them. The advantage that integrated large-scale retailers hold over the independents is particularly marked in transport. By controlling the ordering pattern of their branches they make more efficient use of their storage and transport facilities and the scale enables them to handle larger units loads.

Carriers have actively improved their services. Airline companies are carrying an increasing proportion of goods overseas. Currently some 14 per cent of British exports go by air, an increase from 6 per cent in 1961. The expansion of the motorway network has greatly benefited road hauliers and the maximum permitted size of their vehicles has increased. Labour problems delayed the introduction of containerization at the ports but there are signs that the parties to this dispute are coming to their senses. Various other unit load techniques, such as palletized loads and 'roll on/roll off' road vehicles, are increasingly used.

Inadequate and old-fashioned premises, both at the wholesale and retail level, impede the introduction of modern storage and handling techniques, which are discouraged by low wages. As elsewhere the large firms are the pacesetters, using computers to reorder automatically at retail and wholesale level and replacing old multi-storey warehouses with single-storey automated installations.

Standardization, branding and consumer protection

The annual reports of bodies like the Consumer Council (disbanded by the Government in 1971) and the Consumers' Association are depressing. True, they have been successful in their attempts to press suppliers to improve standards of products, of service and of fair trading. But most of their successes have been a culmination of long drawn-out battles against suppliers' and distributors' trade associations rather than a result of cooperation. It is hard to believe that some marketers have the consumer's interests at heart as they quibble over safety standards and struggle to prevent him from access to informative labels. With certain notable exceptions they have been less than enthusiastic over policing their own voluntary schemes and yet, sadly, when a British Standard is finally forced on them their protests dwindle away to nothing.

Parliamentary legislation is the main method by which standards are set. Recent legislation includes the Consumer Protection Act (1961), the Weights and Measures Act (1963), and the Trade Descriptions Act (1968). The British Standards Institution have been setting uniform specifications for a wide variety of items since the 'twenties, but are concerned with industrial rather than consumer goods. Their Kitemark label is widely accepted as a guarantee of quality. Suppliers often argue that development of grading and the establishment of standards will reduce consumers' choice. In some instances they feel that external standards are well below their own and are reluctant to use a standard mark. Both these impressions may well be true, but justice must not only be done, but be seen to be done.

Branding establishes a standard and at the same time differentiates one's own product from the competitors'. It is now spreading from groceries into most other consumer goods, but the enormous expense of establishing a brand name limits the opportunities. A survey in 1970 of thirty-four grocery products on which consumers spent just under £1,000 m. showed that 60 per cent of this turnover is in only ninety-one brands.

As products have become more complicated the balance of power has shifted towards the manufacturer. A laboratory is needed for adequate testing. Judgement and experience are insufficient. To counteract this shift, the Consumer Association was formed in 1956, and later, as a result of the Molony Report on consumer protection in 1962, the Consumer Council was set up by the Government in 1963. This council operated until 1971. The Press and Government maintain pressure on traders, and there are various voluntary schemes; for example, to have a uniform colour code for bottle tops on various types of milk. Retail Trade Associations have generally been reluctant to support these officially, and honest traders have suffered from the activities of their less scrupulous competitors.

Credit practices

The Crowther Report on credit, published in March 1971, surveyed the whole chaotic field of consumer credit and recommended new laws to govern all credit transactions. In 1969, new consumer credit to the value of £4·3 billion was extended, bringing the total outstanding to £12·8 billion. Building societies provided nearly £2 billion for house purchase, while banks, finance houses and retailers provided about £500 m. each. There has been a rapid rise in recent years in check trading, to £130 m. in 1969, in order to circumvent Government restrictions on instalment credit. Older forms of consumer lending such as moneylending and pawnbroking are falling behind and only accounted for £44 m. between them. Very little use is made of credit cards in the UK, and credit card business is minute relative to cheque business.

Outstanding debt on consumer goods in Britain is, as a proportion of disposable income, less than half of that of the United States. There is considerable confusion in the consumer's mind about true interest rates. A sample of retailers charged from 11 per cent in electrical showrooms to 29 per cent in furniture shops, but consumers almost always underestimated the rate they were paying. The Committee recommended a simplification of the whole system.

The marketers of the United Kingdom

Marketing has been recently discovered by much of British industry. A survey carried out in 1970 for the British Institute of Management[3], covering 500 of the 2,400 companies with an annual turnover above £750,000, showed that senior management in the largest

[3] British Institute of Management, *Marketing Organization in British Industry*, B.I.M. London, 1970.

UK companies knew that there was more to business than production and sales. To quote from the summary:

'Certainly there is evidence that managers in some industries have shown uneasiness and, on occasions, reluctance in the face of the marketing concept. This study, however, has served to demonstrate that the senior managers in a great many of the most important companies have an adequate awareness of the implications of marketing and have shaped their activities into a pattern which reflects the diversity of sophistication implicit in the operational implications of the concept.'

Awareness of marketing concepts has certainly changed over the last ten years, but there is still widespread misunderstanding about marketing. Beyond the pockets of thought among the more advanced marketers of branded consumer goods, it is most common to find marketing viewed as a grouping of the 'downstream functions' of the organization, after the factory has finished the product. Businessmen concerned with introducing marketing concepts into their firms often seize on the single move of changing the organization so that sales, advertising and market research functions report to a marketing director. In most cases there is no intention of opening the firm's entire decision-making procedures to the discipline of the marketplace.

One explanation of this is found in the pattern of professional education in the United Kingdom. For many years the professional engineering bodies provided the bulk of the design and production executives and the professional accounting bodies the bulk of the accounting and finance executives, while for sales and advertising executives is was unusual to find any professional preparation. To many, marketing was simply a new title for the sales and commercial group. The Institute of Marketing, which with about 16,000 members, is the largest professional marketing body, was for many years the Association of Sales Management and its change in title added little to the general impression of what marketing involved.

Within the higher education establishments of the United Kingdom, however, marketing courses are gradually becoming more common. A recent report on marketing from the National Economic Development Office summarized the picture as follows:

'Our overall impression is of a great variety of activity spread thinly over a large number of institutions. With management education taking place in many universities, polytechnics and colleges, and with specialist and professional courses being run on a local basis to cater for day release, part-time and evening students, a multiplicity of offerings is inevitable and possibly desirable.

'More advanced post-experience work, particularly combined with fieldwork in industry, is comparatively rare. In all sectors there is a serious teacher shortage.'

Some thirty universities offer courses leading to a diploma or master's degree which include a marketing component and almost as many offer undergraduate instruction. The polytechnics and colleges of further education offer many more places for those studying either for the National Diploma in Management Studies or for a degree in business studies through the Council for National Academic Awards.

These developments place marketing education in the United Kingdom ahead of the other EEC countries but still not at the point where employers widely require marketing education. The demand for short post-experience courses in marketing reflects a false belief that adequate training involves just a few weeks' study in 'modern business techniques'.

The demand for more marketing men is caused partly by the increased competitive edge of effective marketing, partly because of fashion, and partly from the tendency to change organizations away from a straight functional pattern. For ten years the standard consultant's advice in the United Kingdom has been to reorganize so that profit responsibility is traceable as far down the organization as possible, and to hold executives accountable against detailed profit plans. The resultant divisional and product line posts require executives who understand marketing, to plan their actions successfully and not simply lapse into budgeting figures with minor adjustments to current performance.

In contrast with the inadequate supply of general marketing management, the United Kingdom has many specialist marketers, particularly in advertising and market research. The highly developed sub-culture of advertising dates from the time when Lord Lever determined to copy the American mass merchandiser and Lintas, the Lever Bros. advertising agency, became the largest agency in the world.

The advertising men are concentrated in the central London agencies between the City and Hyde Park. They tend to have been to universities and wear an air of men steeped in culture and quality of life. They tend not to be quantitatively rigorous nor highly profit-oriented. The businessman dealing with them may find that he himself has to introduce all such down-to-earth calculations as the effect of advertising on sales and profits.

There are many agencies, but the top thirty account for two-thirds of the billings. J. Walter Thompson is the largest and, as with most of the leading agencies, now is linked with Madison Avenue in New York, though is almost exclusively British in staff.

With the levelling in advertising expenditure over the last two years, agencies have found business difficult. Mergers and takeovers have been rife among the medium-sized, non-specialist agencies. There is a move away from prestige activities, whether it be Mayfair office blocks or free services to clients, and better cost control. Employment in agencies in the Institute of Practitioners of Advertising has fallen from 20,000 in 1966 to 17,000 in 1970. Fees based on the services rendered are beginning to replace commissions on billings.

Marketing research is, like advertising, very highly developed by world standards. The Market Research Society focuses this sub-culture. Entry is not limited by examination, but the standard of professional competence among the 2,500 members is very high indeed. Market research in the United Kingdom has drawn heavily on economics and statistics graduates, with the peculiar result that competence in researching questions is often higher than the managerial competence in identifying what questions need to be asked. Europeans will recognize a tendency to place a higher value on the rigour of designing and carrying out research than on the apparently 'softer' exercise of wisdom in making a good diagnosis. Perhaps this reflects university curricula that lacked a basis of successful application.

The foreign firm entering the British market should easily obtain the market research competence it requires. Many consulting agencies capably provide services, from audits of television advertising and assessment of channel effectiveness to consumer sampling. Well known names include: Audits of Great Britain, A. C. Nielsen, British Marketing Research Bureau Ltd., Attwoods, and Retail Audits Ltd. If the foreign firm has difficulty it is more likely to be in finding high quality general marketing management to specify the questions – a scarce commodity throughout Europe.

Conclusion

In very many respects, then, the United Kingdom market is not only quite different from that of any of its EEC partners but also it is going through a period of rapid change. Institutions are changing as new forms of distribution and selling are developed to meet customers' needs. Wages and salaries are rising much more rapidly than prices. Increasing pressure is being exerted on manufacturers' and distributors' margins. Unable to pass on all cost increases to their customers, marketers are being forced to be more efficient and to be more cost conscious.

Customers are also becoming more sophisticated. Increased income means increased spending power, and the potential for such things as the more sophisticated consumer durables and leisure products is enormous. As the noise level in the market-place increases, tone and clarity of expression become more important than sheer volume of sound. Perhaps because he is better educated, perhaps because he has never experienced the rationing and queues of the 'fifties, the consumer of today is both more able and willing than his predecessors to discriminate.

The United Kingdom has seldom closed its markets to foreigners. Few countries import or export such a high proportion of their gross national product. As tariff barriers come down and taxation changes, the opportunities are there for those with the imagination to grasp, and the skill to develop, them.

D

The prospects for the UK economy

3

R. J. Ball

The object of this paper is to examine the possible development of the United Kingdom economy on the assumption that the UK becomes a member of the European Economic Community in 1973. This raises a series of questions about the capacity of the UK to deal with inflation and the balance of payments in the longer term, which are potential constraints on the UK rate of growth, as well as the extent to which joining the EEC will have a favourable effect on the underlying growth potential. To reach some answers to these questions it is necessary to understand both the position of the UK economy at the time of writing (March 1972) and the history of the economy in the recent past.

Why has Britain grown so slowly?

It is well known that the growth performance of the UK economy in the last twenty years has been manifestly poorer than the majority of other industrialized countries – certainly a great deal poorer than almost any country of comparable size. Roughly speaking it is worth dividing the last twenty years into two parts, the period up to 1966 and the subsequent six years. One reason for this is that the average growth rate over the first fourteen years was substantially higher than in the last six, something over 3 per cent per annum as against well under 2 per cent per annum.

If we look at the 1950s we see that on balance the performance of the UK was not demonstrably worse than that of the United States. Its subsequent performance was considerably worse than the United States particularly after the American tax cut of 1964. But to put the matter into some perspective it must be understood that in the years up to 1966 the average growth rate of the UK economy was greater than had been achieved over any other comparable period of time during the twentieth century. Indeed there is little evidence that the underlying growth rate was much higher during the period of expansion up to 1870, and considerably faster than that achieved in the period 1870–1914.

It is important at the outset to distinguish between the actual rate at which the economy has grown and the underlying rate of growth of productivity which is related to the potential rate of growth of output. Up to 1966 there is some reason to believe that, on balance, the actual average rate of growth was not far short of the rate of growth of productive potential, although this period was punctuated by periods of slow and periods of relatively fast growth. Since 1966, with the sole exception of 1968, the rate of growth has been unequivocally slow, and throughout this period almost continuously below the rate of growth of productive potential. As a result an ever widening gap has developed between the actual level of output and the potential level of output that the nation's resources can support. Consequently, unemployment has risen to an unprecedented postwar level that would hardly have been contemplated ten years ago.

Growth of productive potential

Even if we take the rate of growth of productive potential before 1966, it is still true that Britain has compared unfavourably with other countries. The explanation of this is not easy. Many economists have advanced particular reasons why this was the case. Some have pointed to the relatively low proportion of output invested in capital equipment. Britain, it is said, has been a society which has both publicly and privately consumed too large a proportion of its output. The solution to the problem is then seen as one of increasing the proportion of output saved in the long run. Others have laid stress on the problems created by a shortage of labour. This, it is said, has two implications. Firstly, as compared with other countries over the last twenty years, Britain has lacked a ready supply of labour that could be transferred from the agricultural and other sectors into the faster growing manufacturing industries. Secondly, the acute shortage of labour over much of the period has meant that the power of organized labour has been augmented and this has made it difficult to introduce labour-saving investments which would have increased the underlying rate of growth of productive potential. Industrialists themselves have often laid emphasis on the disincentive effects of the tax system, which have penalized entrepreneurial effort and influenced the allocation of scarce managerial resources between risky and safe enterprises. In addition, something has been made of the 'early starter' argument, which suggests that Britain has been at a disadvantage because of being first in the industrial field. A heavy weight of outdated capital equipment is seen to act as a deterrent to further investment and modernization. This, combined with a shortage of labour, has tended to mean that much capital investment has had to be of a deepening rather than a widening kind, which has resulted in a high capital cost in achieving given increases in output as compared to other countries.

As is often the case there is no doubt some element of truth in all these explanations. However, the long history of slow growth that has characterized the UK economy since before the turn of the twentieth century suggests that the growth problem lies deeper than any simple problem of investment or tax system, although appropriate changes in these factors may undoubtedly help in the right direction. Perhaps a clue is to be found in the fact that attitudes to change have not on the whole been those conducive to growth and expansion. Britain has been an extremely traditional and conservative society, with a strong anti-professional bias (amateurism being much prized) and in which achievement should be based on effortless superiority rather than the explicit publicity of hard work. In all this, the UK has been in marked contrast to the United States over several decades. What has perhaps been lacking is the flair of France, the self discipline of Germany or the rapid acceptance of new ideas which characterizes the American.

Hopeful signs

It is not important whether these speculations are precisely right. What is important is whether one accepts the proposition that growth is not purely an economic matter, but, as many studies of developing countries have shown, is fundamentally interrelated with the standards and values of society. Growth is therefore a matter more generally of what might be described as social engineering rather than simply of economic carrot and stick. It is difficult, even perhaps impossible, to prove the point, but it is important to bear it in mind. It does mean that simple economic changes will not themselves bring about a change in the underlying rate of growth unless the attitudes of labour, management, the universities and the public service change in sympathy.

My own view is that attitudes are changing in Britain although perhaps not as rapidly as some of us would like. The process of self-examination that started in the early 1960s has certainly led to a reappraisal not only at the level of individuals and organizations but also within government as a whole. But the process is almost inevitably slow. It is a matter not of a decade but of a generation. There is constant friction between older and established ideas and behaviour patterns and the new more technocratically oriented ideas where some general and workable compromise has yet to be achieved. We are still nowhere near equilibrium.

To me this means two things. Firstly, that the economy has great potential because it has such a long way to go in modernising itself in all aspects of business and public life. Secondly, that we cannot expect, in terms of the growth of countries like Japan and West Germany, an economic miracle in Britain in the immediate future. We can look for steady improvement but not for a revolution. But even a 1 per cent increase in the underlying rate of growth would be a welcome achievement. And there is every sign that this is coming. The changes that have already taken place have resulted in some considerable acceleration in the rate of productivity growth in recent years. Admittedly this has taken place in a period of growing and accelerating unemployment and it remains to be seen whether this rise in productivity is largely due to a substantial shakeout or whether it represents a fundamental change in the generation of productivity gains.

Problems with aggregate demand

These remarks apply to the underlying rate of growth. But of course since 1966 the actual rate of growth has been far below that of the potential and, as pointed out earlier, has resulted in substantial unemployment. This situation it must be emphasised has been largely self inflicted. As in the 1920s the preservation of a fixed exchange rate was the start of the trouble. The protection of the balance of payments became for a period the central objective to which growth was completely subordinated. This, added to the cautious attitude of successive Chancellors of the Exchequer to expanding the level of demand, resulted in a slower and slower rate of growth of actual output, while potential continued to rise relatively rapidly. At the time of writing there is no doubt about the enormous reserves of capacity and labour that wait to be activated by more appropriate aggregate demand policies. There is no doubt that in terms of physical resources Britain now has the potential for rates of growth of up to 5 per cent per year for two or three years to come. If all goes well she will enter the EEC on the crest of such an expansion. This will, of course, have implications for the balance of payments which are discussed separately overleaf.

The effect of EEC membership on UK growth

I do not myself believe that the advent of the UK into the enlarged EEC will in itself lead to any material effect on the UK underlying rate of growth of productive potential. Probably the most sensible position to take up is one of healthy agnosticism. I cannot myself find any compelling arguments for accepting that there is any prima facie case for expecting increased growth, and most of those so far put forward are open to severe criticism. It is worth considering some of them.

Much weight is placed on the enlarged market argument that on joining the Market the UK will now have access to a large home market of 300 million people. As a result, not only will there be export growth, but within this market it will be possible to realize greater economies of scale. There are a number of points to be made about this central argument.

The statement itself suggests an optical illusion. The UK is not now barred from this market. The issue is not whether one is in or out, but whether it will be possible for the UK to compete more effectively in that Market when the Common External Tariff is imposed and the UK is in the EEC. Thus the critical question is what is the effect of the equalization of the tariff? Since the average *ad valorem* tariff against the UK is only of the order of 7 per cent, put this way the step of joining the Market does not look in economic terms anything like as impressive as far as UK industry is concerned. The net effect on exports is roughly equivalent to a devaluation of the same order of magnitude which could hardly be described as a major impact. It is interesting that when the pound sterling was devalued by no less than 16 per cent in 1968 no one anticipated that this would have any major effects on economies of scale. Of course it is evident that the tariff change will benefit UK exporters in general, and obviously there will be substantial gains for many individuals. In addition, there will undoubtedly be some realignment of resources as a result of the changes in relative prices induced by the change in the tariff both ways. However, even the most optimistic estimates of these gains from trade, which are the static effects of the change, which have been made in the UK do not suggest that the gains from trade are likely to be very large.

The small size of the gains from trade is further indicated by an examination of the history of the member countries of the EEC since its inception. The economic theory of customs unions tells us the main gains from union will be derived from the increased application of the principle of comparative advantage, i.e. that member countries should concentrate more on those things in which their relative efficiency is greatest. The history of the EEC, however, suggests that both by product and by country the effect of the EEC has not been to concentrate uses of resources, but on the contrary to spread them more evenly throughout the market. Thus in relative terms the major gaining country in the EEC has been Italy and the major loser Western Germany, pivoting around the others. On balance the smaller countries seem to have done relatively better and the others relatively worse. If this pattern were to be followed in an enlarged EEC then one would expect to see Ireland, Denmark and Norway gaining in the market with the share of the UK in trade and production of the enlarged community struggling to keep up. Moreover, even in theory the argument about specialization becomes hard to sustain insofar as it is difficult to see in what one could describe the UK as having a comparative advantage. Important industries in the UK, like motors and chemicals, for example, would find it hard going, since the reduction of import tariffs is likely to have a severe effect on them.

Moreover, if we examine the current structure of British industry there is very little evidence that firms and industries that will be important in relation to EEC entry are actually operating under increasing returns to scale. After all, a genuine home market of nearly 60 million people with a comparatively high level of real income should be sufficient for most purposes. Large multinational companies in which the UK has a substantial stake such as ICI, Unilever and Shell are unlikely to be very much affected at all by the decision to enter the community in terms of scale. The real danger here for Britain is that in the long run entry will result in reallocation in Europe rather than in the UK. This problem is discussed below further.

On the other side of the coin it must be borne in mind that the average rate of protection in *ad valorem* terms for UK industry against the Market is over 11 per cent. On balance the degree of competitiveness of the Market countries in the UK should be increased relative to the UK's competitiveness in the Market. But this is, of course, precisely what many people want – increased competition to be imposed on UK manufacturers. However, as matters have turned out, the long relative recession that has persisted since 1966, has meant that most of the shaking out of labour and the streamlining of firms and organizations has probably taken place. It will go on for some time, but there is little reason to believe that as far as manpower is concerned most of the fat has not now been worked off.

None of this is to say that the UK is wrong to join the EEC– there are many sides to that issue. It is, however, to predict that as far as UK industry is concerned the outlook is likely to be a difficult one, with at best little change in the status quo and at worst an increased competition which will make life difficult for UK firms in the early years. A main concern here must lie in the potential psychological shock that many in the UK will suffer when they realize that joining Europe is not a panacea for all the ills of the UK economy over the last twenty years. Unfortunately, much of the pre-entry discussion has been in this vein. As will be argued later, however, the basic problems that the UK economy faces today will still be there.

What can we do about inflation?

The UK has experienced a rate of inflation since the war that has been substantially above the average of the industrial countries – so much so that the kind of inflation that has arisen is sometimes referred to as the English disease. Both the rate of inflation and the balance of payments have at different times acted as restraints on the rate of growth which has been adjusted either to slow down the rate of inflation or to improve the balance of payments. Manifestly the two constraints are linked together since a continuous tendency to outstrip the rest of Europe with price increases will lead to continuous long-term trouble with the balance of payments. In this section I discuss the rate of inflation and in the next the problem it poses for the balance of payments.

Diagnoses

Since the war, a wide variety of diagnoses has been offered to account for the rate of inflation in the UK. They are similar to those that have been put forward for other countries. For some the basic problem has been that the supply of money has not been properly controlled. For them inflation is in a significant sense a monetary problem which therefore can be solved by the appropriate manipulation of the money supply, following the well-known work of Professor Milton Friedman. A second group of economists and commentators has argued that inflation has been caused not so much directly by a failure to regulate the money supply but by the existence of overfull employment which has created excessive pressure in the labour market. The result, it is said, is that wage increases have

outstripped productivity increases by a wide margin. For the supporters of this view, the solution to the inflation problem is simply to
maintain a larger margin of spare resources and excess capacity
than would be desirable on other grounds. At one time in the middle
'60s this margin was estimated to be relatively small (assuming that
is a meaningful statement) probably something of the order of
$2\frac{1}{2} - 3$ per cent of the labour force unemployed, compared to a
figure of something over 1 per cent unemployed at record postwar
levels. For the advocates of this view a moderately slacker labour
market provided a simple cure to the UK's inflationary ills. Finally
a third group laid the responsibility for inflation firmly at the door
of organized labour which was postulated to exercise a particular
form of monopoly power. This view not only has substantial support
in the UK itself but has often appealed to those outside the UK who
have characterized British industry by its proneness to strikes, the
restrictive practices of trades unions etc., which not only have been
inflationary but which have also led to delay in export deliveries,
particular difficulties for multinational companies such as Ford in
the car market and so forth. Those who give substance to this view
can be divided into those who believe it and are basically sympathetic to the trades union movement and those who believe it and are
not. The first group sees the only solution to inflation coming
through some accord with organized labour while the second is more
likely to be in favour of curbing labours powers primarily through
some form of appropriate legislation whatever that might be. In
this context the Industrial Relations Act passed by the present
Government carries a number of hopes. I doubt myself whether it
is going to have much effect either way.

   Once again there are elements of truth in all the arguments.
Monetary restraint within limits is certainly a necessary condition
for the control of inflation, but it is doubtful whether it can be
effective in any long term sense unless accompanied by a socially
undesirable level of unemployment. Moreover, the experience of
the UK in recent years has cast considerable doubt on the proposition
that only a moderately slack labour market might do the trick,
particularly when we observe a record rate of inflation in 1971
coupled with a record level of unemployment and a 1 per cent rise
in the national output. Proponents of this view have been hastily
looking round for ad hoc reasons to explain this curious situation
while still preserving the view that in the longer run the relationship
between inflation and unemployment that appeared to exist before
will be restored. Thus while many talk of expansion the fear still

exists that it will only refuel the inflationary fire. There is little doubt that prior to 1966 a relationship between unemployment and wage movements existed in the short run, although whether it exists in the longer run is open to substantial doubt.

Possible solutions

My own view about this is that inflation at full employment or a socially acceptable level of unemployment is inevitable in the absence of some accord between organized labour and the Government. The fundamental problem is not simply one of controlling the money supply or keeping a slack labour market, but is related to the problem of equitably distributing the gains from productivity that occur, over the community at large, in a world in which prices are largely inflexible downwards and wages are flexible upwards. With inflexible prices the arithmetic of the problem is straightforward enough – if price stability is to be achieved on average the money wages of those in industries where productivity is rising fastest have to rise less than the increase in productivity, and in those industries where productivity is rising slowest they have to rise faster. This question of equity is not simply a matter of economics, it is a political fact with which governments of all persuasions have to deal. Any solution to it must be as much a political one as an economic one – there are a number of solutions, many of which are relatively arbitrary and most of which are currently unacceptable to one side or the other.

There is, however, another hypothesis which has not yet been put to the test, that suggests that in the longer run, inflationary pressure is the result not of excessively fast rates of growth and pressure on scarce resources, but on the contrary results from a real income frustration derived from the fact that the long term rate of growth has been too slow. This hypothesis may be set out as follows. Suppose that at any given period of time there is some 'normal' expectation with regard to the growth of real wages. If the actual rate of growth of real wages falls below this norm, then organized labour bargains harder for increases in money wages to achieve the increase in real wages required. In 1970, for example, despite the slow rate of output growth, real disposable income actually rose at about twice the rate with a concomitant sharp fall in the share of profits in the national income. Over certain periods at any rate the hypothesis that unions cannot raise real wages holds little water even if in the long run it is true. The rather special circumstances of

1970 may be attributed to the emergence of this real income growth frustration which was given a licence by the withdrawal of the Wilson government from an active incomes policy toward the end of 1969.

As far as the short run is concerned, there is no doubt that faster growth in the UK, with the consequent effect on unit labour costs would help materially to reduce this kind of inflationary pressure. Whether it would do so in the longer run depends on whether an economy with a faster rise in real wages would reduce the scramble for existing productivity increases and therefore serve to keep money wages more in line with productivity. I must confess to being personally very unsure about this outcome, since while faster growth should reduce the general feeling of real income frustration it may also open up the gap between the haves and the have-nots as the dispersion in productivity increases gets larger. For this reason faster growth may not solve the problem entirely, but it would at least serve to provide a better basis on which government might seek some accord with labour. Thus the faster rate of growth to be expected in the UK over the next three years or so should certainly serve to check the record rate of inflation we have experienced recently, indeed the modest pick up in output in the middle of 1971 was associated with a marked slowing down in the inflation rate. One thing I am sure of, in disagreement with many others no doubt, is that a background of faster growth is one which offers the most hope in arriving at more sensible ways of distributing the national productivity gains than through inflation. The period ahead offers, therefore, more opportunity than we have had in the recent past.

What will happen to the balance of payments?

At the the time of writing (March 1972) the UK has just completed a year with the largest surplus on its current account since the war. The turn round in the balance of payments that has taken place is only partly attributable to the devaluation of the pound sterling in 1967. The improvement in the balance of payments is also due to the fact that for the first time since the war the UK has been growing slowly at a time when world trade was expanding rapidly. Thus a large part of the improvement has been bought at the cost of the high level of unemployment that now exists.

A useful concept to bear in mind here, is that of the 'equilibrium exchange rate'. When the IMF charter was drawn up, the equilibrium exchange rate was conceived of as that rate required to balance the books on current account but making allowance for normal long term capital flow. On this definition it is likely that even at the present time the UK balance of payments would not be in equilibrium at full employment, if we define that as being something like 2 per cent of the labour force. The expansion in output to be expected over the next two years or so coupled with the lagged effects of the abnormally high rate of inflation relative to its competitors should see the disappearance of the current account surplus that now exists. If we add to this problem the impact of entry into the EEC on the current balance it is almost certainly true that a deficit in the account would appear at the 2 per cent unemployment level if not before.

The short run

The impact of EEC entry on the balance of payments will, of course, be spread over time, both with regard to tariff changes and with regard to the costs of entry to be paid. The short run effects will almost certainly be adverse, although perhaps not as dramatic as some commentators in the UK have supposed. At best they do not make the problem of the UK balance of payments any easier, the basic immediate problem being related to the possible return to full employment. The question is: given this situation, what is to be done about it?

It should be emphasized that this problem exists quite apart from any ensuing difficulties that may emerge from a failure to prevent UK prices from rising faster than those in the Community at large in subsequent years. There must be some presumption that our competitive position will slowly deteriorate on present policies on top of the full employment problem. The solutions available are probably limited to either delaying or preventing the return to full employment or making a further change in the exchange rate. Each of these solutions, however, presents its own set of problems. If the growth rate is to be once again limited by the need to prop up the current balance the UK will be back in the vicious circle from which it has been attempting to find courage to get out of for the last ten years. To pursue such a policy would in my view constitute a major national failure and would undoubtedly create substantial political difficulties for the government of the day. With an election due in Britain in 1975, or before, it is unlikely that either political party would want to go into such an election on a platform of restraint to protect the external balance. From a domestic point of view the arguments in favour of changing the exchange rate are inescapable.

The long run

The position is, however, complicated by the attitude of the Community to exchange rate changes after entry. It is the declared policy of the Community at present to proceed towards monetary union and France in particular has made clear her opposition to any kind of flexible rate system between EEC members. There is both a short and a long-run problem here. The short-run problem is how to deal with the likely British difficulties that will emerge as a dual consequence of entry and a return to full employment. The longer-run problem relates to how any future balance of payments difficulties are to be dealt with. With regard to the short-run problem, no doubt members of the Community might be prepared to negotiate some transitional arrangement which would involve a once for all further devaluation of the pound. The long-run problem, however, is likely to prove more serious.

Perhaps some of us in the UK are too pessimistic about the long-term future of the UK balance of payments. But it would seem sensible on the basis of historical experience to suppose that the probability of further balance of payments difficulties for the UK after entry is quite high. In a monetary union with the objective of moving toward a common currency there would be no scope for exchange rate changes thereby limiting the ways in which any deficit might be eliminated. Within an area with a common currency potential 'payments' imbalances are effectively met by the transfer of real resources from one region to another. This, of course, gives rise to familiar problems of regional imbalance and development. The worry from a purely UK point of view is that if efficiency differentials cannot be eliminated by adjusting the exchange rate, the problem will be met by a transfer of real resources from the UK to the continent of Europe.

From some points of view, however, it might be argued that this is essentially what being European in an economic sense is all about. If Europe is genuinely to be a single market the flow of resources around that market should be quite free. In one sense the French commitment to a monetary union is a completely logical development if economic union in the long run is to be achieved. Whether it is to Britain's own self interest is another matter. The outsider looking in is more entitled to be optimistic about the capacity of the UK to deal with its balance of payments problems with a flexible exchange rate system than in the context of, at minimum, a fixed rate with other community currencies.

An international problem

It is doubtful if these issues are going to be settled in isolation from the problem of the relationship between the Community and the rest of the world. The UK, unlike other members of the Community, has had substantial interests in other parts of the world particularly in the Commonwealth. The UK record of trade growth with her traditional Commonwealth partners has been extremely disappointing over the last decade. Despite being formally outside the Community of the six, the UK's trade with the Community has been the fastest growing compared with both the dollar area and the Commonwealth. As far as the Commonwealth is concerned the main competition has come from the Japanese and there is every reason to believe that this will continue. Insofar as Japanese trade with the United States is going to be affected by the determination of the United States to put her own balance of payments in order, Japan will inevitably seek to expand its markets elsewhere by way of compensation. Europe as a whole has already shown some nervousness at the prospect of increased Japanese competition and no doubt the UK will come under further increased competition from Japan nearer to home.

The future role of Government

The future development of the UK economy is clearly going to be affected by the way in which Government is going to see its role in the foreseeable future, and as part of the background to the UK economy some comments on this are in order. This is not simply a political matter relating to which government, Labour or Conservative, is in power, since there are forces that operate both in connection with the way that economic decisions are taken and with the fact that the middle ground is where the essential political battles take place. In Britain governments ostensibly of the left start on the left and move to the right and the reverse is true for those that start ostensibly on the right.

Increasing government intervention

Historically the UK economy like many others has passed from the simple view that Government is concerned solely with equity and social efficiency in the use of resources to the acceptance of wider responsibilities for the general level of employment and the rate of economic growth. Government responsibility for the general level of employment is based on the acceptance of fundamentally Keynesian principles relating to the way in which the general level of economic activity is determined at a point of time. The emergence of Government responsibility for the rate of growth is clearly also related to this, but as a specific objective really only stems from the late 1950s.

The emergence of this objective has focused attention, of course, on the fact that general demand management policies may have only a tenuous connection with what determines the underlying rate of growth of productive potential. This fact was partially recognized in Britain by the Conservative government in 1962 when it set up the National Economic Development Council which was intended to look at longer-run issues connected with economic growth. What was partially recognized here was that growth is tied up not only with demand management policies but also with far reaching problems of economic structure. This trend was accelerated by the Labour government after 1964, which began to extend government activity in a more interventionist way into other areas of business. The Prices and Incomes Board and the Industrial Reorganization Corporation are both examples of the product of this trend. The PIB, starting as essentially a body dealing with prices and wages, ended up as a body whose activities extended into making 'efficiency' reports into particular industries. The IRC was set up to promote mergers and industrial rationalization which resulted in some substantial action. All this could be regarded as new in so far as Government was now extending its activities along paths it had not trodden before.

The importance of the 'middle ground'

By 1970 this rather more dirigiste approach to the problem of growth had fallen somewhat into disfavour, and the new Conservative government was pledged to a substantial withdrawal from intervention over a wide front. This applied to the role of Government in interfering with prices and wages, its attitude toward reducing public expenditure where possible, and its broad belief that industry should on the whole stand on its own feet, exposed more to the winds of competition and to the laws of the market place. In practice the familiar process of shifting back toward the middle ground is taking place at the time of writing although no doubt the Government would deny it. The issue is open to further public debate and has not crystallized over the broad front. It is important in so far if one believes that the underlying rate of economic growth can only be altered by governmental intervention on a wide scale then the future drift of events is important in relation to the economic prospects of the economy. The view of these issues given here must therefore inevitably be a personal one.

As pointed out above, the tendency of governments in Britain is to move to the middle ground. Paradoxically some of the most liberal steps have been taken by Conservative governments and on occasion the most conservative actions have been taken by Labour. The present Conservative government was largely committed to some substantial reduction in the role of government against a background of improving the general framework within which private enterprise could flourish, e.g. by reducing the burden of direct taxation. I doubt myself, however, whether any government is going to be able to reduce materially the role of the state. It was, in fact, the last Labour Government that brought public expenditure under control, but already one can see some signs that it is going to be difficult to hold spending steady or to reduce materially its share of the GNP. However much one may be in sympathy with the tax changes that are proposed at present, it is doubtful whether changes of this kind alone can bring about a fundamental shift in the rate of productivity growth. While many of the interventionist policies briefly referred to above were ill thought out and often too ambitious, I believe myself that the climate they generated and the self appraisal that they encouraged in companies may well have had effects in focusing on the need for improved efficiency, some of the fruits of which may now be about to appear.

Given this tendency to the middle ground it is likely that in different forms and guises governments will find it necessary, both because of the political climate and on analytical grounds, to move back to the kind of ideas about structural change that have been common over the last ten years. There is a need to strike a proper balance between the rule of the market place and the social interest in more than just the macro-economics of economic growth. The problem from a British point of view may be that the achievement of the latter will be more difficult for Britain in an enlarged economic community in so far as harmonization of domestic policies (which must emerge if a full economic union is to be achieved) becomes a reality. It is therefore going to be important for Britain that a substantial freedom exists in the hands of government to interfere at a micro economic level if it thinks fit. There is no solid reason to suppose that this will not be the case, but the issue needs to be borne in mind if the UK Government continues to accept a large measure of responsibility for economic growth.

E

Towards the future

Growth

Earlier in this essay the point was made that the expectations of
many with regard to the effects of the UK joining the EEC would be
frustrated in part because the problems that face Britain today
would in large part still exist. It has already been argued that slow
growth in Britain in the last six years has been due to a combination
of deliberately sacrificing the rate of growth of output to the balance
of payments and inflation on the one hand, and the protection of
the exchange rate on the other. Joining the EEC as such will have
very little direct or immediate effect on these issues. The economic
outcome will still depend very largely on the independent policies
pursued by the British Government, in the field of demand management, exchange rate policy and structural change.

The exchange rate

The exchange rate question has been already discussed above, and
it is crucial to the immediate future of the economy. For the first
time in recent years, the Chancellor of the Exchequer in his budget
speech in March of this year proclaimed the intention of making
growth a priority objective not to be constrained by the main-
tainance of an inappropriate exchange rate. He must be the first
British Chancellor since the war to nail his flag to this particular
masthead, and while changing the rate may be easier said than done,
the expressed intention gives one the hope that when the moment of
truth comes, common sense in these matters will prevail.

The structural background

The structural background against which British industry will
operate over the immediate future, its industrial relations, competition policy, etc. are discussed in other papers given to this meeting.
Perhaps, however, what the present government, and the Chancellor
of the Exchequer in particular, may be best remembered for at the
end of the day is as a tax-reforming government and a tax-reforming
Chancellor respectively. There are three aspects of the tax reform
policies that are currently being pursued in the UK and which one
anticipates will continue to be pursued in the near future. The first
of these concerns the general level of direct taxation which is regarded
as inhibiting at the margin to both enterprise and economic growth.
This is essentially an efficiency argument for reducing the burden of

taxation, and there is a large literature on both sides of this question that has grown up over the years. My own personal position is to be sympathetic to the view that current high marginal rates of taxation distort the allocation of managerial resources and reduce their mobility in an undesirable way. It must be emphasized that this view is highly subjective. I find it difficult, however, to foresee any dramatic changes in the impact of such a reduction in the direct tax burden on the rate of growth of output. Secondly, the current tax reform programme will greatly simplify the tax system, a development that is to be welcomed on all sides and from almost every point of view. It should make the tax system easier to understand and easier to administrate. Again, however, it is doubtful whether this will have any dramatic effect on the economy, significant though it is in its own right. Thirdly, the tax reform programme is a first step in the direction of harmonizing British fiscal policy with that of EEC members, notably as a beginning by the introduction of the Value Added Tax which will come into force in 1973. On balance this move is perhaps less revolutionary than it might have been, since the present object of the exercise is to replace the collection of certain sums from one form of indirect taxation by the same sums collected from another. Clearly, the changes in relative prices that will take place will affect both the pattern of spending and the use of resources. But there was also the possibility that the change might be used to change the balance between direct and indirect taxation. On balance more use is made in Europe of direct as opposed to indirect taxation, but there are views in Britain that suggest that a shift from direct taxation to indirect taxation might be better from the point of view of encouraging saving and enterprise even though the move might also be considered regressive. At present, however, there seems no intention to go this far. These changes must be borne in mind as part of the backcloth against which the story of the UK economy over the next few years will unfold.

The prospect

Given a more flexible attitude to exchange rate policy, and the programme of tax reform just discussed, the future will depend on the success of conventional demand management policies, a more satisfactory way of dealing with the inflation problem, and the style of government in dealing with the underlying process of structural change. At the time of writing, the Government has the enormous, if from several points of view unwelcome, advantage of an economy with vastly under utilized resources. The commitment to long-term productive investment by industry will primarily be governed by the credibility of the Government's long-term commitment to steady growth, solving balance of payments and inflationary problems as they arise. Here the exchange rate and a form of incomes policy will be of major importance. As already indicated the latter is as much a political as an economic matter and no one possesses a magic formula for dealing with the problem. To find some acceptable way of doing so is going to depend on the kind of political leadership that the government of the day can give and the recognition that purely economic forces alone cannot solve the problem. This the Government has already implicitly recognized by its support of the voluntary price restraint policy pursued by the Confederation of British Industry. The issue is probably going to turn on whether a voluntary prices and incomes policy can be encouraged without direct Government intervention or whether at the end of the day more direct interference by the government will be required. I believe that a voluntary policy by itself will not be sufficient in the longer run, and that some more formal and official mechanism will be necessary to bring employers, unions and the State, together to thrash out some compromise.

Since so many aspects of these issues are in the political rather than in the purely economic domain, prediction of the longer term future from a purely economic point of view is impossible. Like the Prime Minister, I believe that, for rather different reasons perhaps, Britain stands on the threshold of great opportunity. But it is not an opportunity borne solely of the entry into an enlarged EEC. It derives also from the opportunity for positive economic government based on a large volume of unused resources, and a firm and unyielding commitment to the objective of economic growth in Britain.

Industrial relations in the UK

4

Tom Lupton

Introduction

In the UK discussions of industrial relations are now dominated by speculation about the eventual impact of the Industrial Relations Act (1971). Apparently, the Act signals the end of the 'voluntarism' that has characterized the British system of collective bargaining for over a century, and the beginning of legal regulation. In the following section I examine the structure and functioning of the UK institutions of collective bargaining before the Act, the intentions of the Act and the machinery set up to express them. Events will no doubt confound any estimate of the extent to which the legislation will fulfil its framers' intentions. However, I shall hazard a guess at the future impact of the Act.

Collective bargaining between unions and employers about wages and conditions, whether it takes place on the shop floor or at the national bargaining table, does not exhaust Industrial Relations in the UK (or anywhere for that matter). The nature of the relationships that men enter into in manufacturing and service enterprises, their different jobs, how they are managed, the non-pecuniary rewards they receive, and many other things, influence their content or discontent with their jobs, their productivity and their commitment to the enterprise. Many UK companies have embarked and are embarking on plans to improve job-interest and labour productivity and to enhance the industrial worker's status.

I therefore approach the subject of industrial relations at two different but related levels. I shall show that they are related in many interesting ways.

The institutions of industrial relations
The Trade Unions

British trade union membership is now about 10 million. The largest unions account for about 60 per cent of this membership.

Following the usual formal classification of unions, a *craft union* is chiefly distinguished by its members being workers whose high skills are easily transferable from one industry or service to another; for example fitters, electricians, plumbers and draughtsmen. The *industrial union* organizes all workers in the same industry regardless of craft or occupation. The *general union* is a union which recruits members of any occupation or in any industry.

Although these formal distinctions are still made, the craft union has evolved towards a membership which includes workers other than craftsmen. For example, the largest of them, the Amalgamated Union of Engineering and Foundry Workers, has several grades of membership from the unskilled to the most highly skilled craftsmen and in many companies including clerical supervisory and technical workers. Craft unions in Britain now resemble the general unions' width and scope of membership. The description 'industrial union' still fits the National Union of Mineworkers, the National Union of Railwaymen, and the British Iron and Steel and Kindred Trades Association (BISAKTA).

The formal distinctions are rapidly eroding because of technical change, the emergence of new occupations, and shifts of power among large, and between large and small, unions. Yet each type of union still bears the marks of its past. Craft unions retain their identification with the craft tradition. Their leaders tend still to be skilled craftsmen. The general unions, e.g. Transport and General Workers Union, and General and Municipal Workers, retain the marks of their origins as amalgamations of small unions of unskilled and semi-skilled workers.

Total membership of the trade unions has remained fairly steady for many years; its composition has, however, changed greatly. The textile unions, for example, have declined dramatically, while others such as the white collar unions, have rapidly increased. Miners and railwaymen have lost the commanding position they once had. But the massive changes in the structure of occupations in the UK over the past twenty or thirty years are not reflected exactly in the membership of trade unions, because of the British trade union movement's curious structure and the fact that only half the working force is organized.

The movement still lacks a clear logical framework. Unions have emerged and have responded to technical and economic and social changes by widening their occupational and industrial base. Unions have also tended, and still tend, to merge, to amalgamate and to federate, taking in new categories of occupations and groups from other industries. This has led to a bewildering diversity of organization structures and principles; also a concentration of power.

The theory of union democracy

However much British trade unions differ in their organization structure, origins, traditions and customs, and however much they may compete for increased membership, they are united in adhering to a theory of trade union democracy. In British trade unions, the officers are considered to be the servants of the rank and file members.

The organization structure of unions

All British trade unions have a system of branches, and representatives at the place of work (shop stewards), who may or may not be branch officials. Many shop stewards are members of district committees even though they are not officials of branches.

All except the smallest unions have executive committees at national level whose task is to carry out the members' wishes expressed at union national conferences. Larger unions employ full-time professional officers at every level except, in some cases, at branch and workshop. The officers at national or district, branch, and workshop level, whether full-time or part-time, paid or unpaid, will mostly be concerned with negotiations with employers or with employers' associations, or dealing with their members' grievances.

The Trades Union Congress (TUC)

British trade unions are very jealous of their independence. The unions voluntarily affiliated to the TUC regard it as a servant, not a master; the TUC therefore possesses few executive powers, and is largely seen as a provider of services and advice, and a voice on matters affecting all unions. Formally, the TUC is the annual assembly of delegates from affiliated unions, usually meeting at a British seaside resort in September. The number of a union's delegates relates to its size; the larger unions have a bigger say when the 'block votes' are cast on resolutions before the Congress. These resolutions from the individual unions, express their views on national questions, particularly economic questions. The voting on these resolutions gives a rough guide to the trade unions' mood. The General Council of the TUC is composed of representatives of trade unions from various sectors of the economy.

The TUC administration is headed by a permanent General Secretary, currently Mr Victor Feather. The General Secretary is a powerful figure; he is in close and continuous touch with the Government and with employers of national associations like the Confederation of British Industry. He is not elected but usually appointed after service in the TUC bureaucracy at Congress House in London.

The Economic Division of the TUC is staffed by professional economists. Its views are influential. Other divisions include education, international relations and production. Important is the special sub-committee dealing with disputes between unions, particularly with areas of jurisdiction and the poaching of members. Because of the structure of the movement these disputes occur frequently. There may be many competing unions in a single industry, company or plant; but as we shall see the Industrial Relations Act may change this.

The TUC does not negotiate with employers to establish wages and conditions in the economy or in any particular industry. It does not itself engage in disputes with employers. Indeed, it is often called in to mediate in disputes between unions, and sometimes in disputes between unions and employers. During recent disputes such as the strikes of postmen and miners, Mr Feather often appeared as a kind of conciliator in discussions between the parties.

It would be entirely mistaken then to view the British trade union movement as an authority heirarchy with the TUC on the top and the individual union branches at the bottom, with varying ranks and orders in between. Reality would be more closely represented were the pyramid turned on its head.

Employers' associations

Little is publicly known about the structure of these associations but it is estimated that they now cover more workers than do the unions; their members are companies and not individuals. The Engineering Employers' Federation is the best known and the largest such Federation. Until recently when the national machinery for collective bargaining was dismantled the EEF negotiated at national level with the engineering unions to establish basic wages and conditions for the industry, leaving the districts, the regions and local employers to negotiate special additions to the basic rate. Most employers' associations are known to act in this way; that is, to settle together with the unions a set of minima upon which more detailed local negotiations can be based.

The Confederation of British Industries is a national association of employers and employers' associations which acts for employers in a similar way as the TUC does for unions. It does not negotiate wages and conditions but provides services and acts as a spokesman and representative of the employers in Great Britain. Like the TUC, the CBI is usually consulted by governments about economic policy and it will express what it believes to be the beliefs and opinions of employers as a whole.

Industrial relations and politics

Unlike some of their continental counterparts, the British trade unions have no institutional links with religion; nor have the employers' associations. British trade unions are linked with the Labour Party. The Labour Party grew in the late nineteenth century out of an affiliation of unions and certain small socialist societies. Nowadays individual members of trade unions may subscribe, through their union, to the unions' political fund. The unions are required by law to keep this separate from the industrial funds. They may, by law, subscribe to political parties. Most unions subscribe to the Labour Party and in consequence they have a voice at the Conference of the Labour Party each year; a very powerful voice, in fact.

Unions sponsor Labour candidates for Parliament in the constituencies. Many trade union officers and members now sit as MPs, all of them on the Opposition benches. The employers and their associations are not linked in this direct way to the Conservative Party, but each individual company may subscribe to political parties. In fact, many subscribe to the Conservative Party. Both the unions and the employers are represented in their official capacity in a wide range of government committees; for example, the National Economic Development Council and the Industry Training Boards. At local level it is quite common to find trade union officials on Hospital Management Committees, local government committees and in public administration generally; and in local Government as councillors and aldermen, and as lay magistrates in local courts.

The machinery of collective bargaining

Many industries have national bargaining machinery. Each year, or even more frequently, an industry's union will prepare a claim for improved wages and conditions which they will submit in writing to the employers' association. The parties then meet, usually to discuss the employers' written rejection. Bargaining then begins and continues until some settlement is reached; sometimes, but not often, at the point where unions threaten openly to strike or the employers openly to operate a lockout. The settlement is usually about minimum rates and conditions; necessarily so, since one cannot argue at national level about the details of local payments and conditions. The engineering industry was early to set up a national bargaining system and a national procedure for avoiding disputes, a procedure allowing disputes to be passed from the factory floor to a national body for settlement. However, in large sections of British industry company bargaining is the rule. This also applies now in the engineering industry. Recently, the national machinery has been set aside after a fruitless attempt to get agreement to reform it. The Ford Motor Company, ICI and the British Electricity Authority, operate company bargains where the unions in the industry negotiate with company representatives, not with employers' associations.

Until the recent passing of the Industrial Relations Act, all bargains struck between employers and unions were voluntary in the sense that they did not carry the force of law. Nothing in the old law prevented negotiators from declaring that agreements were contracts enforceable at law, but there are very few examples. The typical British collective bargain, whether struck at national level or local level, does not yet resemble a legal document but rather a set of understandings to guide the parties until the next claim. Typically, agreements do not state a duration. Claims may be lodged at almost any time and frequency. In the past two or three decades, national annual claims have been the rule rather than the exception.

British collective bargaining has much flexibility, since usually minimum wages and conditions only are specified nationally, leaving local bargainers scope to exploit the position they find themselves in. Successful efforts could, of course, become the basis of further national claims. The voluntarism and the flexibility of these arrangements are claimed as virtues by most senior trade union spokesmen and some managers. Union leaders have, almost without exception, resented the moves both by the recent Labour and the present Conservative governments to impose a legislative framework. At this moment the TUC and most of its affiliated unions are resisting cooperation in working the Act.

The Industrial Relations Act 1971

Strikes and the Act

Britain is not near the top of the league table in time lost through strikes but increases in small unofficial and unconstitutional strikes, leap-frogging wage claims from uncoordinated plant bargaining and the growing power of unions in full employment conditions, gave rise to unease about machinery of collective bargaining and the structure of British industrial relations. Those who argued for the introduction of a legislative framework also pointed out that the British system of industrial relations encouraged militants at the shop-floor level to break national agreements. Negotiating minima at national level and leaving local bargainers to make additions led, they added, to a push on wage costs, adding to inflation. This in its turn affected Britain's balance of payments adversely.

Others claimed that union officers had no control over their members and could not guarantee that the bargains that they were making would be honoured. Over to the political right, critics argued that in conditions of prolonged full employment too much power had accrued to the unions, a power used indiscriminately to disrupt industrial life.

All this, it was argued, made necessary a legal framework; some method of establishing legal rules and precedents for bringing order to replace the imputed anarchy of British industrial relations.

Before discussing the Act we must say something of the role played by Government in the system of industrial relations. The British Ministry of Labour (now the Department of Employment), and its predecessors, have for at least seventy years played a positive part in industrial relations, either as 'holder of the ring' or, more recently, under both Conservative and Labour governments, by actively intervening in its processes. The Department of Employment operates a conciliation service and will provide independent arbitrators at the request of deadlocked negotiators. Under the incomes policies operated by successive governments, the Department actively vetted collective bargains submitted to them according to the rules or guidelines laid down by Parliament.

The Industrial Relations Act

Intervention of Government in industrial relations is therefore not new in the UK. Unions and employers have lived through eight decades of more or less active intervention; indeed they have made very full use of the machinery and the expertise provided. The Industrial Relations Act, however, provides new principles to govern the conduct of employees, employers and Unions. The Act is probably best described as an attempt:

(a) to correct abuses; particularly against the individual worker by his employer or his union;

(b) to give legal redress to workers against unfair practices both by employers and by unions;

(c) to promote the legal regulation of collective bargains;

(d) to promote the speedy and just settlement of disputes; and

(e) to improve the practice of industrial relations in British companies.

What follows is a bald, but fairly complete, summary of the main provisions of the Act.

Unfair practices

The Act enlarges some individual rights. Here are some typical examples:

(a) Before the Act, closed shop agreements between unions and companies sometimes required a worker to be a member of a particular union before he could get a job. The 1971 Act confers upon every individual not only the right to belong but also the right *not* to belong to a trade union. It therefore puts an end to 'pre-entry closed shop' agreements.

(b) Before the Act, the individual worker had no appeal in law against his employer if he thought that he had been unfairly dismissed, although he might enjoy the protection of his union. Now he has the right to appeal to an industrial tribunal for redress.

(c) Under The Contracts of Employment Act of 1963 the worker was given rights to notice of termination of his employment; this employer had to provide him with written information about his contract of employment. The amended Act improves these rights.

(d) Before the Industrial Relations Act became law, the employee had no right in law to access to information about the economic performance of the organization which employed him. He has now the right to receive at least annual statements about his organisation.

(e) If an employer attempts to influence an employee not to join a trade union, or having joined not to take part in its activities, he, the employee, may seek redress from an industrial tribunal or from the National Industrial Relations Court set up under the Act.

(f) An employer who attempts to infringe an employee's right not to join a trade union may be proceeded against under the Act; so may an employer who refuses to employ an individual because of his membership or non-membership of a union.

(g) If anyone tries to influence a party to a collective agreement, which is a legally-enforceable contract, to break that agreement his action may be construed as an unfair industrial practice.

(h) Under the Act a trade union is defined rather strictly; it is any organization of workers registered with the Registrar of Trade Unions. Any group of people may, however, organize and not register with the Registrar and still enter into agreements with employers. All organizations of workers whether or not they are, strictly speaking, trade unions may commit unfair industrial practices. For example, they may attempt to induce an employer not to enter into an agency shop agreement after a ballot has shown a majority of employees to be in favour of one.

An agency shop is something quite new in British industrial relations. An agency shop agreement is one which makes it a condition of employment that those covered by the agreement must either belong to the registered trade union concerned or must be prepared to make appropriate contributions to that union, unless they have a conscientious objection both to belonging and contributing to the union. Such an agreement may be entered into voluntarily between one or more employers and one or more registered unions. However, if an employer is unwilling to enter into such an agreement, either he, or the unions concerned, may apply to the National Industrial Relations Court (NIRC) to have the issue decided by secret ballot of the workers to whom the agreement would apply if it were made. The ballot will be arranged by the Commission on Industrial Relations (CIR). Once an agency shop agreement has been concluded it must run for two years before another ballot can be held. Many more unfair industrial practices are defined by the Act; it would be wearisome to rehearse them all.

The judicial system under the Act

We have already mentioned agencies set up under the Industrial Relations Act; they are:

Commission on Industrial Relations

Established in 1969, it orginally investigated industrial relations following reference by the Secretary of State for Employment. It prepared a number of very detailed and useful reports on particular companies and industries with recommendations for improvement. The Act gives the CIR a statutory basis and a leading role in the Act's system of industrial relations as an investigatory and administrative adjunct to the judicial machinery. The CIR cannot enforce compliance with its recommendations by law; voluntary reform will remain its major job.

National Industrial Relations Court (NIRC)

This is the principal new institution established by the Act. It is a High Court and, like any British court, independent of the Government. It is headed by an eminent judge. It was intended to appoint lay members from amongst employers and trade unionists to assist the judge in deciding important cases. The unions have so far boycotted the Court altogether.

Industrial Tribunals

Established by the Industrial Training Act of 1964, their composition is like that of the Industrial Court; legally qualified chairmen sit with laymen who have experience of industry and industrial relations. The Act considerably expands the role of the tribunals. With the NIRC, they will form a two-tier judicial system in cases involving the rights of employees and industrial relations.

Registrar of Trade Unions and Employers' Associations

A new office under the Act. The Chief Registrar and his colleagues keep a new register of trade unions and employers' associations and will ensure that these organizations meet the Act's requirements about their rules and administration. The Registrar has powers to investigate complaints of the treatment of the members of registered organizations and may himself investigate certain suspected irregularities.

Industrial Arbitration Board

This is an old institution (Industrial Court) renamed so as to avoid confusion with the National Industrial Relations Court. Set up under the Industrial Courts Act of 1919, it acted as a kind of official independent arbitrator. Under the Act of 1971 it will arbitrate only on terms and conditions of employment. The Act extends the conciliation services already provided by the Department of Employment. Additional officers will be appointed to try to achieve voluntary settlements, for example, of complaints of unfair dismissal and infringement of trade union rights. Figure 4.1 sets out in diagrammatic form the machinery for administering the legislation.

Collective bargaining under the Act

Unions and employers may still enter into voluntary collective agreements under the Act, but unless they declare, in writing an agreement, that they do not wish it to have legal force, it will be treated as legally binding on the parties. The unions have decided against legal agreements and will press employers to agree to disclaimers. They have also refused (with few exceptions) to register under the Act, and thus have lost tax concessions and their claim to be called trade unions; since, under the Act, legislation defines a trade union.

The refusal to register makes a trade union no less liable for actions taken under the Act for unfair industrial practices. The Court may issue injunctions to restrain unions or their members (whether registered or not) from committing unfair practices. Heavy fines were imposed early in 1972 upon the Transport and General Workers Union (a non-registered Union) for contempt of the Court, when some of its members at Liverpool docks 'blacked' the lorries of a St. Helens firm[1] shipping containers into the docks.

Nor are non-registered unions exempt from orders by the Court to 'cool-off'. Under the Act, if negotiations break down and a strike threatens seriously to disrupt the economic life of the country, the Secretary of State may ask the NIRC to impose a 'cooling-off'

[1] At the time of writing (30 April 1972), the shop-stewards involved have refused to follow advice to end their 'blacking'. Indeed, the 'blacking' looks like spreading to other ports. This looks like becoming a severe test of whether the legislation can be effectively administered.

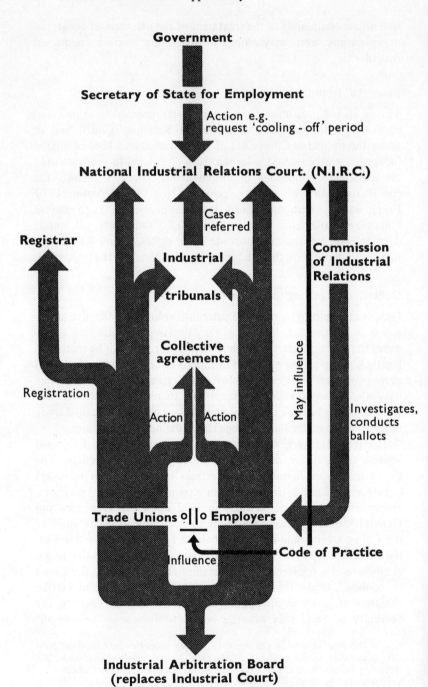

Government

Secretary of State for Employment

Action e.g.
request 'cooling - off' period

National Industrial Relations Court. (N.I.R.C.)

Cases
referred

Registrar

Industrial

tribunals

**Commission
of Industrial
Relations**

**Collective
agreements**

May influence

Registration

Action   Action

Investigates,
conducts
ballots

Trade Unions o||o **Employers**

Influence   **Code of Practice**

**Industrial Arbitration Board
(replaces Industrial Court)**

period, so that work may be resumed and negotiations re-started. The railway unions, not registered, were under orders to 'cool-off' in April 1972. Their members, on the leaders' advice, then stopped a work-to-rule.

The Code of Practice

The Industrial Relations Act is accompanied by a Code of Practice. Failure on the part of employers and unions to adhere to the Code will not render them liable to penalties in law. However, the Code may be invoked in proceedings before the National Industrial Relations Court, or an industrial tribunal. Its purpose is to encourage all employers and unions to follow the standards of the best.

The best way to summarize the Code is to define the salient characteristics of an organization which is thought to have 'good' industrial relations. In such an organization managers will accept that it is their job to promote good industrial relations, initiating arrangements with other employees and their unions for communication, consultation, and negotiation and handling disputes as they arise. Such a management will ensure its own proper training in the industrial relations aspects of work organization, leaving industrial relations to personnel specialists, although it will employ such specialists. It will see also that supervisors are trained properly because they are in a position directly to influence relationships at the working face.

It will also tackle some of the causes of industrial conflict at source, and deal with symptoms as they arise; for example, by trying to organize work so that the employee derives satisfaction from it, and by designing systems of payment which offer a fair reward for work and manifestly do so.

The unions, according to the Code, share responsibility with the management for promoting good industrial relations. They should ensure that, while their members' interests remain their prime concern, these are best promoted by agreed peaceful, orderly processes of argument and negotiation governed by agreed rules.

Employees must, as individuals, find out what their rights and obligations are, and what machinery exists to protect their interests and to handle their grievances.

The managers in the 'good' organization will plan for the procurement and use of their human resources just as carefully and as systematically as for plant and materials; perhaps even more carefully with such a volatile resource. They will use modern techniques

F

of manpower planning, will introduce wage structures and pay systems appropriate to the firm's circumstances; they will select and induct employees with care, and will provide as far as possible stable employment, and good pensions. Redundancy must be planned and executed carefully, fairly, and sympathetically. These managers will also see that the workplace is as safe, hygienic and pleasant as possible. They will take every opportunity to inform employees by word of mouth, or in writing, in good time, of plans and policies affecting them, and will set up committees and councils where employees may air their views.

As for collective bargaining, our 'good' managers will seek to define, jointly with the unions, at what levels what subjects will be bargained about. For example, it might be agreed that holidays and job grade rates will be negotiated at company level in a large company, but an incentive bonus scheme at plant level. They will give union officials of recognized unions the facilities needed to carry out their duties efficiently and ensure that unions have all the information the organization can safely part with, probably well beyond what the Industrial Relations Act strictly requires.

Shop stewards, in our 'good' firm, will be properly accredited, their periodic election will be properly and fairly conducted, they will be well trained for their work and given the facilities they need. The trade unions, of course, should cooperate with management in making sure that the shop steward's rights and duties, are clearly defined, and that he understands them, and where the bounds of his authority lie – or so the Code says. The union should ensure that the work of the shop stewards in an enterprise is properly coordinated.

In the 'good' firm, managers and trade unions will collaborate to decide what training shop stewards need to carry out their duties competently, and to see that they take it. The Code stresses the importance of procedures to redress individual grievances.

Much of the Code's 'good' industrial relations would command wide agreement amongst managers, trade union officers, employees and the public generally. However, some clauses might arouse dissent, especially in the early days of the implementation of the Act.

The Code says that:

> 'A shop steward should observe all agreements to which his union is a party, and should take all reasonable steps to ensure that those whom he represents also observe them.' (Clause 105).

Already, as the Liverpool docks case indicates, it is apparent that shop stewards may regard this clause as restricting their freedom of action to represent their constituents, if employers wish to use the Code to enforce compliance with agreements they consider to be inappropriate to their circumstances, or when the union leadership is pressed by the law to enforce unpopular agreements on its members locally, which local employers refuse to modify. There are circumstances where grass-roots militancy might be thought to be an entirely appropriate tactic to persuade a recalcitrant employer to meet a reasonable demand. If this avenue is closed, then, so the argument might go, the local stewards might seek to 'bend' the agreements to suit their purposes, inviting counter-moves to close loopholes, thus generating a conflict, in which the Code and the Act will tend to favour the employer.

Trade union and other comments on the Act

Many Trade Unionists regard the Act, and the Code, as ill-considered moves by a Conservative government to use the judiciary against the unions; to the benefit of employers, and in order to shift the balance of power in collective bargaining, using the inflationary state of the British economy as their excuse. They do not see employers speaking out against the Act, and they take this as evidence that employers welcome the legislation as in their economic interest. The ground that anything that an employer sees as being in his interest is likely to be against the interests of employees and their unions, confirms their opposition to the Act.

The Labour Party is pledged to repeal the Act when it returns to power. Such is union influence in the Labour Party that, however much some Labour Party politicians may wish to retain the Act or parts of it (and remember, the last Labour government had prepared similar legislation as an instrument of economic policy before it was voted from office two years ago), they will find it difficult to do so.

Labour front-bench politicians have advised unions not to defy the rulings of the NIRC because such actions will bring Parliamentary democracy itself in disrepute and encourage employers and others to break laws passed by Labour administrations in the future.

Inevitably, then, the field of industrial relations in Britain has become in some respects (but by no means all) a party-political battleground. If the framers of Industrial Relations legislation were expecting that the legal regulation of collective bargaining would

remove industrial relations from the political arena they are
probably mistaken, certainly misguided.

The impact of the Act—some personal reflections

The nature of the Contract of Employment

At the centre of the argument about the Act, there is a confusion
about the nature of the contract of employment. The opponents of
the Act regard the contract between an employer and an employee
in a capitalist society as essentially a matter between the company
as a corporate body owning the plant and equipment, and the
individual employee. Since the employee, singly, is at a disadvantage
against a large and powerful employer, he is obliged to organize and
choose a representative to bargain the terms of his employment
collectively. On this view, the representative is the servant of the
employees, removable by them. If the individual, acting alone, or
with his fellows, on-the-job, can exploit local labour market
conditions to improve on what his representative has gained, then
surely he must be free to do so and to withdraw his labour, or
threaten to do so, in support of his claim.

The Act is based, it seems, on a different view, which sees as
anarchic a situation where union negotiators conclude bargains in
good faith and are then apparently powerless to prevent the
apparent breaking of those bargains by their members. Having
elected or appointed negotiators, members of unions should settle
for what the negotiators are able to obtain. On this view the contract
of employment is like a contract of sale, where a representative of a
company is empowered to represent it and to buy or sell goods on its
behalf. The contract, once concluded, will hold up in law if one party
is obviously in breach. Why, then, when a union has negotiated, e.g., a
50p rise with an employers association, should not the union guarantee that its representatives will not ask for more than 50p for the
duration of the contract, and accept the responsibility for the breach
of contract if they do. The increasing incidence of small, unofficial,
disruptive strikes, and large, inflationary settlements, are, on the
first view, indications that, at most, the procedures for voluntary
resolution of conflict need to be voluntarily improved, and that the
Government, the employers, and the unions should work together
to arrive at a just policy for regulating incomes in the light of the
public interest. On the second view, they signal that the voluntary
machinery for conflict resolution has broken down or been flagrantly

abused, and a reminder that it is the Government's duty to define and protect the public interest. Hence the development of a legal frame-work under the Act. The second view, again, was expressed in the proposed legislation of the recent Labour government, and is by no means the prerogative of the political right.

Although I can see merit in both arguments, and justice in some of the provisions of the Industrial Relations Act, particularly those relating to individual rights, and the Code of Practice, I think that the machinery for conflict resolution, and for determining incomes should remain largely a voluntary matter, for the following reasons.

Factory bargaining

Relationships at factory or office level encompass much more than is embraced by the 'pay and conditions' that form the substance of the official collective bargaining we have been referring to. In the British system, even the 'pay and conditions' clauses of agreements concluded by employers and union officials are often regarded as a base from which to negotiate local company or plant additions; in the form, for example, of piecework bonus, factory job rates and long-service awards. These negotiations, usually conducted by shop stewards and managers, may be highly detailed, unwritten, based on custom and precedent and continuous. This would certainly be so in the case of the negotiation of piecework prices and allowances, in conditions where changes are taking place in products, processes and labour markets; but in all cases, factory bargaining tries to arrive at a reasonable or acceptable relationship between effort and reward, in their very broadest sense. Since this relationship may well be crucial to a company and since also it can be rather unstable and potentially explosive, it is central to the concerns of the parties to company and factory level negotiations; i.e. the operating managers and supervisors, and the shop stewards. Their relationship with each other could be seriously worsened by failure to make adjustments.

The process of influencing both the level of reward and the level of effort in ways consistent with the production and sale of high quality goods or service at low cost, plays a significant part in organizational life. The result of such processes might be inconsistent with settle-ments negotiated by official union and employer bargainers. It is difficult, indeed, to imagine how the supply of effort, or time, or competence to an organization could be regulated by an agreement between people who are not involved in the business of designing the jobs and who are not continually and directly seeking cooperation from the people who operate machines, drive trains, assemble components, and so on.

A source of tension

We are faced then, with a conflict, or a source of tension and unease. *On the one hand*, there are problems of enhancing human cooperation in the manufacture of capital and consumer goods and the provision of services, so as to maximize the use of both the human and physical assets of organizations. In organizations that are increasingly more complex and more rapidly growing and changing; and in a socio-cultural climate and at a level of affluence and welfare in which fear of formal authority is diminishing; to promote high levels of cooperation, and commitment at the working face is difficult. It is certainly unlikely to happen merely as a result of periodic negotiations about the rate for the job[2]. The problem of maximizing cooperation is seen increasingly as one of managers influencing the behaviour of their subordinates towards greater commitment to organizational objectives, by such techniques as management by objectives, job enlargement and enrichment, participative management and supervision, improved communication, training for skill in interpersonal relationships (sensitivity training, etc.) i.e. the whole set of techniques deriving from the work of people such as McGregor, Hertzberg, Scanlon and Likert, and labelled behavioural science/organizational development. The objective of these techniques is to maximize economic objectives via enhanced cooperation and commitment, whether that comes from a more interesting and challenging job, a say in determining policies and targets, a sympathetic and supportive boss, or whatever. Some argue that the techniques also promote the individual's satisfaction with his job; or indeed, that the increased commitment arises largely from that satisfaction, and enhances it.

On the other hand, there are the procedures for settling pay and for processing disputes arising from the interpretation, in the workplace, of those settlements. These seem, on first glance, to arise from sheer conflict of economic interest, and to be determined as much by the relative power of the parties as by the notion of a 'reasonable settlement'. Whereas the 'human relations' techniques seem bent on promoting cooperation based on a common interest in the success of an enterprise or an economy, the institutions of collective bargaining,

(2)   Nor, indeed, by setting up the kind of procedures recommended by the Code of Practice, although they might help.

at whatever level, seem intent less on the success, even survival, of a particular enterprise than on the pursuit of a sectional interest: for the employer, whether private or public, to make a profit; for the employees to maximize their pay.

Organizational design and cooperation

A third set of problems arises from the push towards the greater specialization and fragmentation of organizations which arises from the increasingly turbulent environments to which they have to adapt, and to the explosive pace of technical innovation and increasing scale. These are the problems of organizational design for cooperation at the structural level, as against those which are perceived as arising from low motivation, poor communication and the like.

We may regard 'organizational development' mainly as working towards a 'psychological contract', i.e. towards commitment, involvement, etc. as eliciting a contribution from the 'whole' individual, in addition to his time, his physical effort or his competences, in return for inducements such as a more interesting and challenging job, and a say in what goes on. If so, then one might ask whether an 'economic contract' merely stating pay for performance is necessarily complementary or compatible with an approach via the psychological contract. The cynic might point out, indeed, that the psychological contract is only possible when the 'economic contract' is satisfactory, 'gilt on the gingerbread', as it were.

Certainly, British unions would on the whole prefer to confine themselves to the 'economic contract'. They regard themselves as concentrations of labour market power, not as partners with managers of capitalist enterprises in the search for enhanced worker motivation and commitment to the company. They have neither the time, nor the resources, nor the inclination to become officially involved, although they would not usually stand in the way if managers sought the cooperation of rank and file members. British unions claim with great justification that they have an enviable record in the responsible use of power under the voluntary system, as well as success in improving their members' living standards. It is not difficult to understand their resentment at the new laws.

Centralization and decentralization

I personally perceive an increasing tension in the UK between, on the one hand, the pressure towards legal centralized bureaucratic

control of economic life, which arises from the needs that governments perceive to intervene in economic and social processes so as to
maximize objectives such as increased rates of growth of GNP, or
balancing payments, or re-distributing income, or slowing down
inflation; and, on the other hand, the desires of individuals to
escape from the control over their lives which is represented by such
administrative control. At the level of the enterprise, progressive
firms are slackening the constraints so as to promote greater participation and involvement, not only to meet expressed psychological
needs, but because the efficient operation of modern technology
seems to demand such methods of management.

The Industrial Relations Act, however, is, it seems to me, an
example of the first process, i.e. towards greater bureaucratic
control at all levels. Even the Code of Practice emphasizes formal
written rules and procedures, formally instituted committees, and so
on. The implementation of Act and Code could well increase tension
between the two sets of pressures, a tension that could find its
expression in worsened relationships in the enterprise. Many
personnel managers' unease about the Act arises not only because
it might involve them in more paperwork, and committees, but
because they see, I suspect, that it will make their professional task
more onerous. I confess to a difficulty in finding and following a
logical chain which leads from the Industrial Relations Act and the
Code to a real improvement in the quality and efficiency of life in the
modern industrial enterprise. If that is what we are aiming for, the
means to that end mostly lie elsewhere, probably in the more
serious and consistent application of the social sciences to the design
and management of organizations.

Suggested reading

On the Industrial Relations Act

A Guide to the Industrial Relations Act 1971, HMSO.
The Code of Practice, HMSO.
Agency Shop Agreements, HMSO.
This is the C.I.R., published by the Commission on Industrial
Relations.

British industrial relations

ARMSTRONG, E. G. A., *Industrial Relations*, Harrap, 1969.

See also:

FLANDERS, ALLAN, *Collective Bargaining*, Penguin Modern Management Readings, 1969.

MCCARTHY, W. E. J. (Ed)., *Trade Unions*, Penguin Modern Management Readings, 1972.

Management in Britain

John Morris

Introduction

I find it a daunting task to provide relevant guidelines to understanding and working with British managers. However, I shall try to look at, and then beyond, some common stereotypes; and suggest some of the characteristics of British managers in the past, present and possible future.

Although we are obviously concerned to look forward, one does not get far in understanding British managers if one is not willing to glance backward. It might be objected that the greatest weakness of British managers is that they spend too much time looking backwards! This may be so, but is itself worthy of study. Perhaps only Japan among modern industrial and commercial powers has a stronger sense of historical continuity, or has been more a product of its past, even in a period of great uncertainty and change.

The argument

First, however, it might help if I provide a thread through the labyrinth in the form of an argument. I believe that for the greater part of the past century British managers have been seriously lacking in resourcefulness, having lost much of the panache and vigour that characterized the great breakthrough of the world's first major industrial revolution. After the agonizing, wasteful and yet in some ways inspiring drama of two great wars, managerial resourcefulness is now beginning to return, in the mainstream and not only in scattered tributaries. British management now shows possibilities of regaining its former quality. If resourcefulness takes command, some of the positive aspects of the conventional manager in Britain, such as good humour, tolerance and good sense, will become more evident, and a powerful combination of resourcefulness and responsibility will develop, with a characteristic British flavour. This combination is likely to be most evident in such activities as the service industries, organizational development, professional education, and government/business relations.

An important contribution to resourcefulness has been the Common Market issue. Britain has been forced to make the kind of once-for-all decision that she has usually encountered only during a major war. This decision, now being painfully enacted, with many misgivings (in parts of continental Europe as well as in Britain) seems likely to provide an opportunity that I believe will bring the resourceful and the conventional elements in British society together in a major national effort. Since in this case the effort cannot be crowned by a military victory, it will eventually lose impetus and become consolidated in habit and routine. But by that time, there is a possibility that Britain, and especially her management, who are steadily improving their professional effectiveness, will be establishing a reputation as mediators, catalysts, and organizers of complex activities.

Resourceful versus conventional management

Before attempting to spell out the argument, which sounds distinctly dogmatic in summary form, I shall comment on some of the implications of the key terms 'resourceful' and 'conventional'. It may seem odd that I take these two contrasting qualities from all the distinctions that could have been made between Britain's managers. There are obvious contrasts between managers in terms of class origins, the type of enterprise that is being managed, the 'style' of management (such as autocratic or democratic), the kind of education that the manager has received, and the amount of social and occupational mobility that he has initiated or experienced. We shall glance at some of these in this brief survey of British management. But I am convinced that the most significant contrast for Britain, as a country much afflicted by addiction to its past successes and by subtle rigidities, is between those who are able to cope with changing people and situations, and those who are dependent on their social conditioning, whose attitudes and behaviour can be readily predicted from the prevailing habits and customs.

The contrast, then, between the resourceful and the conventional is not quite the same as that between stability and change, or continuity and discontinuity but there are obvious affinities. Resourcefulness is a way in which people become capable of facing uncertainties, of living in a real-life drama rather than running through a well-established routine. Some of the characteristics of resourcefulness have been emotional resilience, decisiveness, a flexible rather than purely analytical intelligence, together with a strong desire for survival and, wherever possible, mastery of one's situation. Since resourcefulness is an instrumental characteristic it is capable of being combined with many basic attitudes and values. In Britain, there has been much concern over the values that are associated with resourcefulness, since the obvious capacity of resourceful people to undermine or even destroy social order is well recognized.

It would not be too much to say that an enduring theme in British social life, clearly reflected in her educational system, has been the 'domestication' of resourcefulness. The concept of the 'gentleman' has linked resourcefulness with such reassuring qualities as modesty, sociability and good manners. Unfortunately, the struggle between social virtues and personal dynamism has often led in Britain to the victory of sociability over resourcefulness. But this is to anticipate some of the points that need to be spelled out in greater detail.

Britain's 'historical dramas'

Each nation has its historical dramas, forming its national consciousness, and providing enduring points of reference for its major careers. In Britain, many of these dramas have focused on war, invasion, or overseas expansion, throwing into prominence the career of the soldier, the sailor and explorer, the trader and the statesman. It is worth recalling, in face of Napoleon's contemptuous comment about 'the nation of shopkeepers', that Britain, a very old country with immense continuity in her major political, economic and social institutions, places the martial values high among her national priorities – patriotism, solidarity, courage and tenacity.

The industrial revolution

Management, which seems the epitome of peaceful qualities, has in Britain been closely associated with the long sustained but unique drama of the 'industrial revolution' of the eighteenth and nineteenth centuries. The success of this drama, judged by its elevation of Britain to a leading position among world powers in the middle of the nineteenth century, has provided the touch-stone by which Britain, and the world, have judged her social and economic performance to this day. British managers, as an occupational class, have moved from a drama in which they had a leading role, to a series of dramas and rituals with different plots and sets of characters, in which their roles are difficult to define. What, then, were some of the characteristics of this central drama?

Any attempt to summarize the key developments that constituted the essence of the industrial revolution, between 1740 and 1860, is in danger of becoming absurd. Forced into a few sentences, the way-wardness and individuality of this unique series of events, still the subject of controversy among historians and sociologists, takes on the clarity and inevitability of a Greek play. Nevertheless, at the risk of tumbling between two stools – the tedious repetition of a familiar story and an absurdly compressed summary – I should like to recall some of the factors that made British society what it is and which shaped British management in both its resourceful and conventional aspects.

Britain's industrial revolution brought closely together the entre-preneurs who took the financial risks (in those days very great because of the lack of joint-stock limitations on commitment), the inventors who made technical breakthroughs and the managers who supervised the day-to-day operations of the new factories and offices. Many of the great men of the period were of humble origins, but enormous versatility. Robert Owen, for example, a poor boy from Wales, became one of the most successful textile manufacturers of the first third of the nineteenth century. An entrepreneur of great coolness of mind, but also an immensely sensitive and effective manager, he engaged in building schools, designing educational curricula, planning and building new towns, developing the socialist programme and establishing new institutional forms for organized labour (his short-lived Grand National Consolidated Trades Union was almost a century before its time).

But a revolution in industry and commerce is not only made by great men, whatever their social origins of enterprise and social vision. It gives abundant scope to many other types – ruthless exploi-ters of opportunity, stupidly rigid followers of others' rules, a whole range of the destructive and the mediocre. The price that Britain paid in the course of its economic and social growth tends to be forgotten because it was so long ago, before the age of mass comm-unications. But the horrors of Manchester in the 1840s, the savagery of penal sentences on poor people threatening the property of the wealthy, and the complacency of the rich forced the mass of the working classes into a complex mix of attitudes – including defens-iveness, guilt, envy, docility, and stubborn pride in manual work – that have not left them to this day.

The 'new men'

The themes that seem central to the revolution are vital to under-standing the place of British management. The revolution was only partly due to the qualities – good or bad, effective or ineffective – of managers. It was partly a matter of good geographical location, central to the trade routes of the 'civilized' world, of a strong navy and a tradition of successful belligerence, of good possibilities of developing a coherent and relatively rapid system of internal trans-port, of a reasonably wealthy and accessible home market, of a social and political system open to economic change. Not least, in the social system, there was an upper class of extraordinary tenacity, ruthlessness, public spirit, intelligence and resilience. Whatever weaknesses one attributes to the upper class during the eighteenth and nineteenth centuries, and there are many (arrogance, stubbor-ness, chauvinism, to name but a few) they knew a good thing when they saw it, and worked vigorously to ally themselves with the entrepreneurs, bankers, financiers; many of whom, one must remember, were firmly established and successful before the *industrial* revolution gave them new opportunities. The alliance would only take place with the outstandlingly successful new men, so there was a state of affairs very close to the Darwinian 'survival of the fittest' before that harsh doctrine became associated with Darwin. The result was the formation of a stable but reasonably flexible 'upper crust' to society, formed of diverse but collaborating elements.

We see, then, the emergence of an immensely complex blend of the traditional aristocrat, the wealthy squire, the prosperous manu-facturer, the ingenious and successful inventor, the banker and the supervising managers who worked with them as their indispensable agents and stewards, in a situation of apparently inexhaustible opportunity as the control of overseas territory followed exploration and military conquest. Opportunities called to ambitious and able men of every social level, and 'management' became the 'melting pot' of British occupational groups.

Britain and the Empire

One of the peculiarities of the blend is that it made Britain and her almost divine mission a meaningful point of national integration, releasing vast energies. Britain was, and is, a small enough country, with a sufficiently long and colourful history, to be captured in the imagination even of those of limited intelligence and blinkered vision. The clear physical distinction of Britain, as a wealthy and civilized country, and the peoples over whom she reigned, enabled vast power to be combined with a simplicity of mission not paralleled since the Roman Empire. A characteristic feature of this separation of 'home' and 'abroad' is that it enabled some of the great polarities of human life to be divided into the convenient compartments of 'us' and 'them'. The British could feel themselves to be peaceful (unless roused by outrageous provocation, of course), civilized, educated, and above all progressive, while those abroad, typically of a different cultural and ethnic status, could be seen as primitive, regressive, childish and violent.

In a quite important sense, Britain's empire was kind of 'collective unconscious' for her middle and upper classes. No wonder that shipping criminals to the colonies was seen as quite appropriate. But the unconcious mind contains more than nightmares: it has experiences that transcend the banality of everyday life, and offer rare delights. India, for example, was seen in Victorian times as colourful, rhythmic and exciting, as well as savage and frightening. The colonies could be a place in which 'men are men', and the young managers, given enormous responsibilities as colonial administrators, could gain experience of a kind and depth that would never have been possible in Britain itself, which through the nineteenth century began to stiffen into an almost Roman severity and gravity. The industrial revolution, then, which formed the profession of management in Britain, also created some fundamental contrasts.

Some relevant distinctions

Class divisions

In this newly powerful Britain, the growth of population and the movement of many of the people into towns, made evident a class system very unlike the functional groupings characteristic of an agrarian economy. The 'working classes' began to be divided from the middle and upper classes, and the owners and their agents began to form a reasonably articulate, prosperous grouping which was fairly sharply divided from the urban workmen in factory employment. Housing, schools (or lack of them) and almost every aspect of the style of life, revealed two social groupings confronting one another, with a great deal of unease among those who were on the boundary – the small shopkeeper, the lower grade of clerk or shop assistant, the technician, the foreman. Although each social grouping showed important differences within its own ranks, the confrontation was sharp enough to make the terms 'manager' and 'worker' the focus of many social issues. Marx, of course, thought that the confrontation would grow to revolution, but the countervailing growth of powerful trade unions, with reasonably effective bargaining powers, combined with moderate prosperity and social expansion to take the edge off social discontents.

What of our chosen qualities of resourcefulness and conventionalism as the nineteenth century drew to a close? Some would argue that the resourceful manager was increasingly frustrated by the under-educated and reactionary masses of the conventional working people, forming a tightly-knit opposition to all forms of social change. But resourcefulness and conventionalism do not divide conveniently along class lines. Much of the resourcefulness of the working classes was, it is true, spent in defensive activity, since the undivided pursuit of power and profit have never been kind to those at the bottom of the ladder. But the history of the British labour movement shows no lack of resource, and the fact that most of it was devoted to evolution rather than revolution is an indication that it was British rather than socialist.

Workers and managers

The growth of trade unions throughout the nineteenth century showed two themes – negotiation with employers for better pay and conditions of work, and the search for social justice. These are themes which can be worked on resourcefully or conventionally. It is a tribute to the organizing ability of the 'common people' that the unions became much more than the piecemeal exploiters of opportunities, but developed into major social institutions, giving birth eventually to one of the two great British political parties – the Labour party.

Profit versus people

It would not be too much to say that this development led to a division in British management into the organization of material and financial resources for profitable production, and the management of people for organizational effectiveness. Management inertia often pushed the trade unions into becoming the virtual managers of the British labour force, negotiating with employers for the terms on which 'their' people would work and the kinds of work they would do. Some British managers, traditionally interested in technical or commercial affairs rather than man-management, were able to maintain an extraordinary insensitivity to the day-to-day lives and aspirations of the people they were supposedly managing.

Organizational scale

This insensitivity, where it occurred, was not helped by the vast growth in scale of industrial and commercial enterprise, outstripped only the growth of the public sector, which gave its name to 'bureaucracy' – the predominant organizational form succeeding owner-management. Although the phrase 'big business' has come to be associated with America, there were a lot of big business and other big organizations in Britain by the close of the century. Resource within big business is either at the very top, dealing with the endless opportunities and problems that are activated by vast size, or in the specialized sections dealing with 'research and development' or 'trouble shooting'. The rest of the organization often flattens into day-to-day routine, far from the traditionalism of the countryman and the craftsman. The routine of bureaucratic organization is rational, orderly, systematic, explicit, and – above all – detached in its objectivity as contrasted with the hopes and fears of those who manage it or are managed by it. Fortunately, the spirit of the British people has proved singularly resistant to such rationality. The God of the British people is reasonable rather than rational.

The qualities of British managers

Perhaps this is a useful point to summarize some of the leading qualities of British management as they had emerged during the breakthrough of the industrial and commercial revolution, and begun to stabilize during the last third of the nineteenth century. First, some of the virtues of the resourceful pioneers had been confirmed by success and become part of the character of management – looking for commercial opportunities in the Empire, using the skills of craftsmanship to the utmost and learning from personal experience. Unfortunately, as these virtues became part of the conventional wisdom, they inevitably lost their cutting edge of intelligence and flexibility. 'Imperial preference' then became an obstacle to looking for markets in other parts of the world; craftsmanship became an idol to be worshipped rather than an instrument of commercial effectiveness; and 'experience' became a synonym for 'seniority' and an excuse for relegating able young people to the lower rungs of the managerial ladder for many years while they learned the job.

Second, the growth in size of many firms, combined with the international trading pattern of Britain as the centre of a great empire, led to a fragmentation of managerial careers into many functional ladders – production, engineering, sales, admininstration, commercial, purchasing and several others. This was, of course, a pattern followed by other large industrial and commercial powers, but in Britain it was marked by a sense that these functional divisions were an outgrowth of natural order, since they grew slowly and with little break in continuity out of the dramatic changes of the first part of the century. The result of all this inner diversity – all of which seemed so 'practical' – was to obscure the recognition that management could be a profession, with a theory of its practice and systematic forms of preparation. In short, managerial careers became almost opposed to the world of education, rather than in sympathetic and constructive relationship to it.

Third, the triumph of continuity over discontinuity – of evolution over revolution – meant that resourceful people had to show their willingness to work in amicable relationship to the growing mass of conventional people. The major decision rule adopted in British management seemed to be: It is unwise to show anyone how resourceful you are, except in a real emergency. Then get back to normal as quickly as possible. The first part was overdone, but there can be little doubt that the second part of the rule, indicating that resourcefulness of the most extreme kind is acceptable in emergency, was fully accepted by all social classes during the two great wars.

The twentieth century

The Edwardian era

Eric Hobsbawm, in his study of 'Industry and Empire', expresses the situation before the 1914-18 war with characteristic sharpness and accuracy:

> 'Britain was becoming a parasitic rather than a competitive economy, living off the remains of world monopoly, the under-developed world, her past accumulations of wealth and the advance of her rivals . . . . And, especially in the Indian summer of Edwardian England, the contrast between the needs of modernization and the increasingly prosperous complacency of the rich grew ever more visible . . . . The prophets already – and not incorrectly – predicted the decline and fall of an economy symbolized now by the country house in the stockbrokers' belt of Surrey and Sussex and no longer by hard-faced men in

smoke-filled provincial towns . . . When the war came in 1914, it was not as a catastrophe which wrecked the stable bourgeois world . . . . It came as a respite from crisis, a diversion, perhaps even as some sort of a solution.'

The reason for this sense of being able to switch to a real emergency was that the major social forces of Britain seemed to have lost their impetus for growth and world leadership, and also their capacity for maintaining internal unity. Resourcefulness came bubbling forth in the long agonizing years of the war, but this same war provided the most brutal and mechanical device for destroying the brave, the energetic, the patriotic, as well as the pathetic, unresisting 'cannon fodder'.

Between the wars

The chequered years between the wars, aptly termed by the British poet Robert Graves 'the long week-end', seemed for much of the time to provide opportunities for frivolity and escapism rather than managerial resourcefulness. The arts flourished, and sport, exploration, and science did well in the nineteen-twenties in a period of acute economic disturbance. But the threat to the stability of the pound in 1931 provided a sense of crisis which brought out the dormant sense of community. At last, in the 'thirties, major steps were taken to bring the relatively inert, dispersed segments of such major industries as textiles, steel and engineering together, until at the outbreak of the Second World War Britain was one of the most effective, concentrated industrial and commercial societies in the world. Management played a vital part in this renaissance, slowly developing a sense of professionalism, associated in part with specialized higher education in economics and commerce. Government was establishing itself in a role that later became increasingly familiar – the source of guidance, financial assistance in times of trouble and occasional strong intervention in the interests of national purpose.

Second World War

During the Second World War, Britain amazed the world (and to some extent herself) by her unique combination of tenacity, ingenuity, aggression and sheer energy – a powerful alliance of the resourceful and the conventional virtues. With inspired leadership, Britain once more had a national strategy and, not less important, a flow of information about what was happening, and what was expected to happen. To use a phrase of the times, people at all levels felt that they were 'in the picture', whether things were going well or ill and their efforts were of enormous significance. In the armed services and on the home front, ability was given its head, and young people who in peacetime would have been in powerless junior positions (unless they had been on the outposts of empire, where young men were given great power) were now found in senior posts, with life-and-death responsibilities.

A point about life in wartime which has been greatly underestimated was the social and geographical mobility it entailed, its dependence on good selection, on individual and collective adaptability, and, not least, a systematic programme of job analysis and training. The war, with all its waste, horror and futility, achieved some good things. Operational research brought scientific ingenuity as well as scientific method to large-scale operations, and became a vital management tool. Industrial psychology, psychiatry and social science contributed significantly to selection and training.

The postwar world

After the war, some of the things that had been learned were put to use. The Tavistock Institute of Human Relations was founded by a group of psychiatrists and psychologists who had worked in officer selection. An Administrative Staff College for management was founded at Henley, explicitly using the experience of the armed services in developing senior management. The idea of professional management, rather than learning solely by doing the job in a particular firm, moving up a ladder step by step, was given more serious attention than it had received for decades.

The pendulum years

But there was also a less happy series of events – food rationing, a recognition of a huge depletion of precious national resources, especially irreplaceable young people, a sense of exhaustion after the years of all-out effort. The Festival of Britain in 1951 made a brave showing for a while, but not until the later nineteen-fifties did some national sense of future possibilities begin to emerge. Britain felt a paralysing sense of its inadequacy, and sent missions throughout the world, not to evangelize as it had done in the nineteenth century, but to find out how to be more effective, in the American or the

Scandinavian manner. In the 'sixties, the invidious comparisons continued, focusing mainly on economic performance. A British journalist, Bernard Levin, in an extended review of the decade of the 'sixties, wrote of 'the pendulum years', with constant oscillations between forward-and backward-looking elements in British life.

The books and articles written during this period questioning the 'state of the nation', usually its economic conditions but also its moral, political and spiritual state, were indicative of a sense of malaise and even crisis. Michael Shanks, a perceptive financial journalist, wrote at the beginning of the decade of 'the stagnant society'; an American business consultant and staunch admirer of many aspects of British life, William Allen, had already written of 'half-time Britain'. In July 1963, the intellectual journal *Encounter* produced an issue, edited by that distinguished bell-wether, Arthur Koestler, called 'Suicide of a Nation?'

The encouraging future

Although not a lot has happened in the last ten years to bring Britain racing into the 'growth league', a number of encouraging changes have taken place. They are all the more encouraging because many of them have been looking at what Britain, Europe and the rest of the world really need, and seeing what can be achieved constructively, rather than taking a single variable such as 'profit' or 'economic growth' as the unquestioned value. I shall take six of the changes which, together, seem to represent a kind of move to resourcefulness, appropriate to Britain.

Research and development

First, came a recognition that much of the basic research being done by scientists and inventors in Britain, much of it distinguished and potentially effective, was not being applied to the advantage of British industry and commerce. The National Research Development Corporation was founded in 1962, and other efforts were made, by government, industry and commerce, to develop research applications. The universities have played an important part in such work, both in diagnosis, prescription and the establishment of development institutions. Among these have been the Business Schools, of particular significance to management. These have all been much concerned with research programmes as well as teaching, and a spate of reports on their effectiveness has encouraged self-criticism and the development of defensible policies.

Marketing

Second, the decade of the 'sixties brought a marked concern with marketing, as the extension of selling and distribution into the area of business policy, looking particularly at new markets and new products. The emphasis of the marketing approach on finding and creating opportunities greatly appealed to the more extroverted kind of resourceful manager, and provided a link with the American examples in the field of creative management of the business environment. It must be admitted, though, that some of the most impressive examples of leadership in Britain in the marketing field came from expatriates (Americans mostly, but also Hungarians, Czechs, Poles, etc.).

Finance

Third, after attempting to improve marketing and the application of research, there has been an even greater concentration on improving the uses of money and finance: in such areas as investment appraisal, capital budgeting and managerial accounting. One of the great trends in board rooms during the 'sixties has been the appearance of accountants and bankers to supplement the views of production and sales people. A transformation in the profession of accountancy is well under way. With management accountancy replacing the traditional emphasis on historical accounting, the provision of information for effective decision and control of cash flows is being given greater weight than the historical balancing of the books.

Organizational design

Fourth, the combination of technical research and development, marketing and finance have placed a great deal of emphasis on the value of a flexible organization of people at work. Many of the jobs done by factory and office workers have been learned by rote from observing and imitating others. Lacking a 'theory of their practice', many British workers have been lamentably rigid in their attitudes to change. Admittedly, much of the change that they have been forced to endure has been for the worse, as far as they are concerned, and it would be seriously mistaken to conclude that opposition to change is always ill-founded. This said, there is a good deal of opposition to change that springs from limitations of knowledge and skill. So the whole question of training and developing people for greater flexibility has been given more sustained attention in the last decade than in any other peace-time decade during the past century, I would judge. There has been a commensurate degree of concern paid to getting agreement from organizations of workers – the trades unions – for increases in job flexibility. This is the other side of the coin of organizational change: it avails nothing for a worker to be more widely competent if his unions will not permit a re-definition of the terms of employment. 'White collar unionism' has been predictably growing through the 'sixties under the idiosyncratic and powerful guidance of Clive Jenkins; and the managerial and professional classes have been learning for the first time that a focus on terms of pay and employment may be very useful for them in a changing, large-scale economy, in which technological improvements can change traditional status lines almost overnight. The clearest examples of such changes are provided by office machine operators, some forms of supervision, and, above all, the clerks.

Organization means all things to all men, since it refers to all the ways in which work is shaped to produce a given outcome, whether this is done explicitly and rationally or (as has been the case in Britain, for the most part) traditionally and implicitly. It has therefore been a continuing question of the decade whether there are general laws of organization that can be used by senior management. The most commercially successful answers to this question were undoubtedly provided by the American management consultants, McKinsey, who became a legendary source of influence on some of the most central British industrial, commercial and governmental organizations during the 'sixties. The Bank of England and the British Broadcasting Corporation joined Shell, ICI, and many other businesses in 'bringing in consultants' to help them re-organize. Ironically, McKinsey gained a far greater reputation for such work than they had ever achieved in their home country. The British, it seemed, were desperate to learn the latest wisdom from the Americans. If this sounds rather sour, it is perhaps because Britain seemed belatedly over-eager to imitate just those aspects of American business life that were beginning, in the 'sixties, to cause sharp criticism and reaction from the Americans themselves – profit at all costs, efficiency as an end rather than a means and over-emphasis on rationality in decision and control. Above all, a high-handed and wasteful attitude to human resources, though there were countervailing tendencies, expressed in concern for 'motivation' and 'communication'.

I shall return to this theme later, possibly because the whole field of organization breaks the bounds of a few summary paragraphs, possibly because I know a little more about it than about the other changes during the decade of the 'sixties. But before we do go on, there are two other factors that should be mentioned as the fifth and sixth elements in this crucial decade of change.

The new agencies

Fifth is the powerful, though by no means single-minded, influence of Government on organizational effectiveness. During the 'sixties, in ways that events have made somewhat similar though they claim to be adopting vastly different approaches, the Labour and Conservative governments in turn have made a great impact on the economy. The Labour government set up agencies for helping the financing and integration of companies, through a whole range of activities from investment grants, funding from government agencies, to mergers and acquisitions. The most striking activities on the Labour side were the ill-fated National Plan, the very active and, I believe, useful IRC (Industrial Reorganization Corporation) and the Prices and Incomes Board. All were inspired by the belief that British industries needed encouragement to grow to a size which would enable them to compete in world markets, against steadily growing competition from Europe, Japan, and America, and the belief that forward planning is a vital element in effectiveness in times of rapid change and scarce resources.

Education

Sixth, and last (though only last because of limitations of space), there are the massive changes in British education that started during and after the Second World War, and now beginning to spread through the whole extensive and complicated system, arriving last at the relatively autonomous and profoundly traditional parts – the public schools, the older grammar schools and the universities. (A brief reminder about the 'public' schools may be in order – they are the schools attended by only about five per cent of the country's children since they charge relatively high fees and are in fact a private alternative to the system of State education.)

The Universities

As a result of these changes, the British manager is now better educated than before. University graduates are now more common in management, and they are not limited to graduates in 'business subjects' like economics or commerce, but graduates in arts, languages, science, law and social science. Technicians, as narrow specialists with little understanding of the theories underlying their practice, are slowly giving place to more broadly educated technologists.

The foundation of many more universities and other institutions of higher education has led to much-needed thinking about subjects and methods of study, with encouraging results on the whole; though the limitations of academic expertise have led in some cases to a yawning gulf between students and faculty, over which students who know that they are not getting what they want glare angrily at their mentors, who are decidely unclear about what to put in the place of their traditional subjects and methods.

The business schools

In this predicament, the newly established business schools (which are really broader in interest than their names imply, with much concern for the management of the public sector) have been picking their way very carefully, under close scrutiny from the whole of the management world. The British zest for self-criticism, which we saw earlier in the discussion of 'The State of the Nation' in the 'sixties, has focused with special relish on the business schools, and it must have seemed occasionally to the hapless faculty as though the frustrated need for higher productivity were being channelled largely into the writing of reports on the shortcomings of management education in general and the schools in particular. Nevertheless, partly because of this close attention, and resulting funds from Government and business, Britain can take pride in the fact that it must now have the most fully developed system of management education outside the United States and Canada, in relation to its population.

The virtual revolution

When these six sets of changes are squeezed together in a rapid survey, they give the impression of a virtual revolution within the last ten years. Certainly the pace has been hot for Britain, and has undoubtedly opened up the possibility of a large-scale recovery of resourcefulness. A major factor bringing all these changes into focus has been the great issue of the British entry to Europe. After muffing the opportunity offered immediately after the war to be a partner in European integration and recovery, Britain is now formally committing herself to entry, but with considerable doubts and anxieties. Some of these, of course, are legitimate concerns about the price that will have to be paid in Commonwealth commitments, as well as in the increased price of agricultural and other commodities. Outside the purely economic realm, there are fears of the centuries-old vision of a United Europe petering out in a morass of bureaucratic rationalization, compared with which the so-called amateurism and bungling of British management at its worst would be a kind of bliss.

But when all has been said about hesitations and reservations, it is difficult to avoid the feeling that Britain is not just being forced into a decision by a powerful government, but is at last recognizing that something needs to be done.

To conclude this brief survey of changes during the 'sixties: it was a period of self-criticism and breakthrough in many areas, with the decade ending a switch to a right-wing government, under Edward Heath, and a decisive move towards European entry. From the management perspective, although the desired major improvement in economic growth did not take place it was a decade of increasing awareness of development of opportunities – in the applications of research, in marketing, finance, and, not least, the development of the skills and motivation of its working population.

Education was one of the major institutions to be seen as a contributor to this new state of affairs, though by many traditionalists it was seen as distinctly subversive. It is these linked themes of improvements in education and emphasis upon development of resources and resourcefulness that now lead us into the 'seventies.

Into the 'seventies

Although the pace of change in the 'sixties was something of a revolution in British life, there have been a number of world-wide social revolutions in which Britain has been very much on the sidelines. I have in mind at least four such revolutions; that of the working classes against the propertied classes; the young against the old; those with black or brown skins against the white; and women against men. Seen together, they are revolutions of the 'have-nots' against the 'haves'. The aims are often varied; but they always include a more equitable distribution of power.

In Britain, with a few exceptions (most obviously the judiciary, who are professionally highly sensitive to any threat to social order), the attitude to each of these world revolutions has been a mild public interest and a widespread assumption that 'it won't happen here'.

Some problem areas

There is, of course, one major exception to this statement – Northern Ireland. Ireland has for centuries been treated by the British as a somewhat incomprehensible foreign country, embarrassingly placed on their doorstep. The violence that has now broken into virtual civil war has astonished the British, who have done their best to keep the whole thing at arm's length. On the whole, the effort has been successful, because Britain is relatively free from civil violence. But I may be seriously underestimating the vulnerability of Britain to these revolutionary influences, since I am writing these notes at a time (spring 1972) when the trades union movement is mobilizing itself, both officially and unofficially, to cope with what it sees as a serious right-wing threat to their traditional liberties. This is the use of the new Industrial Relations Act as a weapon for restricting strike action. This matter is discussed in another conference paper (by Tom Lupton) but I must note that the very factors that are leading towards enhanced responsiveness and resourcefulness can well bring instability and conflict into the heart of British life.

In this context of social instability, British managers would do well to feel seriously worried about their relative failure to bring people into a cooperative relationship with organizational goals. The developments of the 'sixties will need much managerial skill and energy to bring them together into some simple and unifying ideas and programmes. An abortive example of what I have in mind happened a few years ago with the 'Backing Britain' movement, supposedly begun by a small group of typists in a London suburb who offered to work extra time for nothing. For a few weeks, the pent-up desire of people to find some practical way of helping their country burst into an astonishing series of activities. But the spontaneity of the activity did not find institutional support, and it died as quickly as it had begun. In the future, I think there is much more likelihood of a gradual and varied set of activities being established, all with realistic links with powerful institutions. Possible examples could be the newly formed British Overseas Trade Board, which is working hard to develop an acceptable national strategy for overseas trade which will prove acceptable to the diverse governmental and business interests; the relatively newly formed Confederation of British Industry, which is providing a focal point for the hitherto very scattered enterprises of Britain; the Trade Union Congress, which is currently under great internal and external pressure to reform; and the growing set of education and development centres.

Changing views of efficiency criteria

In this last connection, the business schools, although at an early stage of their development, are beginning to establish sound working links with similar institutions throughout the world, particularly in Europe, through the European Foundation for Management Development. Since the schools organize both full-time and part-time programmes for managers of all levels and ages, they gain a revealing impression of managerial characteristics and expectations, in the public as well as the private sector. Despite many individual differences, there is a clear underlying theme – the desire for a 'dynamic balance'. These managers feel that many of the managers in countries with which British managers are unfavourably compared – Japan, West Germany, Sweden, and above all the United States – have a somewhat narrow outlook, and give growth and profitability an inappropriately central place in their lives. These British managers believe that the economy of a country must be an instrument rather than the centre of life. That is, they are men and women first, and managers second.

This said, they are eager to improve the performance of their organizations. At the moment, many of them are vigorously pursuing 'management by objectives'; experimenting with operational research and management information systems; exploring some of the contributions of the behavioural sciences. In each of these areas of management thinking and activity, they are looking for effectiveness by a balance of alternatives: in management by objectives they want both organizational effectiveness and individual satisfaction with a job well done; in the field of management techniques, they want to be assured that these new methods can be adapted to the particular requirements of the organizations in which they are to be applied. No doubt the supporters of dynamic management at all costs would criticize them for their belief that the eternal contrasts and contradictions of the human condition can be held together in some kind of balance.

Preserving a balance

But British society has been able to preserve an unusual balance between these diverse goals. The price has been high: the over-all level of effectiveness has been disappointingly low. But many firms are working hard to raise the energy level of their balance: such as ICI, Shell, British Petroleum, Pilkingtons, United Biscuits, Marks and Spencer, British European Airways and Fisons. All of these organizations are committed to making work more satisfying, as well as achieving the usual commercial objectives of growth and profitability.

In recent years, powerful outside pressures have reinforced the efforts of the more enlightened managers. After experiencing the ravages of industrialism in its early stages – slag heaps, grimy factories, archaic and dusty offices, hideous textile mills, rail sidings, slum houses, towns for working in rather than living in – Britain has been among the world leaders in conservation of the environment. Her young people in particular have seen the vulnerability of their small and still astonishingly varied and beautiful country to further assaults on her natural and human resources. More than many other countries, Britain has preserved her fondness for small things and, despite her industrial and commercial concentration and concern for competitiveness, there are loud and influential voices declaring the superior advantages of small units, dispersed control and the encouragement of individuality.

New opportunities

As Britain moves firmly into the 1970s, the nature of her managerial contribution becomes increasingly clear. First, there is the concern for integration, appropriate to an old country with limited resources living somewhat precariously in a world of giants, not all of whom are benevolent. Integration has many aspects, but I have in mind the integration of the present and the future with the past, as a deep sense of continuity, together with the effective integration of many objectives into organizational life. Perhaps the term 'balance' is better than integration in this context. The combination of continuous growth and organic balance is the aim of organizational development as a planned activity, intended to achieve effective results without threatening the quality of life.

Second, Britain is becoming increasingly aware that she has much to offer Europe and the rest of the world in such service industries as banking, insurance, tourism, fashion, mass entertainment and education. Some of these industries were well known before the industrial revolution: banking and insurance, for example. An advantage of service industry is that it often fits in better with the needs of conservation than many of the extractive or manufacturing industries. It may also enable an advantage of experience, education and skill to be exploited, rather than depending on the accident of physical location of material resources.

Third, Britain for generations played the role of educational leader to the Empire, later the Commonwealth. Educational institutions are highly complicated establishments, sensitive to most of the conflicts experienced within a society. They take many years to develop, are vulnerable to age and sickness, especially the insidious sickness of complacency and routine. Britain's universities and professional schools, after years of near-stagnation, are now presenting an exciting picture of innovation and imagination, related to the fundamental issues of social, economic and political life. While it cannot be claimed that Britain's managers are themselves adequately educated, despite the mushroom growth of management education centres in the last decade, the way is now open for her to contribute research findings and teaching expertise to Europe and the rest of the world.

This achievement is partly due to relationships between Government and business, both of which are still groping for a constructive path between the subordination of individual enterprise to the imperatives of national strategy, and the laissez-faire abandonment of business to the operations of the market place. Britain is by no means free of the unholy trio of organizational controls – autocracy, bureaucracy and paternalism. But the dangers have been recognized and the development of institutions that respond both to general and particular interests has been rapid and effective.

Britain in Europe

Britain in Europe, the catalyst that is most likely to accelerate these positive influences, will be in some ways a microcosm of Europe herself in the world community. Europe is attempting to find a meaningful place among the great power blocs: Britain, after much vacillation, is committing herself to a place in Europe. Europe is struggling with the social revolutions of the 'under-privileged': Britain has held these at arm's length for many years, but finds them coming increasingly close to home. Perhaps the most powerful link between Britain and Europe is that they both have a feeling for greatness, and an anguished awareness of the terrible pitfalls into which national ambitions can lead. If British managers, compared with some of their continental counterparts, are rather more traditional, pragmatic, democratic, and yet bafflingly ruthless and elitest, these are not differences so great as to preclude fruitful cooperation. With the increase of professional education and mobility within multi-national organizations, we can confidently expect the emergence of a truly European, if not international, management.

Developments in the British capital market and some questions on Britain's entry into the EEC

Harold Rose

Historical differences between the British and other capital markets

The British capital market has traditionally been described as differing from those of most other countries, particularly of continental Europe. The range of financial institutions is wider in Britain: its short-term money market is highly developed and open to the influence of international funds; the London stock market and new issue market play a more important role in the long-term financing of business than do stock markets on the Continent; British banks are much less involved in long-term finance for industry; and financial institutions as a whole have been subject to less formal governmental control.[1]

If all of these factors are considered it is no great exaggeration to say that the British capital market has been unique in the financial world. One contention of this paper, however, is that this distinctiveness has been reduced by postwar changes.

Historical factors

The character of the British market arises basically from Britain's economic lead in the eighteenth and nineteenth centuries. Together with its concomitant industrialization this lead provided a fertile soil for the development of financial institutions and closely influenced their character. The international aspects of Britain's economic growth until the First World War not only stimulated the

[1] For a full discussion of these differences see *Capital Markets in Europe*, Economic Research Group of: Amsterdam-Rotterdam Bank; Deutschebank; Midland Bank; S. G. de Banque Generale Bankmaatschappij, March 1966.

H

London short-term money market, through the role of sterling in general and the 'bill of London' in particular, but also provided a function for the London Stock Exchange as an international new issue market, giving London pre-eminence as a market for securities in general.

This development of the securities market in particular, together with sterling's role in the finance of international trade, enabled British banks to confine themselves to the traditional banker's philosophy of providing working rather than fixed capital.[2] Banks abroad, in contrast, in the absence of an adequate stock exchange at a time when rapid industrial development called for the large-scale supply of long-term funds, had to undertake functions of external long-term financing reserved mainly for the securities market in Britain.

This early development also meant that the irregularities to which most new types of financial institution are subject after their first rapid growth occurred when direct Governmental control was still relatively unpopular. Legislation to regulate financial institutions differed from that later introduced in other countries in bearing lightly on banking and in general basing itself on disclosure rather than on control. Certain types of institution, e.g. the building societies and savings banks, were subject to broad rules defining their lending, but the investment policy of life assurance and private sector pension funds was quite unrestricted. This also helps to explain the vitality of the British new issue market.

Freedom from Governmental control too, was facilitated by the early development of a broadly based securities market. The breadth of the market in Government securities assisted the finance of the growing public sector, making it easier for the Government to pursue its monetary policy by open market operations, for example.

Governmental influences

Since the Second World War Government intervention in this sphere has greatly increased, as a consequence of Britain's balance of payments problems and of the difficulty of containing inflation. Government intervention has therefore aimed at control over the international movement of capital and of the flow of internal lending. The Government, especially through the Bank of England, has

---

[2]   British banks will certainly lend for the purchase of fixed assets, but the amount they will lend normally depends on the net current asset position of a business and its cash flow in the relatively short-term.

often put informal pressure on financial institutions. This ability to exert informal influence is due not only to the ultimate threat of legislation but also to the concentration of financial institutions in London and their social cohesion. The City, at least, is a social as well as an economic system, led mostly by men of similar origins and outlook. Its relative homogeneity has in many respects helped the capital market, not least in making possible a degree of mutual trust and informality of operation that exists nowhere else on a similar scale; but it has enabled the authorities to exert influence without the legislation that would be needed elsewhere.

Between the wars Government influence took different forms. In the depression the Government sought to broaden the supply of finance to industry by reducing, or encouraging the City to reduce, the degree of imperfection of the market at several points. Hence the Government's concern with long-term finance for companies too small to use the new issue market economically; although only a small beginning was made in this field until 1945. The Government also sought to provide finance for especially depressed industries like shipbuilding and agriculture, in the form of official encouragement for and, via the Bank of England, participation in new institutions in these industries. Its traditional desire to foster personal saving also led the Government to extend the tax reliefs to life assurance and the building societies which it had introduced before the First World War.

Government intervention was also undertaken in support of its macro-economic policy. For example, in 1920 the banks were first induced to agree to limit advances to restrain the immediate postwar inflation. In the early 1920s informal restrictions were also placed on new foreign issues in support of the return to the gold standard. Such restrictions were later intensified in support of the policy of cheap money in the early 1930s and to protect the balance of payments during rearmament in the later part of the decade. From 1937, too, control over domestic issues was introduced, leading to the formal establishment of the Capital Issues Committee in 1939.

Postwar developments

The formation of Government-sponsored institutions

The policy of the first postwar Labour government was broadly to attempt to contain inflation by means of fiscal policy and direct controls over private sector expenditure and over capital issues. But its concern with the efficiency of the capital market and full-employment also led the Government to extend the pre-war policy of sponsoring or establishing new institutions. The Bank of England, for example, participated in 1945 in the establishment of the Industrial and Commercial Finance Corporation, (ICFC) whose other share-holders are the clearing banks and which is designed to provide long-term finance to companies too small to resort economically to the stock exchange. Another institution was the National Research and Development Corporation (NRDC), set up in 1945 as a Government-financed body to support the development of promising inventions. Later, in 1962, Technical Development Capital Ltd. was formed as a subsidiary of ICFC as a private institution with the comparable aim of financing new high-risk projects.

The Bank of England also sponsored in 1945 the Finance Corporation for Industry (FCI), financed mainly by insurance companies and investment trusts and designed to provide very long-term finance to capital-intensive industry, where a long gestation period might discourage private investors. Unlike ICFC, the role of FCI has been small; but this has not been due only to the greater efficiency of the capital market in full employment conditions. The nationalization of large sections of transport, steel and fuel and power removed from the private sector those industries which the philosophy behind FCI had most in mind; and large firms in other industries have in several 'strategic' cases been provided with direct support from both Labour and Conservative governments. An early example of this – to save foreign exchange – was the formation of the National Film Corporation in 1949; but assistance has since been given to individual firms like Rolls-Royce, Upper Clyde Shipbuilders and International Computers. The Industrial Reorganization Corporation (IRC) was set up by the Labour government in 1966 to facilitate and promote structural change in industry by mergers and other means, backed by a £150 m. credit facility with the Central Government. The Corporation was disbanded by the Conservative Government in 1971, but there are signs that the latter intends to revive some of its functions within the Department of Trade and Industry.

New structural developments in the 1950s

The passing of immediate postwar problems and the election of a Conservative Government in 1951 led to the relaxation of most direct controls over the economy, including those over domestic (but

not overseas) capital issues. In the following decade many new financial institutions in the private sector were established and existing ones
expanded. Two broad factors can be seen. First, the gradual reduction of excess liquidity strengthened the demand by business for
external finance. This led both to greater activity in the new issue
market and to the development of forms of financing of plant and
equipment such as leasing and hire purchase, undertaken partly by
companies already active in consumer credit. In the field of working
capital the device of factoring, whereby companies devolve credit
control to specialized institutions, took new root, and finance by
way of commercial bills expanded once more.

The second broad development was the 'cult of the equity',
the increase in the demand for ordinary shares by investors in
general and life assurance and private sector pension funds in
particular. This response to postwar full employment and inflation
led to a sharp rise in ordinary share prices during the decade,
facilitating the financing of industry by new issues and stimulating
the growth of institutions such as investment trusts and unit trusts.
Another aspect of this, and of their ability to respond to new developments, was the emergence of the merchant banks as managers of
large investment portfolios on behalf of pension funds, investment
trusts, unit trusts and wealthy private clients.

These developments took place when official monetary policy,
especially from 1955, was seeking to control inflation partly by
pressing the banks to limit their advances and generally by attempting to restrain the growth in the money supply. The latter policy was
made increasingly difficult, however, by sales of Government
securities by private investors, including investment institutions,
which sought to reverse their wartime accumulation of gilt-edged
securities because of fears concerning inflation and the balance of
payments and the attractions of ordinary shares. The authorities
nevertheless felt obliged to support the gilt-edged market to sustain
the marketability of Government debt, which they regarded as
essential to both the stability of private financial institutions and to
the operations of government finance.

The Radcliffe Committee

The ineffectiveness of monetary control led to the inquiry by the
Radcliffe Committee in 1957 into the workings of the monetary
system. Although minor structural problems existed, the Committee
found that the increasing variety of institutions and the tendency for

most of them to become rather less specialized, together with the active new issue market and the general financial confidence that full employment policies had created, had led Britain's capital market to become a highly integrated one. In it the relative importance of the banking system had declined. (By 1960 the liabilities of non-bank institutions were nearly 80 per cent larger than those of banks and discount houses, whereas in 1945 they had been only some 20 – 25 per cent higher.) It therefore concluded that control over the money supply in general and of bank advances in particular could play only a minor part in short-term demand management, although it did see monetary control and associated interest rate levels as useful in determining the longer-term financial climate (or general 'liquidity position', as the Report called it).

Changes during the 1960s

Monetary policy and the banking system

Governments after 1960 followed the advice of the Radcliffe Committee in concentrating on fiscal policy to manage demand, but monetary policy has continued to occupy their attention. Although not accepting the extreme version of 'monetarist' prescriptions, the Treasury and the Bank of England have come to emphasize the need to contain the growth in money supply whenever demand must be held down. The growth in bank deposits has therefore been held back relative to the liabilities of other institutions in periods of high demand. However, this policy itself was for some years handicapped by the official practice of acting as 'buyer of last resort' in the gilt-edged market whenever the latter was under serious pressure from sales by the banks and other investors. Until recently control over clearing bank advances was therefore exercised by directives, and although these were accompanied by similar requests to non-clearing banks and consumer credit companies in recent years, they tended to limit competition between the clearing banks and other institutions and indeed, between the clearing banks themselves.

Because more open competition in the financial system was desirable, but within the context of a more effective monetary policy, the authorities' policy has changed over the past five years, especially as it became evident that the clearing bank cartel on interest rates was already being weakened by institutional changes.

Increased Competition

Foremost among these developments was the growth of a 'secondary' banking system, a complex of overseas banks, merchant banks and the subsidiaries of the clearing banks themselves. This growth was originally due to two main factors, the emergence of the local authorities as large short-term borrowers in the middle 1950s and the role of British clearing banks, merchant banks and the London subsidiaries of American banks in the growing Eurodollar market following the relaxation of exchange controls from 1958. This secondary money market was first an intermediary between the movement of overseas funds in general, and the Eurodollar market in particular, and the short-term borrowing (in sterling) by the local authorities. Later the system came also to embrace term lending and borrowing for domestic funds and domestic industrial borrowers. Although this market only accommodates relatively large deposits, the open competition within it clearly threatened to undermine the cartel operated by the clearing banks, whose 'bidding subsidiaries' became just as active in the new market as the merchant banks and overseas banks. Increased competition within the banking system and between banks and other institutions also stemmed from: (*a*) the creation in 1966 of a National Giro system; (*b*) the development of the inter-company loan market, in which the clearing banks may act as intermediaries; (*c*) the agreement by the clearing banks in 1969 to make a fuller disclosure of their profits; (*d*) the continued expansion of non-bank short-term and medium-term lending practices such as leasing.

Greater competition within banking was paralleled by the further development of the official view that effective control of the money supply required withdrawing support from the gilt-edged market[3] in times of pressure and, therefore, necessitated wider fluctuations in interest rates, which were also seen to be needed to induce shifts in bank asset portfolios. Greater interest rate changes would have further strained the clearing bank cartel, but in any case the authorities came to form the view that the abolition of the lending ceilings applied to the banks and instalment credit houses was necessary for a more visual and innovative capital market, a condition, perhaps, for Britain's success in the European Economic Community.

The new arrangements

Accordingly, in September 1971 the Bank of England announced

[3]   This support began to be modified in 1968.

far-reaching changes in the monetary and banking policy. These can be summarized briefly as follows:

1. The Bank of England no longer provides outright support for gilt-edged stocks having a maturity of over one year.

2. The clearing banks have abandoned their collective agreements concerning interest rates on both borrowing and lending.

3. Lending 'ceilings' by banks and instalment credit companies have been abolished.

4. In place of the previous minimum 'liquid asset' ratio (of 28 per cent) to which the clearing banks only were subject, *all* banks, including merchant banks and the British branches of overseas banks, now maintain a new minimum 'reserve asset' ratio (of $12\frac{1}{2}$ per cent). 'Reserve assets' are defined more restrictively than the old 'liquid assets'.

5. The discount houses will keep at least 50 per cent of their borrowed funds in certain categories of public sector debt. The Bank of England continues to confine lender-of-last-resort facilities to these institutions, so that the latter will continue, as their side of the bargain, to cover the amount of Treasury bills on offer at the weekly tender. But the discount houses will no longer tender for these bills at an *agreed* price. The Treasury bill rate, and even Bank rate, is likely to fluctuate rather more than in the past.

6. Instalment credit finance houses are subject to minimum reserve asset ratios of 10 per cent.

7. The Bank of England may now call for 'Special Deposits' from all banks, not just the clearing banks, and from instalment credit finance houses. Different rates of call may be applied to overseas deposits (so as to influence the movement of international funds).

The effects on competition

How far the new system will affect competition in the capital market has still to be seen. The banks have undoubtedly sought to raise their advances in general through more forceful marketing and new forms of personal loans, to which the previous restrictions had been applied most forcefully. Greater competition has led to a new flexibility in the banking interest rate structure; in the slack conditions of the winter of 1971 – 72 both borrowing and lending rates were reduced in relation to Bank rate.

Nevertheless the incentive to compete has been restrained by the weak industrial demand for advances in the slack economic conditions of 1971 – 72. How far the clearing banks will actively compete for small deposits when the industrial demand for advances recovers is debatable, especially now that the clearing banks are reduced to four large banks plus one smaller group. Price competition in oligopolistic industry is usually restrained, and in banking such restraint, which goes back for about a century, may well prove to have outlived the formal cartel. Price competition for large deposits, whose supply to the banks as a whole is elastic, is understandable. However, except for savings-type deposits at present held with the building societies and the National Savings movement, the supply of small deposits to banks collectively is relatively inelastic, so that a rise in deposit rates on the part of the banks as a whole might simply reduce banking profits. To compete effectively with other institutions the banks would also have to match any capture of their deposits by a similar capture of their lending, by making loans of a greater riskiness or of a form different from those in the past. Moreover, the authorities have given notice that they would not look with favour on a transfer of deposits to the banks from the savings institutions.

In general the new policy strengthens the position of the clearing banks as against that of the 'secondary' banks and the instalment credit houses (several of which, however, are the subsidiaries of the clearing banks themselves).[4] Whether the ending of the cartel will be sufficient to offset these gains to the clearing banks is doubtful, especially as the fuller disclosure of profits in clearing bank accounts has led them generally to pursue the goal of higher profit margins by one means or another, and competition from banks outside the clearing banks is not – or not yet – acute as far as any but large deposits are concerned. Nevertheless, Britain's banking is clearly entering a new phase, in which greater flexibility of interest rates and greater competition for new business are likely to lead partly to innovation and greater operating efficiency in the clearing banks. Certain forms of banking service previously offered as a substitute for price competition are likely to be trimmed, but other activities will almost certainly be widened. The clearing banks are likely to take advantage of their new freedom by developing new forms of lending such as terms loans and by increasing the range of their 'non-banking' services, especially as this remains a more tempting

---

[4] Some instalment credit houses are also seeking to be officially recognised as 'banks'.

method of attracting new business than raising deposit rates. British clearing banks are thus likely to depart from the specialization to working capital finance that was once their distinctive feature and so should develop closer similarities with the 'comprehensive' banking typical of other countries, especially those in continental Europe.

Other developments

The company sector

Many developments outside the banking system clearly discernible in the 1950s have gone further during the past decade. Pressure on company liquidity has been aggravated by a fall in the share of company profits in company sector factor incomes[5] and by the

TABLE 6.1　*Eligible liabilities* and reserve assets of banking groups and finance houses*

	Eligible liabilities (£m.)	February 1972 Percentages of total	Reserve assets (£m.)	Reserve assets ratio (%)
1. London clearing banks	10,865	59·2	1,557	14·3
2. Scottish clearing banks	1,038	5·7	150	14·4
3. Other deposit banks	271	1·5	42	15·5
4. Accepting houses	1,054	5·7	223	21·1
5. British overseas and Commonwealth banks	1,346	7·3	270	20·0
6. American banks	1,132	6·2	229	20·2
7. Foreign banks and affiliates	356	1·9	105	29·5
8. Other overseas banks	112	0·6	29	25·9
9. Other banks	1,460	7·9	247	16·9
BANKS – TOTAL	17,633	96·0	2,852	16·2
10. Finance houses	727	4·0	37	5·1
TOTAL	18,360	100·0	2,889	15·7

*　'Eligible liabilities' are those against which minimum required reserve assets are calculated and differ from the total liabilities of these institutions by only a small amount.

[5]　The share of company gross trading profits in factor incomes generated in the company sector, excluding stock appreciation, has fallen from 27·8 per cent in 1960 to 19·0 per cent in 1970, roughly comparable years of the economic cycle. The exact balance of causes for this decline is debatable, but the pressure of wage awards is probably one explanation, contrary to earlier views about the constancy of labour's share in national income.

restrictions on bank advances. The company sector has responded by restricting capital outlays and partly by resorting further to external financing outside the banking system. Relatively new developments such as leasing and trade credit factoring have accelerated and the new issue market has been busy. The 1965 Finance Act replaced the previously relatively neutral system of Profits Tax by Corporation Tax, which discriminated against the payment of dividends, causing a switch of emphasis towards loan stock financing, leading to an increase in the degree of gearing of British companies closer to that typical of the USA and continental Europe.[6]

TABLE 6.2 *New capital issues* 1961-71*

	Total (£m.)	Ordinary (£m.)	Ordinary (%)	Preference (£m)	Preference (%)	Loan stock (£m.)	Loan stock (%)
1961	629·4	446·2	70·9	−1·1	−0·2	184·3	29·3
1962	573·0	261·6	45·7	2·7	0·5	308·7	53·9
1963	540·6	193·3	35·8	10·0	1·8	337·3	62·4
1964	613·3	223·4	36·4	7·5	1·2	382·4	62·3
1965	629·1	87·5	13·9	−14·9	−2·3	556·5	88·4
1966	845·9	158·6	18·7	28·4	3·3	658·9	77·9
1967	704·5	77·4	10·9	−2·4	−0·3	629·5	89·3
1968	716·3	374·4	52·3	−10·0	−1·4	351·8	49·1
1969	684·3	210·5	30·8	−0·6	−0·1	474·4	69·3
1970	363·6	83·2	22·9	12·4	3·4	268·0	73·7
1971	745·6	226·2	30·3	11·4	1·5	508·0	68·1

* Quoted companies only; issues less redemptions.

Another consequence has been the spread of sale-and-leaseback operations, whereby industrial companies sell freehold property in exchange for a long-term rental agreement. This shift of external financing away from ordinary shares towards all kinds of fixed-interest finance coincided in the 1960s with a further shift in investors' asset preferences *towards* ordinary shares. The latter can be explained partly as a long-term adjustment by investors to the forces of inflation and economic growth, but it was also accentuated by the Trustee Act of 1961. The latter allowed trustees to invest trust funds in ordinary shares up to certain limits even where no express provi-

(6) The 1972 Finance Act, however, has replaced the Corporation Tax system by a company tax structure similar to that of France and which is relatively neutral as between dividends and retentions, at any rate.

sion about this was made in trust deeds. The general enlargement of the demand for ordinary shares, together with a reduction in the proportion of external company financing taking this form, caused a sharp rise in ordinary share prices to levels at which price-earnings ratios were comparable with those in the United States and in some European countries.

The Institutions

Another consequence, naturally, was a further increase in the share of institutional portfolios, i.e. life insurance and pension funds, represented by ordinary shares and a further decline in the share taken by government securities in particular. The demand for ordinary shares also favoured, at least until recently, the expansion of the unit trust movement. One aspect of this development was the spread of life assurance policies linked to unit trust holdings, a device favoured by the tax relief accorded to life assurance and by the freedom with which life assurance can be sold, in contrast to the statutory conditions on the direct sale of unit trust shares designed to protect the public from fraud and excessive management charges.

Since 1968, however, the experience of industrial recession, in combination with serious cost inflation, together with the sharp fall in share prices in 1969 – 70, has clearly weakened the interest in ordinary shares shown by individual investors. Instead, one consequence of inflation has been the development of a new type of unit trust, the property bond trust, whose assets take the form mainly of real property, largely commercial and residential property. This development has coincided with an unprecedented rise in house prices over the past two years.

These developments in property no doubt reflect a new attitude on the part of the public towards the effects of inflation, but they have also been accentuated by the expansionist monetary policy pursued by the authorities to check the industrial recession, by the aggressive lending policies of the banks with the removal of official ceilings, and by the unprecedented flow of funds into the building societies. The latter have enjoyed the benefit of relatively low short-term interest rates, a high level of personal saving and the diversion of that saving away from ordinary shares to less risky forms of invest-ment during the economic recession.

Increased emphasis on equities

Other features of the capital market during the past decade deserve

TABLE 6.3 *The assets of life-assurance offices** – 1927-70

	1927	1937	1948	1965	1966	1967	1968	1969	1970
TOTAL ASSETS (£m.)	1,064	1,655	2,724	10,979	11,788	13,109	14,382	15,621	16,997
Percentage held in:									
Mortgages	12	11	7	14	15	14	14	15	14
Loans on public rates, British municipal and county securities, public boards (UK)	5	7	4	2	2	2	2	2	2
Loans on policies and personal securities	5	3	1	1	1	1	1	1	1
British Government securities	26	22	40	16	15	16	14	14	13
Commonwealth Government provincial and municipal securities	8	7	4	2	2	3	2	2	2
Foreign Government and municipal securities	7	5	4	3	3	3	3	3	3
Debentures	15	16	9	16	17	17	16	16	17
Preference shares	5	8	8	4	4	3	2	2	2
Ordinary shares	5	10	11	22	21	21	24	25	25
Real property	5	5	5	9	9	9	9	9	10
Agent's outstanding balances and accrued interest	4	3	5	7	7	8	8	8	8
Cash	2	2	3	2	2	3	3	3	3

* Offices established in Great Britain only, but including their assets held against overseas and non-life business. The figures relate to balance-sheet and not market values and understate, at market value, the proportion held in ordinary shares and real property and overstate that held in fixed-interest assets.

mention. As one aspect of their equity-mindedness, many institutions have shown a special interest in investment in relatively new and smaller companies. The development of new specialist institutions in this field in the 1930s and immediately after the war has been taken further with the interest shown in small companies by merchant banks and other institutions, some of which are subsidiaries of the merchant banks or clearing banks. This interest is particularly great in companies which might be groomed for public flotation. The emphasis has therefore shifted from fixed-interest finance to equity participation. As far as small companies with a record of profitability and good management are concerned, the 'gap' in the capital market which the Macmillan Committee discerned in 1931 has been filled by these new institutions and by the increased efficiency of the new issue market itself. The Macmillan Committee placed the minimum economical level of new stock exchange issues of new capital at £200,000, equivalent to £1 m. at today's prices. Issues of this size by newly-floated companies can today be made with little difficulty in London or on the provincial exchanges. As in all countries, however, the finance of completely new ventures where there is no relevant past record and where the risk of failure is high, remains a problem. Taken as a whole, however, the supply of 'venture capital' today probably exceeds that of *realistic* propositions by small companies seeking finance. The capital market has thus come to adapt to the diminished role of personal wealth in the supply of risk finance to new business.

Accountability

A second aspect of the relative ease with which most companies can obtain finance in modern conditions is that the Government and the Bank of England have continued to be concerned at the separation of ownership from managerial control in the private sector. The desire to give greater recognition of the interests of shareholders in this context and to make competition for finance more effective has led to further legislation requiring a fuller degree of disclosure by companies in general. The 1967 Companies Act requires standards of disclosure surpassing in many respects, with the main exception of 'insider trading', those even on the New York stock exchange. In general British company accounts are far more informative than those of EEC countries.

Another aspect of this problem, but in a different context, was the establishment of a City Panel in 1959 to frame rules of conduct for the financial conduct of take-over and merger operations. Since

1967 there has been a particularly high level of acquisitions, and the City Panel was set up on behalf of issuing houses and other institutions as an alternative to the establishment of an official body comparable to the SEC in the United States. The City naturally prefers a watchdog of its own breed to one imposed by the Government, and although problems undoubtedly persist the Panel has succeeded in terminating various abuses in acquisition tactics with the help of the cohesive quality of the City already referred to.

The Bank of England was active in spurring the City to establish the take-over panel. The Bank's concern with the problems raised by the separation of ownership from control and the need to apply more effective sanctions to inefficient management reflects the traditional unwillingness of institutional investors like insurance companies to interfere with boards of directors except at times of crisis or when the rights of particular *classes* of shareholders are involved, as in a company reconstruction. This remoteness has undoubtedly decreased in recent years, but it contrasts with the more active role played by European banks in company affairs. In March 1972 the Bank of England expressed its concern with these problems by suggesting that institutional investors set up a joint working party with a more positive role than that so far played by the trade associations or 'investment protection committees' of these institutions. The implications of this policy have still to be seen.

Entry into the EEC

Developments in banking and the formation of government or government-sponsored agencies have given the British capital market features characteristic of the capital markets of continental Europe. Nevertheless, in its range and in its wealth of experience and still acquired in both overseas and domestic finance, London probably remains unique in Europe. Despite the increasing role played by Government, British institutions are less encumbered by direct restrictions than are their counterparts in other countries. And despite the expansion of direct contact between financial institutions and industrial companies the London stock exchange and new issue market remain relatively more important than similar institutions in other European countries.

The capital market

Although Germany in particular among EEC countries has grown in influence, especially in the Eurobond market, the London capital market, by virtue of its institutional maturity, is the natural candidate for financial leadership within the Common Market. Because of its size, its range of institutions in the fields of both short-term and long-term finance and its skills, the London capital market is still without a single large rival within the EEC.

The Stock Exchange

This is particularly true of the London stock exchange. The market value of quoted industrial securities is roughly comparable with that of EEC countries as a whole and the volume of activity is almost certainly much higher. Moreover, the London Stock Exchange has long had experience of international securities, which as far as equities are concerned already exceed in market value the total of purely British stocks, thanks to the importance of international mining houses etc. Most large British stockbrokers already have well developed international connections.

It is therefore not difficult to envisage the development of London exchange as the heart of an EEC securities system, especially as the Government has said that it intends to remove all exchange controls on the movement of capital between Britain and the EEC within five years. Optimists see London, indeed, as becoming eventually the basis for a unified EEC stock exchange network. Nevertheless, institutional obstacles must be removed if the role of the London market is to grow. First, the disclosure rules for European companies are much less demanding than those of Britain. Secondly, the London Stock Exchange system of fortnightly settlement (for non-Government securities) contrasts with the more or less immediate settlement typical in Europe. Thirdly, in Britain the registered stock procedure prevails, whereas in Europe bearer securities are more common. Fourthly, the system for charging for security transactions in London differs from that followed in the EEC. British maximum commissions, on relatively small transactions, tend to be higher, but in Britain there are no supplementary 'service' charges (e.g. for safe custody, divided collection) typical in European centres. Questions such as these will have to be resolved if harmonization of practice is to be secured.

Life insurance

Problems of harmonization also exist in life insurance, where

British companies have a history of relative freedom from Governmental control over premium calculation, valuation practice and investment policy that has enabled them to innovate in a way that is difficult on the Continent and that has encouraged the development of a conservative but sophisticated actuarial profession unrivalled in most European countries. British life insurance companies are likely to resist any attempt to 'harmonize' on the basis of European practices involving the need for actuarial reserves unnecessary in British conditions and will undoubtedly resist equally unnecessary restrictions on investment policies. The basic issue is not that of competition with Continental insurance companies but the adverse effect that any such restrictions would have on the growth of life insurance in the United Kingdom.

Banking

Although British banking differs from that on the Continent in several respects, no technical problems of harmonization exist in banking, which is already in some respects an international business; although it must be admitted that the existing overseas interests of British banks lie mainly outside the EEC. It is not easy to discern the course of future developments here. All EEC countries already possess mature banking industries with relatively little room for international competition in routine *domestic* banking business. Most large banks in Britain and on the Continent already have a small number of branches in other member countries of the Community, together with well-developed correspondent facilities; international banking, indeed, does not require a large network of international branches. Perhaps the most likely development is the further extension of consortium banking, to match the development of large multi-national companies. Such developments would probably accelerate the movement of British clearing banks in the direction of 'comprehensive' banking, which has already begun for domestic reasons. One interesting question concerns the future of the merchant banks, which took advantage of the once relatively narrow specialization of the clearing banks to develop as issuing houses, investment houses and international financiers. Their adaptability has been facilitated by their relatively small size. It remains to be seen how far they will prosper in a multi-national European context calling for large-scale operations, in which they will be faced both by large and experienced European rivals and revitalized British clearing banks.

I

The role of sterling

Finally, it must be emphasized that important aspects of the role of the British capital market in the EEC will depend on the position of sterling inside the Community. The British Government has announced that it intends to reduce the part played by sterling as an international reserve currency by working for a gradual running down of *official* sterling balances (which are largely those of other sterling countries). This decision reflects a developing view that to a relatively small country like Britain, with low liquid international reserves, being a minor international reserve currency in a world dominated by the dollar is a net disadvantage. The phasing out of this role appears to be welcome to the French Government, in particular; but recently other voices have been heard arguing that there could be a special reserve role for sterling within the EEC. For sterling would be a natural pivot on which to base a system of relatively fixed exchange rates within the Community, alongside a more flexible relationship with the dollar.

Such wide problems are outside the scope of this discussion. It should be stressed, however, that the British Government's decision to curtail the part played by sterling as an official reserve currency is not in any way intended to restrict its role as an international medium of exchange, which involves a network of sterling flows and the holding of sterling balances by private holders in Europe and elsewhere. This has always reflected Britain's position in world trade and in private international finance, and the development of sterling as an international reserve currency has been a consequence rather than a cause of this position. This is likely to continue to hold good in the future. The role of sterling as a trading currency in the widest sense will depend on the economic health of Britain and the vitality of its capital market within a European setting. Although it is possible for London to develop financial entrepôt facilities, as in the Eurodollar market, even if Britain's underlying balance of payments position is uncertain, in the last resort the bounds to the development of London as an international financial centre will be set by the strength of Britain's balance of payments as a whole.

Management of research and development

A. W. Pearson

Introduction

The rate of growth of expenditure on research and development has received considerable attention over the last few years in almost all countries. General economic factors have stimulated the reappraisal coupled with a more specific feeling that larger R & D budgets do not necessarily lead to a proportional increase in profitability and growth. Many reasons are given for this, not least of which is the difficulty of arriving at adequate definitions of R & D, covering as it does a range of activities from basic research to troubleshooting, quality control, and even market research in some cases. But the problem will not be solved by simply drawing up more explicit definitions of R & D. Much more important is the way we choose to use the technological resources which are available to us and in particular how we integrate these into the organization as a whole. Some organizations, and countries, which undertake considerable amounts of R & D do not seem to be able to turn it to useful advantage; others with much lower expenditures not only succeed in capitalizing on their own but often make considerable use of work undertaken by others.

Recent changes

It is easy to put forward the argument that this apparent anomaly is due to the lack of definition of objectives and to the lack of coordination between R & D and the rest of the organization, but it is not so easy to set about correcting this situation or to establish mechanisms which will enable these deficiences to be overcome. However, very serious attempts have been made over the last few years to do just this, and Britain has not been backward in this respect. We have seen very substantial changes made in a short time both in the attitudes to, and practice of, the management of R & D, and this is now resulting in a new and exciting set of opportunities for forward-thinking companies.

This has not simply been brought about by the introduction of formalized techniques, although these have a part to play in certain areas, but by a change of policies of organizations and a change in attitudes of people within these organizations. Attitudes have changed towards the use of external facilities on a contract basis, the introduction of external finance for joint development activities, the selling of internal technological skills to outside bodies, and the exploitation of 'by-products' of R & D through venture management and through the formation of new companies. These changes have not been brought about painlessly. Some pruning and redirection has been necessary, but this has been generally welcomed once it has been acknowledged that change is necessary, and more important once the decision has been taken that it will be made. R & D is now a more streamlined activity, it is managed as well as, if not better than, other parts of the business, and it is poised to make a significant contribution to profitability and growth by a variety of means.

'Marketing R & D'

One of the most significant results of this rethink is the development of a 'market' for R & D capability in its own right. More and more organizations have seen the potential for selling their technological capability to a range of interested parties. In some cases this has been brought about by sheer necessity, in others by a deliberate change of policy in the light of perceived opportunities. In almost every case it has resulted in benefit to all parties. It is this development with which this paper is particularly concerned because it is one which must inevitably increase in scope as more and more organisations realize that trade in R & D can be a two-way process; that is, they can now buy in from outside and/or sell their own facilities in what is rapidly becoming an open market. However, if organizations which do not already do this are to enter the arena, they must be prepared to change their policies and to adopt new management practices which will enable them to make the most effective use of the opportunities which are available. Many of these changes have already been made in Britain and will be discussed in this paper. Examples chosen from a range of environments will be used to point out the facilities which are being offered and how particular situations are being handled. These will serve to illustrate the range of opportunities which is available to any organization and suggest ways in which it might take advantage of them for its own purposes.

European firms coming into closer contact with Britain in the next few years will find in the area of R & D a keenness and interest which will be on the one hand a challenge to those who will have to compete and on the other an opportunity for those who are able to take advantage of the available skills. The choice is for each company to make, and it has never before been so wide-ranging. Britain views Europe as a market opening for its scientific/technical skills and many organizations are already extending their activities to take this into account, in some cases modifying their charters and in most cases changing old-established policies.

This paper aims to examine these trends and show how European companies can make use of the skills and the opportunities which are now available. It briefly looks at the situation with regard to the possibilities for financial cooperation in the exploitation of new technology and at some of the facilities available for setting up research establishments in the UK, and then concentrates on the major area of developing activity – contract research. Finally, some consideration is given to the way in which management practices are currently changing and how this development is encouraging better links between R & D and the market place and increasing the opportunities for exploiting technology.

Cooperative ventures

One method of exploiting research, particularly in areas of high uncertainty, is through cooperative arrangements with other bodies, which will enable the risks to be shared. This is becoming more and more important as the size of investment required to develop and exploit new technology increases while the size of the market is not increasing proportionately. In certain areas this has long been recognized to be the situation, notably the aircraft industry. The experience to date indicates that the progressing of projects which involve different parties is not always easy, but it is clear that collaboration may be worthwhile if organizational problems can be overcome.

Cooperation in Europe

Other areas where European cooperation has been encouraged for some time are well known, for example space research through

ESRO, and high energy physics through CERN. Other cooperative ventures have been, or are being, encouraged – some very successfully and others less so. It could be argued that many of their problems have arisen primarily because of their international nature.

However, this is not preventing attempts at further collaboration. In 1970 the Brussels Commission proposed the setting up of a European Research and Development Committee, which would put forward proposals for projects, and a European Agency for Research and Development, which would have executive and financial powers as distinct from the political ones vested in the Council of Ministers. A step in this direction was taken in November 1970, when the science ministers of nineteen European countries (participants in the Organization for European Cooperation in the Field of Scientific and Technical Research – COST) agreed to fund seven collaborative projects, totalling about £8 or £9 million. The individual projects will be in the areas of communication systems, metallurgy related to gas turbines and desalination plants, and three projects in the field of pollution. These are not surprising activities to choose, particularly the last, as they are problems which are common, and of increasing importance, to all industrialized countries.

Cooperation in areas such as these is likely to continue and may well increase. Proposals for the launching of common industrial, scientific and technological policies in the enlarged Common Market were aired at a conference in Venice early this year, one of the points under consideration being the possibility of setting up a European research and development committee.

Cooperative financing

Activities such as this are of obvious importance to many organizations, but are likely to have much longer-term implications and be less under their control. Of more immediate and practical importance are the possibilities of introducing external finance into the organization for supporting technological developments, particularly where the risks are high and the funds required are large. The need for this type of cooperative arrangement has been anticipated and there has been a considerable expansion of facilities for entering into joint ventures.

Public Bodies

Public bodies have been active in this area for some time. In the UK the Government established in 1949 the National Research Development Corporation, (NRDC), with the object of licensing to industry the results of research financed from public funds, supporting inventions arising from private inventors, (projects which appeared to NRDC to be of major national interest), and assisting industry by making available finance for ideas or projects originating within industry.[1][1]

The scale of NRDC's licensing activity is indicated by its royalty income in excess of £4 m. in 1971-72, some of which is derived from overseas licences. NRDC has a number of agreements for interchange of licensing situations with organizations conducting a similar kind of activity abroad. In Europe an agreement has been signed with the French National Agency for Research and Development (ANVAR) and such arrangements may well be extended. In addition to this NRDC's investments in joint ventures with industrial companies amounted to £19·3 m. at the end of 1971. This type of finance is unique in the UK in the sense that NRDC seeks to recover its investments primarily by a levy on sales. If the project does not succeed the Corporation loses its money, and conversely it shares with the firm in success if large sales materialize.

Private Organizations

A number of merchant banks and city organizations have also entered this field making available finance, usually in return for equity participation. The recent interest of city institutions tends to ensure that finance will be available for any organization which has an approved record, and wishes to exploit technology and to open up new markets in the UK whatever the country of origin. A variety of methods of funding and profit sharing arrangements is possible.

The 'innovation broker'

Finally it would be a serious omission in this section if reference was not made to a method of exploiting research, or perhaps more correctly ideas, which is now emerging in the UK. This is through the use of an 'innovation broker'. Such an intermediary either sells the ideas to interested firms or arranges for the product to be manufactured and then markets it. Individual financial arrangements are made in respect of each idea on a mutually agreed basis, including (if this is thought desirable) equity participation by both parties.

(1)   Figures in square brackets indicate references listed at the end of this chapter.

This type of operation is significant because it offers any organization the opportunity to exploit ideas which are either outside its own sphere of operation or which it feels unable to handle with its own resources. The importance of this cannot be underestimated. The direct profitability which might arise as a consequence of using this method is unlikely to be large, particularly for the bigger organizations, but it may well help to create and sustain an environment which is productive of new ideas for the very reason that attempts are made to exploit them, even if by external means.

The location of research facilities

Many companies may not wish to become involved with outside finance and cooperative arrangements for a variety of reasons. In this case it is sensible to consider what advantages there may be in locating research facilities in the UK.

The larger multinational companies have long recognized the value of spreading their technological capability throughout the world, locating their laboratories where the necessary skills are available and close to the markets they serve. Key variables in determining the location of any type of facility are the costs of production at the alternative centres and the costs of distribution of the product between the centres and the ultimate markets. In the case of R & D, UK skills in science and technology are second to none and the cost of transferring technological information between centres in different countries is not significantly greater than between separate locations in the same country, or even sometimes between groups and divisions on the same site, communication often being promoted through the mobility of people.

This interchange of personnel between countries is becoming more commonplace and will inevitably increase in scale in the future. However, it is not always possible. In some areas of activity we have already reached the point where it is unlikely that particular skills and facilities can be made available in sufficient quantities in more than a limited number of locations. Hence an ability to link into these as and when required is most important. This can be done in a variety of ways, some more permanent than others. Possibilities of a longer term nature are being increasingly offered through the creation of 'science parks' or areas of land which are set aside for development as centres of technological excellence, usually (but not always), associated with existing facilities, including universities. Cambridge has recently established such an area which has obvious attractions, and a significant step in this direction has been taken by the Electrical Research Association (ERA), which has allocated part of its site for occupation by small technically-advanced companies. Already three such companies have moved into this 'science campus' and are taking advantage of the facilities offered which include on-site expertise on a contract basis from ERA itself. Similar developments are likely in other areas, but may not provide the flexibility which can be obtained through purchasing research skills as and when required on a contract basis.

Contract research facilities

The EEC

The EEC's efforts at a multinational R & D programme with a full budget of its own have so far made little progress, but there is every indication that the COST programmes mentioned earlier, will be a viable proposition. They are completely flexible, involve no joint funds, and are open to participants on what amounts to an *à la carte* basis.[2] Admittedly the COST programme is not as ambitious as the EEC proposal, but the method by which cooperation is proposed must affect their relative attractiveness, and in particular the way in which the former allows individual countries to opt into or out of particular areas of interest. The net result is that the number of participating countries differs between the various projects. For example, at the present time France has opted for six projects and 3·34 million units of account, and the UK five projects and a contribution of 2·98 millions.[3]

This means that each country is free to choose the areas in which it wishes to be involved, and its contribution directly reflects its interest in the various research activities. This method of cooperation is, broadly speaking, a form of contractor – customer relationship, and operates along the lines of the general principles which have been widely discussed following the publication in the UK of the 'Rothschild Report'.[3] In fact this document followed a trend which had been expressed in an earlier publication[4] in which it was stated that 'as a general rule only the "customer" knows what he wants, and by his readiness to pay for it makes the "supplier" aware of his requirements'.

This general principle is not universally accepted by the scientific community or even by non-scientists in some organizations, but it is the one which largely determines the method of operation of establishments which offer facilities on a contract basis.

This type of activity is increasing in volume involving many more types of organizations than was common in the past. For example, universities, Government establishments and even industrial companies are entering this field in addition to the research associations and independent research establishments.

Providing expertise

The employment of research on a contract basis is now being seen by many organizations as an excellent means of buying in expertise in a way which complements their own in-house technology. Fortunately recognition of this has come about almost exactly at the right time, when expert skills and facilities are being made available on an increasing scale. Organizations like the Fulmer Research Institute whose expertise lies in the materials science area, are now well established as independent research establishments working on a contract basis, mainly for individual companies but also undertaking background work for groups of companies which have similar problems. Such organizations are becoming increasingly involved with European companies.

In addition Government establishments are becoming increasingly concerned with this activity. For example, Harwell and Culham with long traditions of fundamental research of high quality in a limited field have now a well-established industrial research section which will undertake contract R & D,

Not surprisingly it has been found that the specialized skills which have been developed in nuclear work can often be readily transferred to other areas of technology: the computer logic developed to follow the complex movements of atomic particles, for example, can be modified and applied to the movement of other particles, be they people, machines, goods or vehicles, and thus to solving problems in scheduling movements in many areas of industrial companies. The variety of industrial companies with which Harwell has worked indicates the range of expertise they have available, covering producers of consumer products such as ballpoint pens, kitchen cabinets, golf clubs, glass bottles and soft drinks, through such diverse industries as electronics, instrument manufacture, chemical production, shipbuilding, motor cars and aircraft to heavy engineering, mining and quarrying.[6]

Recent contracts negotiated with European countries include one from DISA (Denmark) for development work on a laser anemometer, and one worth about £250,000 has been received by Culham from the Institute for Plasma Physics in Holland. This latter contract indicates the sort of capacity which is available for research in this special area of application.

Other groups work on similar lines; International Research & Development Company Ltd. (IRD) which is the largest private multi-disciplinary contract R & D laboratory in the UK, has considerable expertise in such areas as materials technology, mechanical engineering, applied physics and superconducting electrical machinery (d. c. and a. c.) where it is the acknowledged world leader, having produced the first superconducting electrical machine in 1966. It also maintains a techno-economic evaluation unit, consisting of staff with backgrounds in economics, science, engineering and modern languages (and able to draw on the skills of other departments), which can appraise a potential market for a product before money is invested in 'hard' R & D.

Britain's 'research associations'

Other organizations are also increasingly looking further afield to exploit their expertise. For example, many of the research associations in the UK are encouraging overseas organizations to become members. This has been made possible by changes in policy which have been generally agreed by individual RAs and which have been incorporated into their Articles of Association where this was necessary. A recent survey undertaken in the UK[7] showed that in 1970 only four out of a total of forty-three research associations did not have overseas members and that between 1968 and 1970 the overseas membership as a percentage of total membership rose from 6·5 to 7·7 per cent with the percentage of non-commonwealth membership rising even faster.

The strength of overseas membership of such bodies obviously differs from country to country and depends upon particular circumstances. The Shoe and Allied Trades Research Association (SATRA) has in membership almost the whole of the Dutch shoe manufacturing industry. It is interesting to note that SATRA is in a very strong position in the industry, as the UK shoe manufacturing members generally like all new materials they are considering using to be backed by a SATRA report. This is obviously of considerable importance to any European company which is thinking of entering British markets in the footwear field, and no doubt encourages them to take out membership of the research association.

Educational institutions

Educational institutions have not been slow in responding to this rapidly expanding and exciting area. Many have realized that they have very valuable skills which are of interest and use to a variety of organizations, and their ability to encourage customers for these skills is enabling them to develop their own facilities as well as improve their relationship with industry. The form of organization which has been adopted by such establishments varies from place to place; in one case a limited company, Loughborough Consultants, has been established to make available to industry the expertise and facilities of the Loughborough University of Technology on a sound commercial basis with the acceptance of the necessary professional responsibility. In the year 1970 – 71 its turnover doubled to £100,000 and in one area, the Noise Consultancy Unit, projects have been undertaken in Germany, Israel and Ireland as well as for local authorities in the UK. A recent initiative has led to the sponsorship by nearly 100 companies of a joint-development programme intended to reduce the drawing office costs of those engaged in civil engineering construction.

This year the University of Manchester is establishing a new post of Research Contracts Officer whose responsibility will be to act as an interface between the expertise which lies in the University and organizations which would like to make use of it. Such arrangements, which will inevitably be developed further in the future, will help to forge better links between the universities and the community and should facilitate the diffusion of technology as well as providing more immediate benefits in the form of contract research.

Changes in the 'research associations'

Research associations in Britain have for a long time provided development and testing facilities for both members and non-members as part of their service to industry. However, more recently many of these organizations have been completely rethinking their policies and have made considerable changes in the methods of operation and in the services they offer.

One of the most dramatic changes was made by the Electrical Research Association (ERA), which made a considerable shift in direction and moved from an organization essentially serving the electrical engineering industry (with its finance mainly derived from membership fees and Government grants) to an independent research institute now deriving about 80 per cent of its income from individually negotiated contracts, including some on a multi-client basis. It now has over 100 members outside the UK and expects cooperation with Europe to increase in the future.

Another research association, that serving the textile industry and commonly referred to as the Shirley Institute, has set up a separate company, Shirley Developments Ltd., the primary aim of which is to exploit the knowhow of the Institute through the licensing of scientific instruments and machinery arising out of the research programme. The route from research to economic benefits through scientific equipment is an interesting and fruitful one to be looked at, and one which is being increasingly seen to be important. Shirley Developments has widened its terms of reference to enable it to exploit this outlet for other people. Agreements have already been made with the Dutch fibre producer AKZO and with two organizations in France. At the present time a total range of about sixty instruments is being handled and income from royalties and other fees to date has totalled well over £500,000. This may well be a way in which European companies could capitalize on some of their technical knowhow in Britain.

Management and organization

It could be argued that the growth of contract research facilities, some of which have been mentioned in the previous section, is fine on paper, but that they are difficult to make use of in practice mainly because of management and organisational problems.

Project-based organisations

The latter cannot be underestimated, but in the last few years significant progress has been made in management practices which suggests that arrangements for handling projects undertaken externally can be as satisfactory as for those undertaken in-house. At the same time as the growth in the availability of contract research facilities there have been considerable changes made which have brought significant advantages to all parties. The majority of organizations have moved, or are in the process of moving, over to a project-based structure in which responsibility for all aspects, both technical and commercial, are vested in the same person. This person will draw upon all the skills of the organizations as required but in dealings with the client he carries total responsibility. The customer communicates directly with the appropriate person in the organization who is the expert in the particular problem area, and he does not get involved in administrative details with which he does not normally want to be concerned.

The changing economic climate

This might appear to be asking a lot of the individual scientist, and indeed would have been so until quite recently, but very important changes have occurred in the management of R & D which have made this possible. The first of these is concerned with the different attitude which has been introduced into laboratories in the UK – brought about in part by the changing economic climate but interestingly enough welcomed in most cases by an enthusiastic research community, which has become just as keen to demonstrate its managerial abilities as its technical skills.

The profit centre

In many establishments these developments have led to the formalization of the project leader role and an introduction of the 'profit-centre' concept. This has led to a recognition that if R & D personnel are to assume responsibility for the progressing on both a cost and time basis of the projects which they direct they must have suitable tools for assisting them in this work. A variety of aids to management have been proposed in the literature over a considerable period of time, but the general experience appears to have been that they have rarely been effectively used in the past. However, the recent changes in attitudes and philosophy have clearly demonstrated the need for such procedures and over the last few years a number of organizations have developed and introduced very interesting methods of planning and monitoring which they have found to be of considerable help.

Planning

The Fulmer Research Institute has found particular benefit in a method based on computer programming flow charts.[8] Called research planning diagrams, this method offers a number of advantages over the more conventional arrow diagram or PERT type method for R & D situations. It is particularly useful for discussing costs and timescales with potential customers and as such acts as a very effective communication mechanism. This is a major advantage, particularly in situations where the R & D department or establishment and the customer are some distance apart. Fulmer has found European companies are used to a more formalized approach to contracting out work and that research planning diagrams have been very readily accepted by them as a means of progressing projects.

Marketing

A more recent development in organizations has been the introduction into many R & D establishments of a person or group with specific responsibility for marketing the scientific and technical skills. Many larger organizations and in particular the multi-national ones, have for a long time made use of interface or integrating groups to link R & D to the different parts of the business as appropriate, but in the main these have performed a coordinating function rather than being primarily concerned with marketing of the R & D capability. The recent trend is therefore interesting, but not perhaps surprising. It has been most marked in the organizations which do not have a well-defined customer, or which wish to extend their activity outside their normal sphere of operation. In almost all cases the group concerned with marketing has considerable technical skills but does not generally continue to practice these skills, rather concentrating on introducing potential customers to the people in the organization whose expertise is most likely to satisfy the customer's needs.

The role of senior managers

These developments have also to some extent modified the position of the director of an establishment and also of his senior people. They are now more concerned with longer-term planning, and with encouraging the development of appropriate skills, which will enable the organization to open up new opportunities for growth and diversification. What was essentially a technical role in many organizations is now rapidly changing to an active involvement in the more commercial end of the business. However, this has not reduced the need for senior management of an R & D establishment, whether it is an independent institute or part of a large organization, to keep an oversight on projects which are being progressed. In fact, if anything, the need for this has increased with the acceptance of a tighter control of time and cost schedules which is generally agreed to be necessary if an organization is to remain viable in the present economic climate.

When one considers the large number of projects which most establishments are progressing at any one time this would appear to be a difficult task. The introduction of the project type structure and the subsequent development of management skills in senior personnel has helped to reduce this problem, but not entirely overcome it. There is still a need for senior management to be able to see the position of the laboratory at any one time with regard to the number of projects in hand and to have information about the anticipated forward loadings on individual sections and on central services. Many organizations have looked at this problem and have introduced systems designed for their own particular purposes. The Knutsford laboratory of The Nuclear Power Group has done just this, and by progressively developing their system over a number of years has now produced one which is very simple to operate and yet effective.[9] It operates on the principle of defining milestones or stages in the life of a project and estimating the date and cost at which it is anticipated these will be reached. These estimates are provided by project leaders who are now fairly skilled at the operation and the estimates are updated at specified intervals of time. This process of updating enables a history of a project to be built up, and enables all interested parties, for example the group leader, research director and the client, to be kept informed of the state of progress of the work. It also provides valuable information about the likelihood that any particular project or programme of work will be completed in time, enabling corrective action to be taken if this is considered necessary. This particular method is being continually kept under review and modified in the light of experience of its use. At present it is possible to use some of the information to provide forward-loading information for the laboratory as a whole and this is extremely valuable as an aid to management in planning future resource requirements.

Equally important, it indicates whether or not resources are adequate for progressing the current work load and for entering into new agreements. The need for information of this latter type cannot be over-emphasized. No R & D establishment with a commercial market in mind can afford to contract for work which cannot be progressed satisfactorily with the available resources, whether this is due to lack of appropriate skills or simply an overload on existing staff. If this situation is allowed to arise it is likely to lead to very undesirable consequences and it is not difficult to see why many organizations are now re-examining their organizational structure and their planning and information aids as a matter of urgency.

General discussion

More professional management

This paper has pointed out some of the developments which have taken place over the last few years in Britain, many of which have opened up opportunities for companies both here and in Europe. In particular the considerable growth in the amount and extent of resources which are available on a contract basis has been emphasized. Alongside these developments, although not necessarily caused by them, have been changes in the management of R & D which is now becoming increasingly professional. Britain has for a long time had a reputation for the quality of its research work, but it is frequently being pointed out that we have not been able to turn this to advantage at the commercial stage. Times are now changing, competitive pressures have forced all organizations to look more closely at the various parts of their business and R & D has not been eliminated from this scrutiny. In fact it could be argued that it has received more attention than other parts of the business and the resulting changes both in attitudes and practice have made it an area which is now very progressively managed.

A challenge

This poses a challenge in other countries which may not, as yet, have undergone this streamlining operation. Organizations will, of course, respond to this challenge in different ways. Some will already be undergoing similar changes, perhaps even more dramatic; some may decide, as has already occurred, to take advantage of the technical skills of Britain by locating some of their research facilities over here, either as completely new developments or possibly attached to one of the 'science parks' which are able to offer many advantages. Cooperative arrangements between industrial organizations are also possible.

International aspects

European, and indeed international cooperation in R & D has, of course, been with us for some time, the emphasis being towards industries where either the size and cost of the inputs required is beyond the financial capacity of individual countries and/or the potential market size has been too small to encourage more than one entrant into the field.

However, these are exceptional situations, although their numbers may grow in the future. At the present time it would appear that the greatest opportunity for European countries is to make use of special expertises which are available on a contract basis. They will find few problems here. The paper has indicated that these are available from a wide range of organisations, from universities to independent research institutions and Government establishments. A register of the facilities available in Britain has recently been prepared, and a centralized service exists to put prospective customers in touch with the most appropriate body of skills.[10] A useful summary of the contract research facilities available in the UK has also been prepared by Dr H. Rose and has been incorporated as a chapter in a recently published book.[11]

Opportunities for business

However, there is good reason to suppose that if current trends continue industrial organizations could offer similar services to companies on a fee-paying basis. There are very few organizations which can be completely self-sufficient in all their research requirements. As R & D becomes more expensive, and in particular where specialist skills and facilities are involved, this will become increasingly so. The end result of this must be the development of a market for research on a large scale. Every organization must consider the implications of this for its own activities. There is a two-way process involved; one can sell as well as buy and there can be value in both transactions.

A rethink of policy about R & D can bring out so many opportunities for exploitation, and European companies may well feel that they are not making the best use of their own facilities. There is no shortage of people and organizations in Britain which are interested in assisting companies to exploit new technology through licensing agreements and through joint ventures, and the capital can be made available. Some organizations have already done this. In the contract research field Britain is a potential buyer as well as a seller, as some European organizations have not been slow in finding out, but there remain many areas which are relatively untapped.

Conclusions

The challenge to R & D management in any country now is to ensure that maximum recovery is made from all its activities. It must be concerned with exploiting new technology, as well as generating new ideas. It must be interested in new ventures, if necessary being prepared to become heavily involved in the production and marketing stages. Looked at as a profit centre, R & D must be efficient, it must expect to be judged in the light of alternative ways of achieving the desired outputs. There can surely never have been a time when so many opportunities existed for making use of technology and when the management of the activity was being developed in such a way as to give us confidence that R & D, whether internal or external, could be successfully integrated into the company structure.

In addition there are many new avenues opening up through which R & D, right from the idea stage, might be exploited. The coming together of these with the increasing availability of 'venture capital', is altering the pattern of activity in many organizations.

This is therefore a time when management should, if it has not already done so, be rethinking its policy towards R & D and exploring the ways in which the most effective use can be made of both its own resources and those of other organizations.

References

1. Haigh, G. E., Pearson, A. W., Watkins, D. S. and Gibbons, M., 'NRDC and the Environment for Innovation', *Nature*, Vol. 232, 20 August 1971.
2. Reports in depth 2, The changing pattern of research and development from nationalism towards supra-nationalism, *European Trends*, February 1972.
3. European cooperation in research projects, *Science Policy*, January/ February 1972.
4. A framework for Government Research and Development, Cmnd 4814, HMSO London, November 1971.
5. Industrial Research and Development in Government Laboratories, *A new organization for the 'seventies*, HMSO London, February 1970.
6. Marshall, D. W., 'Harwell's work with Industry' *National Westminster Bank Quarterly Review*, May 1971.
7. *Research Associations – the changing pattern*, Centre for the Study of Industrial Innovation, March 1972.
8. Davies, D. G. S., 'Research Planning Diagrams' – *R & D Management*, Vol. 1, no. 1, October 1970.
9. Hardingham, R. P., A simple model approach to multi-project monitoring – *R & D Management*, Vol. 1, no. 1, October 1970.

10. *Register of Consulting Scientists and Contract Research Organizations*, March 1972. Fulmer Research Institute, Stoke Poges, Bucks.
11. *Industrial Innovation through Contract Research*, Peter Peregrinus Ltd., Stevenage, Herts.

Government/business relations in the UK

8

W. G. McClelland

It is impossible in a brief paper to give a comprehensive and detailed survey of Government/business relations in the UK. It is therefore necessary to be selective, and this paper ignores, for example, the impact on business of the British fiscal system and of other measures for managing the economy and for regulating business behaviour in the interests of other parties. Instead, it concentrates on two themes.

First, it examines the way the interface between Government and business varies between two extremes, which might be called respectively arm's length and symbiotic; second, consideration is given to the way in which business can and should predict, adapt to and influence government action.

A mixed economy

In one extreme conception of the Government/business relationship, represented in Britain most purely and prominently by Mr Enoch Powell, Government should simply determine, promulgate and police the rules of the game business plays; hold the ring of the market-place within which businesses interact with each other and with consumers in the pursuit of their honourable though selfish ends. The opposite extreme is represented by a fully socialist economy as in Eastern Europe, or perhaps by the sort of symbiosis between Government and business which exists in contemporary Japan. In the first case, the relationship would be an arm's-length one and the interface clear and simple; in the second, the interface is so blurred that the very concept has become without meaning. The actual situation lies between the two extremes, nowhere more evidently than in Britain. Our economy, like others, is mixed. The Government/business relationship is less arm's length than in the United States, less symbiotic than in France.

Legislation

Certainly, legislation is enacted. It is made known by Her Majesty's Stationery Office and by *Hansard*, via the Press and many other derivative publications and channels. It is interpreted for businesses by their legal and financial advisers, its implications for them are studied by their executives, and they adapt their behaviour accordingly. The same applies to ministerial orders and other forms of delegated legislation. Compliance is assured more or less effectively, by a corps of inspectors, the local police force, or the public prosecutor. Infringements are dealt with, and clarification in the last resort provided, by the Courts. The arm's-length model works and these, in this case, are the institutions of the interface.

This is, however, by no means the whole story. Extensive consultation and lobbying precede most new legislation. At this stage, therefore, business influence is possible and legitimate. Moreover, legislation gives greater or less discretion to the Minister charged with implementing it, and here again influence is possible and proper, in respect of individual cases and classes of case. Finally, there are many forms of Government/business interaction other than those directly concerned with legislation.

For example, Government is not only a law-enforcer and a tax-gatherer but also a participant in the market. Its procurement activities are immense. It is sole owner of a large section of British industry. It is intimately involved with a number of independent companies to which it has provided finance or other forms of assistance; and it has, directly or indirectly, relationships with business at large on a number of issues and in a number of ways which cannot be characterized as 'arm's length'.

Government procurement

In theory, Government procurement activities might well be, perhaps should be, as much at arm's length as any other commercial transaction. In some respects and in some cases this is so. The need to get the best value for money on behalf of the taxpayer has normally in the UK been regarded as the predominant and sometimes the sole consideration. But Government's other responsibilities, and the sheer weight of public sector purchasing power, make the picture more complicated. Without an even flow of orders, a supplying industry or enterprise, heavily dependent on Government purchasing and possibly of strategic significance, may cut back capacity or even go to the wall and be unable to fulfil requirements later. Without reasonably profitable orders it may fail to maintain R & D expenditure and again be unable to fulfil later requirements. And what if – as has been the case with telecommunications equipment for the Post Office – there is a conflict between the best bargain for the taxpayer and the interests of the balance of payments? Should Government purchasing benefit from sweated labour or should it set an example by making its contracts conditional upon suppliers maintaining fair employment practices? (The British Government does the latter.) Can public sector purchasing power properly be used to promote standardisation, productivity, technological advance, exports, and a better geographical balance of employment? For products like computers, motor vehicles, aircraft, how far should it favour the home manufacturer? And does that mean the company manufacturing in the UK or the company that is UK-owned?

In general it may be said that, with certain important exceptions, (such as support for a home-owned computer industry), Parliament has favoured the paramountcy of short-term, value-for-money considerations. Attempts in the mid-'sixties to bring Government procurement into the service of comprehensive policy considerations did not succeed. More recent attempts, however, to improve Government purchasing practice within the conventional philosophy are meeting with success. These attempts were partly fuelled by some notorious cases in the mid-'sixties of grossly excessive profits being made on Government contracts – those of the Ferranti Bloodhound missile and the Bristol Siddeley aero-engines. In terms of institutions, the observer may note, arising from these cases, the existence of an important Parliamentary watchdog on public expenditure, the Public Accounts Committee; the use in both cases of a special independent committee of inquiry; and the subsequent establishment of a new piece of machinery, the Review Board on Government Contracts, with equal membership from Government and industry, under an independent chairman.

Nationalized industries

Even the public ownership of nationalized industries might in theory be compatible with an arm's-length relationship, that of shareholder and company. In fact, that is impossible. It is true that the underlying philosophy of nationalization in Britain has emphasized the concept of relatively independent corporations, commercially and managerially orientated, free from day-to-day interference through, for example, Parliamentary questions and enabled in consequence to take risks and back their judgement. The relevant Acts lay down the objectives of the corporations and define their formal relationships with the relevant Minister – the appointment and tenure of Chairman and Board members, the matters requiring consultation, the provisions for issuing directives, and so on. Successive White Papers have succeeded in clarifying and rendering more rational their financial objectives and criteria. But most of them have a monopoly in the UK of their own product, each of them has pervasive effects on the economy, each of them is potentially a party political football. Their capital expenditure plans must fit into that for the public sector as a whole – being revised upwards to lend credibility to a National Plan, or suddenly downwards to free home manufacturing capacity for exports. They have return on investment objectives, but cannot in practice meet them by a price increase without Government sanction. Nor can they concede a wage increase before Government has weighed the repercussions. They cannot close a pit or a branch line without Government consideration of the social consequences – though the principle of separate reimbursement in respect of non-commercial activities is now established. Nonetheless they have considerable *de facto* power and governments must struggle hard to develop a national fuel policy, or a national transport policy, amidst their warring fiefdoms. The result of all this is that the interface is densely populated by interviews between chairmen and ministers, by directives that are not directives, by work duplicated in the industry headquarters and in the responsible Ministry, and so on.

The private sector

Even outside the nationalized sector Government can no longer disengage itself from industry. If this could have been done, it would have been done by the present Conservative administration. The most spectacular instances of necessity being the mother of a volte-face have been provided by Rolls-Royce and by shipbuilding on the upper Clyde. In both cases a 'lame duck' could not stand on 'its own two feet', but the public interest required Government intervention to save it. The private financial reward was not large enough or secure enough to call forth the necessary financial resources other than from Government. The social cost-benefit analysis showed that from a national standpoint the costs of collapse in terms of unemployment, loss of exports, etc., would be greater than the costs of providing public finance. Such cost-benefit analysis is now well developed in central government administration, the most elaborate example being that applied to the problem of the siting of a third London airport. At the same time – as that example itself shows – major decisions of this sort cannot be taken without consideration of political as well as social and economic factors.

Joint involvement

But even these examples fail to bring out the full extent of the mutual involvement of government and business in Britain, indeed their collaboration. For companies seeking Government financial assistance are clearly suppliants; they propose, Government disposes. And the location of a third London airport was a clearcut major Government decision. But in addition to cases of this sort, Government seeks the advice of business in a multitude of matters, large and small, where business interests are at stake; and it actually delegates part of its discretion and authority – and the use of funds – to bodies on which business men serve.

The NEDC

The National Economic Development Council, for example, meets monthly under the chairmanship of the Prime Minister or the Chancellor of the Exchequer. It is serviced by its own secretariat with a budget approaching £1 m. per annum. It includes six representatives of business, including the Director-General and the current President of the Confederation of British Industry. It provides an opportunity for the leaders on both sides of industry to discuss matters of national economic policy with senior Ministers in the presence also of two independent members and the NEDC Director-General. The body is essentially deliberative rather than decision-making; nevertheless it brings together the major decision makers and undoubtedly they influence each other.

Little 'Neddies'

There are somewhat similar bodies – 'little Neddies' – for the principal individual industries, and Regional Economic Planning Councils to examine regional matters. In each case business members are invited to serve as individuals, not as the nominees of trade associations. And there is a plethora of other consultative or executive bodies on which businessmen serve, principally financed by Government funds, and concerned with exports, consumer protection, industrial development, research, location and a variety of other matters.

Membership

These various bodies, occupying part of the borderland, or constituting part of the interface, between Government and business have several common features. They are composed of part-time members (receiving little or no remuneration) drawn by invitation (not by election or formal nomination) and serving as individuals, but as a body representing a broad balance of different geographical, occupational or other interests. (A sure way to be deluged with invitations to serve on such bodies would be to be a Scottish, Roman Catholic, woman trade unionist!) The net is not always cast as wide as it might be and one sometimes gets the impression of a stage army of overworked carpetbaggers looking after everybody else's business but their own. On the other hand, a degree of overlap in membership between such bodies is useful for informal coordination.

Results

These bodies are effectively serviced by established civil servants, or by staffs otherwise recruited to a structure of posts (or 'establishment') in most cases agreed with the Civil Service Department. In some cases they run an operation of their own, with a good deal of freedom. More often, they are expressing views which have then simply to be 'taken into account' by the departmental decision-makers. They are treated with the greatest respect by Ministers. Often it is difficult to know whether – adopting Bagehot's distinction – they are amongst the 'useful' or merely the 'dignified' parts of the constitution. Something must depend on how closely and effectively each member is in touch with his informal 'constituency' – in the case of a business member, how reliably he can, or at least is perceived to, represent the views of wide and important circles of his fellows, and how frequently and with what weight and standing he speaks *to* his fellows in the light of public policy considerations he has encountered as a member. On balance, these bodies probably make a useful contribution to sustaining a web of relationships without which Government economic policy would more often be misguided and would work more creakily even when right. Certainly, there has been at times in the past a marked antipathy amongst British business managers towards civil servants and all that they stood for, which is much less noticeable today.

Costs

Involvement in consultative machinery can take a heavy toll of the time of some of a company's most able and senior executives. To the question of whether they, their company and the nation would be better off if they were spending that time directly managing their own company's affairs, there is no simple or universal answer. Some of the experience is interesting but frustrating for the individual, of no direct or immediate benefit to the company, and an expensive way of performing the necessary task of educating civil servants in the facts of business life. But despite the plethora of bodies of many different shapes and sizes, the need for close mutual understanding and collaboration between government and business is undeniable and the UK has probably not yet reached the stage of diminishing returns.

Predicting Government action

The problem

A business firm prospers to the extent that it is able to detect and exploit opportunities in its environment. The increasing rate of change in the business environment, coupled with the lengthening time lags involved before a business can adapt to change, have put a premium on predicting the future environment and indeed on influencing it.

In any modern economy, Government is an important part of the business environment. It is therefore important for business to attempt to predict governmental action and its effects, and if possible also to influence it. It is equally important to know how best to adapt to it.

Increasing Government intervention in the economy, and the increasingly sophisticated nature of that intervention and the decision processes which determine it, also result in that intervention and its effects being increasingly difficult to predict.

Stable features

Beneath the turbulence and uncertainty of changes in the structure of the fiscal system, of changes in exchange rates, or of general elections, there are, however, certain relatively stable features of the UK scene. There is a steadily increasing amount of regulation of business behaviour in the interests of other parties. There are also certain constant governmental objectives in the management of the economy, and a limited variety of measures which can be used to affect business behaviour.

The term 'Butskellism' was coined in the 'fifties to describe the common ground in economic policy between the progressive Conservative Chancellor of the Exchequer, R. A. Butler, and his by no means extreme counterpart in the Labour Party, Hugh Gaitskell. It is important not to be misled by party political oratory into exaggerating the differences between the two parties when in office. Major improvements in social security introduced by the immediate postwar Labour government, and their enlargement of the national-ized sector of industry, were with few exceptions maintained and in some respects extended by their Conservative successors. The same principal economic objectives, of full employment, faster growth, stable prices, and a satisfactory balance of payments, are common to both parties. (To be sure, these objectives appear to be mutually incompatible, but since all of them continue to be pro-claimed and pursued it is difficult to detect real differences of priorities.)

There are certainly differences in style, and in the methods of achieving economic objectives, on which each party lays most stress. In general, Labour stands for interventionism, discrimination, and egalitarianism. Conservatives stand for *laissez faire*, equal treatment and across-the-board measures, and a removal of fiscal disincentives to individual effort.

A new policy

In the thirteen years of Conservative rule from 1951 to 1964 no administration proclaimed this philosophy so loudly, or acted to implement it so radically as the Heath government in its first year or more of office after June 1970. Indeed, in the early 'sixties Mr Selwyn Lloyd, as Chancellor of the Exchequer, was establishing NEDC and the Little Neddies, and a National Incomes Commission, whilst his colleague at the Ministry of Aviation, Mr Julian Amery, was negotiating an open-ended commitment to supply Government money for the development of Concorde. In 1970 Mr Heath presided over the abolition not only of the Labour-created Industrial Re-organization Corporation and the Prices and Incomes Board (which was, in effect, a successor to the NIC) but also of the small but useful Consumer Council which a Conservative President of the Board of Trade had established in 1963. The Government was to disengage from industry. There would be control of monopoly and enforcement of competition, but no money for 'lame ducks' – companies would have to 'stand on their own two feet'. There would be legislation to regulate industrial relations, but no national incomes policy. The reversion to *laissez faire* went well beyond anything which observers of the election had thought likely.

Two years later the Industrial Relations Act is in being, but the need for a national incomes policy is becoming increasingly accepted. Competition policy has still to be unveiled, but tens of millions of pounds have been committed to a shipbuilding firm, the major part of Rolls-Royce has been in effect nationalized, and with the introduction of the 1972 Industrial Development Bill the doctrine of letting every private enterprise sink or swim has been explicitly abandoned. An organization for industrial development has been created with marked resemblances to the IRC.

The pressures for stability

The moral of this is not that the Conservatives are uniquely ineffective or fickle. Equally dramatic changes of word and deed could be quoted from the other side of the political fence. The moral is that radically doctrinaire policies – whether of left or right – are alien to the British tradition of empirical pragmatism even when sincerely intended and buttressed by logic that, in its own terms, is impeccable. Faced with the realities and responsibilities of office such policies are quickly abandoned and from a forecasting standpoint should therefore be regarded as a temporary aberration. It should facilitate business decisions and reassure those who make them to know that not everything hangs on the result of a General Election.

Party differences are therefore mainly ones merely of emphasis. Across-the-board measures – affecting the exchange rate, the supply and price of money, the inflationary or deflationary impact of the fiscal system – remain in the panoply of economic measures used by all governments. Specific, discriminatory, direct administrative measures will also continue to be used: Industrial Development Certificates, discretionary loans or subsidies, and so on. In a two-party system, upheld as it is by the system of single-member constituences, each party, to win and retain office, must win and retain the support of the 'floating voters' who adhere to neither extreme.

Sources of variability

If, then, we attempt to list sources of variability in Government action, we may begin by saying that the effects of whichever party is in power are easy to exaggerate. Intra-party struggles, moreover, are of greater importance in determining a party's policy when in opposition – and in determining whether or not it will succeed at the next General Election in turning out the party then in office – than in determining its policy as a Government.

In office, a major question is how far it will succeed in imposing its will on the civil service. Formally, and in general, the civil service effectively serves the government of the day, advising and implementing; in advance of a general election it has worked on the problems of implementation of the policies of both the major parties, and when a different party comes into office it locks away the records of its predecessors' ministerial deliberations and itself moves swiftly into a different mode. In practice, however, there are some deeply entrenched attitudes identified in particular with different departments. The Treasury, for example, has been thought to have taken an extremely cautious view about possibilities of economic expansion, and this has led politicians of both parties, up to now unsuccessfully, to a number of structural devices – one thinks in particular of the establishment from 1964 to 1969 of the Department of Economic Affairs – in an attempt to offset the predominance of this view in the determination of policy. The Board of Trade (now part of the Department of Trade and Industry), similarly, has taken an uncompromisingly *laissez faire* view about measures to assist the British balance of payments, a view which has been strongly criticized in other quarters. Changes in the personnel or structure of Government departments may therefore also have some effect on policy.

When all is said and done, however, the principal source of variability in government action lies right outside Government, in the circumstances with which Government has to grapple. These circumstances may be internal or external. The Korean War in 1950 led to a rearmament programme which overloaded the economy. A victory for a Scottish Nationalist in a by-election in 1967 led to a reappraisal of policy towards the regions. Steps have been taken in order to influence the climate of the EEC entry negotiations which might not have been taken on strictly economic grounds. A change in the terms of trade, the growth of popular concern about the physical environment, the discovery of North Sea gas, the need to placate our EFTA partners, these are the events which help to determine Government action. Certainly, these events have to be perceived, filtered and appraised by men and women at Whitehall and Westminster, but the appraisal and consequences of such an event are often much easier to predict than the event itself.

Some further points

This said, let us list five further points to be borne in mind when attempting to predict British government action:

1. Political speeches – on party occasions as distinct from Ministerial statements give little information. They are means of encouraging supporters, not statements of intention. The presence or absence of an escape clause can sometimes be a clue.

2. Political intention is no guarantee of effective action. The 1964-70 Labour administration failed to simplify the system of personal taxation, being told by civil servants that difficulties of changeover made it impossible. The succeeding Conservative government, however, did so. This was partly due to the volume of detailed preparation done in Opposition, but partly due to some unpredictable alchemy of personal dominance.

3. Political power bases are important but not decisive. Labour's dependence on the miners probably affected the decision to sanction an Alcan aluminium smelter in North-East England in 1968, drawing electricity from its own coal-fired power station, though the Government's plan for smelters had been intended to exploit the low marginal cost of nuclear power generation under continuous load. In 1964, on the other hand, Mr. Heath's need to prove himself a strong reforming President of the Board of Trade carried the Resale Prices Act against the opposition of his own backbenchers.

4. The date of the next general election is important. A newly elected government with an adequate working majority can do unpopular things; as the end of its five-year maximum life approaches, an upswing in economic activity and particularly consumption, becomes ever more important to it.

5. The placing of ministers in departments can be important. The appointment of Sir Keith Joseph to Health and Social Security in 1970 meant that the new Government's policies on Industry and Trade were freed from the constraints of what he had been saying on these subjects as Opposition spokesman on them.

Adapting to Government action

Changes in Government measures, like other changes in the business environment, create new opportunities and enhance or limit old ones. If they can be predicted successfully, so much the better for planning and for certain sorts of action, such as buying and selling shares. Other sorts of action must wait until the expected changes are fully known and one can with reasonable safety predict no further relevant change for the relevant period.

The need for continuity

The fact that business needs to be able to rely on a degree of continuity if its own planning is to be undertaken with confidence is now well accepted by Government. Over the last five years or so governments have emphasized the need for steady and continous economic growth, even if initially at a somewhat lower rate, rather than further 'go-stop'. Particularly in respect of incentives to undertake capital expenditure in development areas, this need for continuity has been recognized; for example, whilst wishing to phase it out subsequently, the present Government has recognized and upheld its predecessor's commitment to maintain the Regional Employment Premium at least until 1974.

Problems of adaptation

But even where Government action is dependable, this does not mean that there are no problems in adapting to it. In markets other than the stock market, there is no immediate adjustment of prices to expectations. Different companies are differently situated and only one or a few may be rightly placed to exploit some new opportunity. Many opportunities go unexploited because companies are too sluggish or unsophisticated to exploit them.

For years, for example, there have been very substantial financial advantages from locating new plant in the development areas. Many British companies are footloose enough, in terms of markets and raw materials, to move there, yet do not do so because of the reluctance of senior executives to move themselves and their families to a different part of the country. Conversely, many companies already lack the managerial capacity to move into new growth industries from the declining industries, such as shipbuilding and cotton textiles, in which they have remained so far. In consequence, much of the Governmental financial assistance is enjoyed by foreign-owned operations, and from an employment standpoint still more are needed.

Reaction to Government action

So much for sluggishness. As for sophistication, with two principal exceptions, Government encouragement to incur capital expenditure, particularly in the regions, has affected, and will in the future affect, post-tax profits but not pre-tax profits. It has been given, that is, by way of tax allowances. It is regrettable but true that many British businessmen have until a few years ago thought in terms of pre-tax rather than post-tax profits. They have based their decision making on non-rational calculations and an incentive based on the assumption that they would act rationally has failed to have its intended effect.

One of the difficulties in adapting to Government action is, of course, that of predicting or calculating its effects so far as they are relevant to your own company. As regards sheer calculations, for example, some tax changes can have extremely complicated effects, particularly where capital expenditure is concerned. A colleague at the Manchester Business School, Professor G. H. Lawson, provides a relevant service in the shape of appropriate tables immediately updated after the announcement of changes in rates or allowances. As regards prediction, economic commentators are ready enough to predict the effects so far as the economy at large is concerned but to get a breakdown for your own sector or industry or region gets increasingly difficult, the greater the disaggregation required. Government statistics have improved steadily and substantially over the past decade and the Government Statistical Service is often able to provide, for a fee, finer breakdowns, or different tabulations, than those published. The work of the little Neddies (Economic Development Committees for particular industries) has included a good deal of prediction relating the future of one industry to that of the economy at large. Similar industry-specific forecasting goes on at the National Institute for Economic and Social Research, in trade associations, and at a number of universities. The position is much less satisfactory with regard to geographical areas.

Response to Government action is not always a matter simply of predicting its effects on the individual company situation and then pursuing the same company objectives single-mindedly in the altered situation. An eminent British economist once suggested that the Government could urge on the donkey of the British economy by using either the carrot or the stick. But he added that there was a third way, which he called 'the stroking of the ears'.

Responding to exhortation

There are situations in which legislation or mandatory action would be impracticable or injudicious, and a Government may therefore find that all it can do is to appeal to business to take some action, or to refrain from some action, *pro bono publico*. Where this conflicts with the apparent interests of its shareholders, what should a company do?

On the one hand it may be argued that its Board has a legal and moral obligation to the shareholders, which it cannot properly avoid so long as discretion is left to it. 'Order us, and we will, of course, obey; otherwise, we have no alternative but to do what we would have done in any case.' Furthermore, it can be urged that if only British business were more single-minded in the pursuit of shareholders' interests, and less susceptible to appeals to the public interest, the British economy as a whole would be in much better shape.

On the other hand, it can be argued that the managerial revolution has long since taken place; that the monopoly power of many major companies means that they no longer need to, and demands that they no longer should, pay exclusive attention to their shareholders' interests; and, furthermore, that the survival of a mixed economy and a democratic society requires that companies recognize their social obligations and be responsive to Government suggestions and appeals even when it is impracticable for these to have the force of law.

In the first two decades after the Second World War this issue has emerged mainly in the context of the priority to be given to exports. The appeal varied from straight exhortation to a Prime Ministerial suggestion that 'Exporting is Fun!' In the later years of this century it may well be that the issue will be seen mainly in the context of business's obligation to respect the physical environment, for it is not yet clear how far this can be fully protected by fiscal measures and outright prohibition. In recent years and in the immediate future, however, the arena for this debate is provided by the question of wage and price increases.

This question puts the issue very sharply. It is practically impossible to control wage and price increases by legislation in peacetime. An individual company, on its own, has every reason to put its selling price up if the market will bear it, and every reason to concede wage demands if it is highly capital-intensive and the alternative is a stoppage. Yet each such instance stimulates others and thus has repercussions which, from the standpoint of the economy at large, can lead to disaster.

'Voluntary restraint'

The most recent example of voluntary restraint is also the most interesting, since it was the most purely voluntary and at the same time explicit and formal, and it embodied a unilateral initiative by industry, rather than a response to any appeal by Government. It was the Confederation of British Industry's price restraint agreement of 1971-72, signed and adhered to by the great majority of the largest companies in the country, and incorporating an undertaking not to raise prices except in defined justificatory circumstances, and even then by not more than 5 per cent. It was for twelve months initially.

At the time of writing it has not led to comprehensive tripartite agreements such as might enable the problem of the wage-price spiral to be resolved by consensus. The TUC has, perhaps, less influence over some of its largest members than the CBI. But the agreement has shown what can be done in this 'grey area' between governmental fiat and *laissez faire*, where each can benefit if only all or nearly all will agree. Similar choices, to accept or reject an avoidable constraint, will have to be made by businesses in the future, and the right answer will depend on their individual circumstances, on the impact of public opinion, on the probable action of other parties, and on the value to them of the prize to be collectively won.

Influencing Government action

There is a whole hierarchy of possible Government actions, ranging from major steps with pervasive effects, like altering the exchange rate of sterling or raising new taxes, to minor and specific administrative decisions concerning, for example, the precise definition of a class of goods or activities to be exempted from some levy or prohibition or requirement, or the interpretation of a regulation in the context of its application in a particular instance. Corresponding to this hierarchy, there is a hierarchy of responsible persons, ranging from the Cabinet or a senior Minister, to a junior civil servant in a regional or local office. Thirdly, there is a hierarchy of means of influence. The Confederation of British Industry is the most substantial of many organizations which make representations annually to the Chancellor of the Exchequer when he is preparing his budget. A major lobbying campaign, aimed at both Houses of Parliament as well as the government of the day, attended the introduction of commercial television in 1955. At the other extreme, tens of thousands of professional auditors negotiate with Inland Revenue officials the tax liabilities of small firms, and thousands of architects seek to persuade local authorities to grant planning permission for proposed factory extensions or new shops or offices. Between these extremes, hundreds of trade and professional associations represent the interests of their members, both at their own initiative and as a result of their being consulted by Government.

The Civil Service

Recruitment to the central government civil service in Britain has been by competitive examination since 1870. The top echelons consist of extremely able, dedicated, hardworking, high-principled, versatile and incorruptible men and women. There have been changes in recent years. The base of recruitment has been broadened, with the 'public' schools, 'Oxbridge', and the classics or humanities supplying a decreasing proportion. The need for specialist competence in economics (though hardly yet in the other social sciences) and in statistics is increasingly recognized, and some training in these subjects is now being given to many of the most able younger civil servants. The formation of larger Government departments has reduced the need for interdepartmental committees and thus has given hope of reducing delays in reaching decisions.

From the standpoint of business there are, however, still many weaknesses. Senior civil servants with previous business experience are few; the occasional 'industrial adviser' is often on short-term secondment and few have made much impact on the machine. The civil servant's normal training and experience leads him to consider every possible aspect of each problem, and to consult widely within the civil service, before coming to a decision, and in particular before saying 'yes'. The risk of a Parliamentary Question challenging the decision and the danger of political repercussions are particularly important delaying factors.

These characteristics impair effective and fruitful relations between Government and business, and this has led to a number of recent changes. The importance of knowing how the machine works has led to the recruitment by business of middle-ranking or senior civil servants, often on early retirement. On the Government side, the most significant attempt to break away from traditional attitudes of non-discrimination was the establishment in 1967 of the Industrial Reorganization Corporation, whose role I have elsewhere[1] described as:

> '. . . active, initiatory, discretionary or discriminatory, non-bureaucratic, commercially-orientated, change-producing, almost, if you like, free-wheeling, wheeler-dealing and buccaneering.'

How to influence decisions

For businessmen, the following prescription for influencing civil service decisions emerges. First, identify the probable decision process: the positions, relationships, and, if possible, character and attitudes, of those who will be involved, and the sequence and timing of the stages. Identify the parties, inside or outside Government, likely to be interested and therefore consulted, and consult them first. Ascertain the arguments against your own proposal, try to appreciate how strong they will seem to those concerned, and if necessary be prepared to modify your proposal, recognising that half a loaf is better than no bread. Accept that dubious or intemperate argument will weaken your credibility. Relate your case, if possible, to known Government objectives or policies. Use a mixture of face-to-face meeting and written submission. Refer only warily to possibilities of seeking support at higher levels or to pressures that could be brought to bear.

Where the Government is actively seeking the opinion of business, the likelihood of effective influence is, of course, greater. Some of the above considerations still apply, but the context and atmosphere are different. The more thoroughly prepared and sophisticated the case, the more seriously it will be taken and the more likely it is that subsequent advice will be sought informally from the same quarter. Civil servants simply do not have access to many of the facts with which interested parties are quite familiar, and many of the considerations uppermost in business minds may just not have occurred to them. Their decisions are taken on the basis of a written case, as coherent and complete as may be, and worthwhile grist to that mill is received with gratitude.

[1] *The Three Banks Review*, June 1972, p. 23

Means for the consultation of business by Government have increased in recent years. Not only have the number and importance of interface bodies, such as those described earlier, increased. In addition, over the last six years or so, the publication of Green Papers has put consultation over impending legislation or major policy matters on a more public and formal basis; a Green Paper sets out proposals (in some cases with alternatives) which the Government is inclined to favour but to which it is not finally committed. Clear changes of the Government's mind as a result of public discussion of a Green Paper have been recorded (e.g. in the 1972 Budget speech).

Summary

This paper has made the following points. Any British Government is heavily and intimately involved with business, and necessarily so. The nature of the Government/business interface varies greatly with the circumstances, for example according to whether the relationship is one of law-enforcement, procurement, ownership, discretionary financial assistance, or persuasion. The borderland between Government and business is studded with deliberative or executive bodies which bring civil servants and business managers together and thus help to improve mutual understanding.

In attempting to predict Government action, differences between the two major political parties as to their behaviour in office can easily be exaggerated. Other and sometimes more important sources of variability include the ascendancy of different viewpoints within the civil service, the proximity of the next general election, and the events and circumstances with which the Government has to deal. In determining how to adapt to Government action, there are difficulties in predicting how it will affect the situation of the individual firm, and how other parties will react both to the Government action and to any action by the firm in question; a particular dilemma may be posed in respect of action which is encouraged without being mandatory. Finally, it should be noted that there are many and increasing opportunities for Government action to be influenced by firms, individually or collectively, in small matters and in great.

Competition policy in the UK

M. E. Beesley

Introduction

Ideas of competition policy

Competition policy in the UK as elsewhere, is concerned to promote competition and so further economic growth. The meaning of 'competition' has always been disputed wherever a policy has been implemented. Perhaps there are three main strands of thought:

(*a*) competition as an ideal structure for industries, stemming from the requirements for the optimal allocation of resources in the whole economy;

(*b*) the deconcentration of economic power in an economy – the preference for more, not fewer, centres of decision making;

(*c*) rivalry – the belief that economic progress is best served by preserving the possibilities of market challenge to established firms.

Sometimes a governmental action to affect firm behaviour – always the proximate objective of competitive policy – can be consistent with all three notions. Very often it cannot, as when effective market rivalry involves a merger, and so greater concentration of power. There is some scope for reconciliation in identifying the *results* of an ideal competitive system, e.g. lower prices, higher output with practical steps to increase market rivalry. But potential conflict of objectives in 'promoting competition' always remains; the UK has not escaped this in developing a competition policy.

The first anti-monopoly legislation was the Monopolies Act 1948, passed by the Labour government, when the principal instrument for industrial change was nationalization. Socialist thought was extremely sceptical of 'anti-trust' legislation. Yet here was an Act implicitly accepting and hoping to improve on, free enterprise. The apparent anomoly is largely explained by the fact that the principal sponsor of the Act within the Labour party was the Co-operative movement. The Co-ops had had unfortunate experiences with manufacturers' collective agreements, which regarded the Co-ops as price cutters. Thus UK policy arose from the desire pragmatically to remove obstacles to free trading. Policy has continued essentially to judge specific pro-competitive action on the merits – the prospective costs and benefits – of particular situations. Any general attitude to competition, approximates to our third concept – that of preserving rivalry, or 'effective competition'.

A desirable industrial structure

Nevertheless the developing policy, under all governments, has embraced wider fields of commercial action; issues of what is a desirable industrial structure have become more prominent. A proposed merger now may pose the need to trade-off a possible stronger competitive challenge in foreign markets against possible detriments, through increased domestic market power, to UK consumers. Also, because they are predictive, judgements in individual cases must have a theoretical framework; and they must be reasonably speedy. So, in recent years, the UK machinery has provided a cost-benefit analysis where the balance of advantage of a merger is in doubt. Such an analysis must be simplified and somewhat abstracted from reality. More important, the appraisal must rely on broad judgements of the relation between industrial structure and performance. These in turn are much influenced by general economic arguments about competitive conditions for the best allocation of resources. The notion of an ideal structure still enters what aims to be a pragmatic approach.

The difficult cases do not comprise the bulk of activities associated with competition policy in the UK. With certain anti-competitive activities by firms, e.g. collective price agreements, the issue of whether net benefits ensue is in effect settled; partly because, there, all three ideas of competition and its benefits seem to run together. Condemning a cartel usually is seen to provide a competitive structure; rivalry and decentralization of decision-making are also promoted. While UK policy continues its piecemeal development, consensus over those anti-competitive actions that should be proscribed has widened.

The policy structure

Since establishing the Monopolies Commission in 1948 with broad powers of investigation but little provision for follow up, the UK has erected a considerable array of legal and administrative machinery. Two systems execute competition policy – the Restrictive Practices Court machinery; and the Department of Trade and Industry's administrative system. The Monopolies Commission is effectively part of the latter. The two systems are independent, though subject to influence by the common stock of ideas about competitive policy; and there is informal collaboration. The decision to create separate arms for the expression of policy reflects the broad judgement that certain forms of anti-competitive agreement and action are *a priori* against the public interest, though exceptions may be deemed 'justiciable' and thus appropriate for formal court procedure. This disengages the executive from control of outcomes thereafter. Other anti-competitive manifestations, and study of the proper scope of policy, are deemed appropriate for Departmental action, with the assistance of the Monopolies Commission, for here the more controversial economic issues are foreseen, and the rights of subsequent executive action preserved.

The two 'systems'

We now consider the two UK 'systems'. The first regulates mergers, 'large firm' behaviour, and investigations and the scope of competitive policy. A 'large firm' is one whose share of the UK market exceeds one-third; mergers come into the system if one of the firms has a one-third market share or more than £5 m. in assets.[1] We call this system 'DTI/MC'. The department responsible for this area of policy, is the Department of Trade and Industry; the Monopolies Commission is an independent body, of nineteen members at March 1972, under Sir Ashton Roskill. The second system was set up by the Acts of 1956, 1964 and 1968.[2] This legislation covers agreements between firms in restraint of trade, the exchange of information and individual retail price agreements. We call this the 'RTPC' system. Its main elements are a special High Court – Restrictive Practices – and an independent Registrar whose duty is to register specified agreements and to activate the Court's processes (see Appendix 1 for details).

[1]   See Merger and Monopolies Act, 1965.
[2]   These are respectively the Restrictive Trade Practices, Resale Prices and an amending Act.

The large firm and merger control system

'Trigger'

In the DTI/MC system, the trigger is activated by DTI, acting on, for example, external representations, knowledge generated by the system, systematic surveys of market shares and merger notifications. It disposes of most cases departmentally, without public enquiry and often by informal understandings with the firm concerned. The DTI need not defend these actions formally in Parliament, so nothing can be definitively said of these cases. Probably sufficient cases are made public to reveal the broad parameters of informal control. Where, prima facie, there is potential detriment to the public (UK citizens) sufficient to offset the benefits in prospect, a reference will be made to the Monopolies Commission (MC). This may concern the activities of a large firm, a prospective merger or a class of activity heretofore not within the ambit of competitive policy action. So the MC is now (May 1972) considering eight 'monopolies', one merger and a general activity – 'parallel pricing'.[3] The MC can investigate services. It will then conduct a cost-benefit analysis, taking up to four years, except with mergers, where a time limitation has kept the average period to 4-6 months.

Investigation

The MC's views will be formed from evidence obtained in response to a preliminary investigation and a set of consequent questions devised by its secretariat, normally civil servants on loan from DTI. Firms involved are usually represented at formal hearings by counsel. There is, however, no controversy procedure, no direct confrontation of firms with different views, and the MC is not bound by its previous findings. It need not, but often does, allow firms to comment on its draft findings; and there is no appeal from the published 'verdict'. While safeguarding confidential information, this usually details those aspects of the firms concerned that are relevant to the Commission. (The reports are an important source of industrial information. With mergers, the parties acquire new

---

[3]   The monopoly references are: Fire Insurance, referred to the MC in Dec. 1968; Asbestos, August 1969; Ropes, March 1971; Connection charges for electricity and gas, June/July 1971; Cereals, June 1971; Shoemaking machinery, June 1971; Drugs, Sept. 1971. Primary batteries, Feb. 1972. The merger case is Glaxo-Boots-Beecham referred in Feb. 1972. Parallel pricing was referred in June 1971.

information, sometimes with substantial effect on their perceptions of the benefits in prospect). There is no formal appeal mechanism.

Findings

The MC's findings, though made public, are in effect advice to DTI, though the DTI usually accepts it. However, there is scope for negotiation in principle about precisely what the firms should do, and the MC's findings may be followed by protracted discussions with the DTI. An outstanding example was in the detergents case; radical measures proposed by the MC to cut advertising and other 'wastes' led to rather minor action, as indicated below, by the firms.

Recommendations:	*Action:*
(i) *Short term*	(i) *Short term*
Reduce wholesale price 20 per cent suggested	Alternative product range, less advertised, 20 per cent cheaper.
Encourage reduction of at least 40 per cent in selling expenses.	
(ii) *Long term*	(ii) *Long term*
Consider disallowing excessive selling expenditure for tax purposes	General research on advertising.
Board of Trade to survey but not regulate prices.	Formal review after 2 years.

However, in other cases, e.g., the BICC – Pyrotenax merger, the firm accepted quite stringent 'undertakings' as a condition of proceeding with the merger.

Two general assurances were extracted:

Para. 146; 'that the future commercial development (including the necessary research) and exploitation of mineral insulated cable in the UK and overseas would not be hampered by other BICC interests.'

Para. 149; 'that the cost reductions achieved as a result of the merger will be used to promote the use of and expand the sale of mineral insulated cable, and to reduce net selling prices to customers (or to avoid increases that would otherwise have been necessary).'

Particular assurances were requested by interested parties who feared the market power created by the merger in the production and distribution of mineral insulated cable (mic). Most of these were accepted in more specific terms by both the Commission and BICC:

Para. 150; 'that BICC will continue to supply wholesale distributors with mic on normal commercial terms.'*

Para. 157; '(i) that BICC will continue to supply other cable makers with mic, and will do so at prices and on terms,* and with service and continuity of supply, which will make it commercially practicable for them to participate in sales of mic.

(ii) that BICC will not give its own electrical contracting organization more favourable prices, terms,* service or continuity of supply for mic than it gives to other comparable electrical contractors.

(iii) that BICC will not offer specially favourable prices or terms* for mic to customers for the purpose of winning business in other types of cable.

(iv) that BICC will not offer uneconomic prices or terms* for mic to customers calculated to drive competitors out of the business of supplying mic.

(v) that BICC will publish its list prices and will make available to each category of customers its terms* for mic appropriate to that category.

(vi) that, if at any time, the Board of Trade should so request, BICC will grant licences under any patents relating to mic, including accessories, on reasonable terms.'†

These undertakings may cover virtually any aspect of commercial behaviour, and reflect the wide powers of control (theoretically) applicable to the DTI. These include specific price controls, or the lifting of import duties[4] (see appendix 2). Obviously, DTI considers general economic, indeed international, policy in carrying out these duties and rarely invokes its full powers. Most important here is equity between firms; if a firm objects to an 'undertaking' required of it, DTI will be acutely aware of seeming to discriminate unfairly against it. So the undertaking must be defensible in other cases too. A general review of outcomes of such negotiations is published in a DTI annual report to the House of Commons. Any detailed bargains remain confidential.

---

* 'The word "terms" here includes terms and conditions as to discount, rebates, and credit.'

† All quotes are from the Commission report, op. cit.

[4]   The following are the chief price or duty regulations enforced (since 1965):
In the case of *colour film* (Report, April 1966) the BOT enforced a reduction of $12\frac{1}{2}$ per cent in price to retailer, and a reduction of 20 per cent in price to customer.

In the *Cellulosic fibres* case, the BOT stated its intention 'to make a reduction in the duties on man-made cellulosic staple fibre, and to continue reductions in the duties on tow in line with those which we shall be making on staple fibre *under the Kennedy Round Agreement*'.

In the *Clutch mechanisms* case, a 'surveillance of price policy' by DTI was announced.

Enforcement and monitoring

It follows that both enforcement and monitoring of actions after a decision are informal. No outside commentator can say what internal steps are taken to secure compliance with 'undertakings', under continually changing circumstances. The law does provide for a second reference to the MC, but this rarely happens.[5] Most cases do not directly concern the MC at all. It is kept as one means of bargaining with firms; failure to reach informal agreement at an early stage may result in reference to the MC. At the very least, this imposes high costs on firms in top executives' time, and uncertainty from the prospect of a sharp increase of information reaching the public and commercial contacts. In effect, the MC currently plays a dual role. It sets standards for judging the public interest and is an element in the informal system for scrutinising and enforcing firms' actions. Feedback is complicated by the formal division between DTI and MC. There is no automatic way of subjecting the whole system to continual management appraisal. There is much concern for the way in which the system works, but it finds expression in periodic changes of legislation like the one now mooted.

The 'restraint of trade' control system

The second system – RTPC – gradually widened in scope as further commercial agreements with anti-competitive elements became justiciable. The practical working of the system has necessarily de-emphasised the role of the Court – partly because its precedents now govern future actions; partly because of changes initiated by the Registrar.

The two Acts

The 1956 Act prohibited agreements for collective enforcement of resale price maintenance; the 1968 Act extended this to individual enforcement, with some exemptions. Agreements to restrain trade in goods had to be registered with the Registrar (under the 1956 Act), who had then to initiate action to determine their status in the Court. Such agreements are presumed contrary to the public interest; the

[5] The examples of follow-up references are:
Timber – 1953
　　　 1958 – to determine if conditions had been complied with.
Electric lamps – 1951
　　　 1968

Court may 'licence' an agreement if certain criteria enshrining the public interest are satisfied.[6] Thus, after 1956, the Registrar acted as prosecutor, aiming to show the Court that the 'public interest' would not be satisfied by granting the 'licence'. Contrary to usual legal practice in UK, the burden of proof did not fall on him, but on the respondent firms. They had to show that agreements were in the public interest and this burden of proof has proved onerous. To May 1972, only ten agreements have been licensed.

The legal process

In a contested case, the Court performs a cost-benefit analysis where the antagonists rely heavily on general notions about the relation of agreements to expected firm and industry performance. The Court relies on its own principles in interpreting the evidence and has shown great respect for the benefits of competition, though often unclear about its connotations. Most legal commentators agree that most of the Court's work of interpretation in this area is finished. With few exceptions, agreements under the 1956 Act will *not* be licensed; what constitutes an agreement is interpreted strictly. Much the same holds for resale prices work under the 1964 Act. (Appendix 3 lists the few 'successful' cases.) Precedents are heavily against success in obtaining a licence for a restraint of trade. Interest has now shifted to the 1968 Act, which brought information agreements into the Court's scope, and emphasized not how an agreement will be evaluated but whether it is registrable. The Registrar is thus responsible for triggering action from a defined set of possible cases. The Court focuses a cost-benefit analysis on the issues – the agreement *between* firms – before it. The traditional controversy procedure, formal rules of evidence, etc., ensure that evidence is probed in depth. Yet the scope for interpretation is much less wide than with the MC – the Court cannot go where the economic argument listeth. Speculation about economic alternatives (e.g. what mergers might ensue if competitive pressures are enhanced by refusal to licence an agreement) is necessarily judged by their nearness to the specific issues. The Court looks for evidence of benefit in two senses – of gains expected to flow directly from the licence and, indirectly, that these must outweigh other detriments to the public. The applicants face a double hurdle in an area notoriously difficult for applying

---

(6)   These criteria are listed at Appendix 3. The most important in practice has been the most general – the second 'gateway'. Appendix 3 also lists 'licensed' agreements.

positive evidence. (The MC cost-benefit appraisal, by contrast, usually looks for evidence only of benefit sufficient to offset anticipated detriment; if there is little detriment, benefit may be virtually ignored.)

The decision–to license or not–is subject to a formal agreement system. The Registrar must monitor agreements removed from the register to see whether agreements 'to like effect' are substituted. For this, the Registrar relies on commercial intelligence, no doubt informally reinforced by official contacts. If they are so found, the Registrar must apply to the Court for a hearing. The Court has been strict in defining 'to like effect' – as the Tyre conference and Galvanised Tank Manufacturers found.[7] Enforcement here raises the protection of the Law's majesty; the offence is against the Court. It is no longer concerned with fine issues of costs and benefits, but rather with ensuring obedience to the Law. The Registrar also may revive a 'licensed' case if circumstances have changed substantially. He is thus formally charged with recycling the system.

Substitute agreements

The relative toughness of the Court (though somewhat dependent on the President of the moment) has naturally led to attempts to find substitute agreements as much as possible like the original one but which are not of like effect; and to the issue whether agreements are registrable. Most future work in the RTPC system will concern information agreements (brought under the Court in 1968) and determining such issues as what constitutes an independent, and so potentially registrable, relationship between parties. The Court has assumed more and more the role of final arbiter; most work now centres on the Registrar.

The 1968 Act relaxed the Registrar's duty to refer registered (including information) agreements to the Court; it also tightened up provisions for registration. Details of new information agreements must now be referred to him *before* they take effect or within three

---

[7] *Galvanized Tank Manufacturers Assoc*, 1965. Total fines of £102,000 were imposed; the Court warned that it would not hesitate to imprison individuals who wilfully participated in breaches of undertakings – this would be contempt of court.

In the *Mileage Conference Group of Tyre Manufacturers*, 1966. The Court imposed fines on each of the companies of £10,000. This case was too close to the above case to make the warning effective.

(Also in the *Motor Vehicle Scheme Agreement*, the Society of Motor Manufacturers and Traders was fined £3,000 guineas (to be paid to Registrar as costs) for unreasonable delay in provision of information.

months of making them, whichever was the earlier.[8] An agreement not duly registered becomes void and is unlawful to enforce.[9] Thus the Registrar has enchanced discretion under the authority of the Court. He has also acquired something similar to the negotiation functions of the DTI in the first system. With information agreements, for example, he reported in 1970 that he would have to make 'detailed enquiries' about an agreement before deciding whether to refer it to the Court. He might then seek 'assurances' from the parties as safeguards against reduced competitive pressures, with prejudicing the increase in efficiency likely from certain information flows 'thus obviating a reference to the Court'.[10] The Registrar has thus taken on the cost-benefit analysis of information agreements. He does not anticipate taking many to the Court – even though the 1968 Act gave the Court more criteria than the 1956 Act did for dealing with information agreements. An agreement can now be approved if it does not 'directly or indirectly restrict or discourage competition to any material degree'. No such agreements have yet been contested. Similarly, the Registrar negotiates with firms over whether an agreement is registrable. They may well accept modifications to make agreements innocent, as perceived by the Registrar, who is here performing evaluatory and negotiating activity similar to that of the DTI/MC.

A summary

To sum up: firms should seek informal clearance for any action likely to be touched by either control system. However, while the consequences of ignoring the Registrar's advice are fairly clear cut, with the DTI/MC there is likely to be less certainty. To the citizen at large most evaluation in both systems seems to be informal and private; however, if the DTI/MC system invokes the MC, evaluation is made public whereas the Registrar's evaluations are subject to public scrutiny only if he chooses to discuss them in a periodic report to Parliament, or refers a case to the Court.

Because the RTPC system is relatively coherent and self-

[8]   The Registrar may represent to DTI that an agreement is not of such significance as to call for investigation by the Court. The DTI may so order. Under this section (9.2) ninety cases have been exempted.

[9]   One of the difficulties with the 1956 Act had been that failure to register carried no penalty beyond the risk that, when discovered by the Registrar, he could *then* take steps to enforce registration. When the attitudes of the Court in deciding cases became clear, it often seemed the lesser evil not to register.

[10]   Report of the Registrar 1966-69, March 1970, Cmnd.4303.

contained, it is a powerful advocate for changing its own functions. Suggestions for change are made in the Registrar's reports to Parliament, where he has discretion and usually reports on two to three years' work. Many of the 1968 changes were foreshadowed by his earlier comments; he was also influential in determining the treatment of resale prices under the 1964 Act. The reduced formal Court activity since the first years of the 1956 Act is not a measure of the future importance of the RTPC system.

Present concerns of policy makers

The UK systems, though formally distinguishing administrative and legal approaches, and maintaining clearly separate entities, do not give would-be reformers choice between truly alternative principles of procedure. In particular, the RTPC system does not operate in the traditional fashion of the US antitrust law. There is no general offence of 'monopolization'. The Court attempts to balance economic interests; weighing costs and benefits, not inferring whether an offence has taken place which is the task of the US courts. True, one can see application of the rule of reason in US antitrust cases; and, in the UK court, concern for defining monopoly power. But the judicial tasks are essentially dissimilar. No official thinking about reform of the UK system seems to have seriously considered the classical 'antitrust' model. Consequently, whatever improvements ensue, the classical US virtues of comparative certainty and equity before the law will in the main have been foregone. Yet, the UK RTPC system has proved durable. Recent discussions have questioned it only as noted later, and the questioning promises simply to extend its functions. Official concern has focused on the monopoly-merger system.

A new commission

This was considered in the House of Commons by the responsible Minister, Mr John Davies and his Parliamentary Secretary, Mr Nicholas Ridley.[11] Mr Davies outlined changes to 'strengthen the machinery' for 'promoting competition in industry and for providing safeguards against the abuse of market power'. He promised a new Commission – an 'authoritative source of information and knowledge of imperfect competition', publicly recommend-

[11] Respectively: *Hansard*, Vol. 808 Cols. 1577, Dec. 1970 and *DTI Journal* 30 Sept. 1971.

L

ing possible subjects for enquiry to the Minister, the Minister retaining formal powers of reference. To shorten enquiries, the Commission's investigations could look at specific issues, e.g. particular company or industry practices. The Minister also hoped to explain the principles governing reference to the MC; and to use the powers in the 1968 Act to ask the Commission to report on the nationalized industries. Mr Ridley explained that references (June 1971) to the MC were becoming more specific in content, e.g. connection charges in the (nationalized) gas and electricity industries. The Government wished to 'get away from' the situation where 'the use of the MC was intermittent, and no solid body of knowledge or principles were built up'. He hoped to build up expert knowledge of industry in the MC, and 'to find a way in which expression can be given to a single competition policy'. For this to be fully effective, he said, new legislation would be needed, but this is still awaited (May 1972). The Minister would also be considering the case for extending RTPC legislation, and 'making it more effective'. In particular, 'we shall be considering the case for bringing services within the legislation, for making negotiable anti-competitive devices by single firms'.

There are here three major concerns: making the trigger mechanism of the DTI/MC system more effective; making MC enquiries more efficient; and moving towards defining 'abuses' of monopoly or large-firm power for action by the separate RTPC system. The first reflected a Conservative suggestion, when in opposition, to make the trigger more effective through a Registrar of Monopolies and Mergers with independent powers of reference. It was later decided that, lacking a judicial framework like that of the RTP legislation, he would 'lack responsibility to anybody'. This, and self-reference, would raise constitutional problems of accountability. Again, in our terms, a third independent centre for preliminary cost-benefit analysis would not help clarity or consistency!

So far, in the DTI/MC system, a trigger mechanism for prospective change in market shares, such as the Department of Justice applies to merger cases in the US, has been rejected in UK – though there must be some principles for activitation, making broad cost-benefit appraisal. The Department of Trade and Industry's published criteria for merger appraisal contain over 100 questions, many implying contrasting benefits and costs. No answers are provided, nor weights attached; the actual criteria used are obscure. Too few cases have yet been referred to the MC to permit inferences about the future. Probably referencing will, in the end, incorporate something like the US approach, with more-sophisticated market-share or firm-size criteria.

Dealing with 'abuse'

The second concern reflects an alternative way to increase MC output, to supplant the traditional one of increasing MC membership (as in the 1965 Act). However, the third concern – new ways of dealing with 'abuse' – is potentially very significant, marking both an extension of anti-competitive control and a move towards the EEC position. Such 'abuse' was not effectively dealt with by the 'investigation and assurance' mechanism. The reference to the use of the RTPC indicates a choice highly constrained by the existing systems. On our analysis, to place within the RTPC system, as opposed to the DTI/MC system, hardly promises improved cost-benefit treatment. Perhaps the thought is that 'abuses' could be defined, declared in principle against the public interest and then made subject to exceptional treatment against specific criteria, as in current RTPC approach. This would encounter much opposition. It is one thing to put the burden of proof on individuals for collective action, as RTPC cases have demanded; it is another to make an individual firm show substantial benefit from its own commercial policy, or be confirmed as 'guilty'. The evidence is that much harder to get; commercial disadvantage in disclosure is higher; and the procedure would be inconsistent with the Courts' traditional treatment of individual firms. Inevitably, as in the present RTPC concern over registration, there would be a growing function of appraisal for a Registrar to discuss and trigger consideration of 'abuses'. This would compound the difficulties of accurate, predictable and equitable treatment. By contrast, defining specific abuses, making them illegal *per se*, subjecting them to prosecution in the courts, and perhaps awarding exemplary damages *would* probably be more effective and equitable. But this means not an extension of the RTPC system but its reform – not apparently contemplated at present.

Finally, there is little concern here for issues of enforcement and so of effective monitoring and learning. The MC has a vast and growing knowledge of industry. To put it to better use means revamping the whole DTI/MC system rather than part of it. The dilemmas of organization, consistency and effectiveness are still unresolved; and the difficulties of effective reform within the existing system must partly account for the delays in revealing the detail of the new Competition Commission.

Current attitudes to monopoly, mergers and restrictive practices

We now attempt to answer questions which a newcomer to the UK might ask. A firm entering the UK market may wish to consider a merger, the status of competitors' defensive actions via merger or the use of existing market power and, in the longer run, possibilities of engaging in market agreements. We comment on these in turn. The evidence must come from public sources which do not make up the total relevant environment for a firm working in the UK. In both the short and long run, however, these attitudes will be important elements in that environment and will strongly influence how the machinery that is set up will work.

Monopolies and mergers

Because the independent entry of an overseas firm into the UK would in general decrease concentration, such entry would be favourably regarded. That it might eliminate weaker competitors and even lead to increased concentration has never been seen as a major drawback in MC cases. The absolute size of the firm is rarely considered; nor is the industrial deployment of the entrant. Competitive methods, once a firm is established strongly, are quite different. With entry by merger, there is little in UK competition policy to inhibit the foreign firm, though this may well concern other forms of economic policy – e.g. in granting loans to the remaining British motor car concerns to help stave off a US challenge.

Foreign involvement

The MC considered foreign involvement in British firms in several cases. Witnesses often urged foreign acquisition as a potential detriment for mergers. The Commission has been little impressed; however, it attempts to analyse the consequences. In the BMC-Pressed Steel Case (Jan. 1966), no advantage was seen in the fact that the merger would avert (American) acquisition, but specific benefits were–'we think that B.M.C. may . . . show more consideration for the needs of Pressed Steel's existing customers than a foreign principal would necessarily feel obliged to do'. Acquisition of Pressed Steel might also lead to questions about 'remittances abroad and perhaps about "rationalization" of Pressed Steel's exports to fit in with a pattern which better suited the foreign principal'. In the G.K.N.–Birfield case (Jan. 1967) the MC argued only that Birfield would probably not remain independent and that this merger was as good as any; the MC did not object to a foreign take-over as such. Most important, over an American rival bid for the Dental Manufacturing Co. (August 1966), the MC confined its analysis of the 'foreignness' of one bidder to a neutral appreciation of the commercial gains and losses expected from foreign control and found much in favour of the US bid; both bids, US and British, were approved. However, the prospective effects of the rival bids on UK overseas trade and the balance of payments, though considered in detail, were secondary to analysis of the likely effect on UK consumers. Since US-based bids have frequently led to mergers since 1965, there have been many other occasions when such phenomena could have been tested, had this appeared essential.

The MC's attitude to defensive action by large firms in strong market positions is also potentially encouraging to prospective entrants to the UK. The MC typically investigates structure, behaviour and performance. It is loath to draw conclusions from structural factors alone – market share or concentration. Thus, in the Flat Glass case, the 90 per cent share of Pilkingtons was not seen as objectionable *per se*; nor was its considerable vertical integration. The MC is more concerned with 'things done' by dominant sellers to enhance and protect market positions, particularly 'discriminatory' behaviour. The MC has condemned agreements between home producers and foreign suppliers to restrict UK competition (Cellulose Fibres); artificial restraints on competition discriminating between customers, e.g. refusal to supply non-approved dealers (Colour Film, Infant Milk Foods, Wallpaper); price discrimination between customers (Cellulose Fibres); undue restriction of supplies to potential competitors (Cellulose Fibres, Cinemas); tying the processing of a good to its sale (Colour Film); aggregating discounts to customers (Metal Containers); and 'fighting companies' to remove or restrict competition (Industrial Gases). The remedy has been to negotiate individually and with, for example, refusal to supply, to order a general survey. A codification of discriminatory practices may emerge, backed by systematic appraisal, monitoring and sanctions. Meanwhile, the MC has generated a considerable climate of opinion against such behaviour. This may help an entrant to the UK in a tough market. He may be confident that if he complains of discriminatory competitive action there will be a response.[12]

(12) See page 182 for footnote.

Criteria for evaluation

If an entrant to the UK finds a new market, becoming the dominant supplier, what other features of his operations and commercial policy may find favour or disfavour with the MC? This is important. Whatever the structure emerging from current discussions on the proposed Competition Commission, increased activity like the MC's is fairly certain. In evaluating large firms, the MC has largely considered performance as shown by profits, costs, output and innovation. The appropriateness of an attempt to infer 'high' profits or costs from any data and the methods of doing so, are often disputed by economic critics of the MC. Our concern here is what the MC's attitudes are; performance is very difficult to predict or evaluate.

The MC's attitude to price/cost margins have been less consistent than its attitude to profits as a return on assets. Sometimes an unfavourable comparison is drawn between the price/cost ratio in a firm's monopolized market compared with the ratio it secures elsewhere (as in Colour Film, and Cellulose Fibres); in comparable cases (e.g. Flat Glass) there was no such unfavourable comment. But an approximate standard has emerged, since 1964, for approval of profit rates on assets. In 1964-9, the MC commented as follows on its cases, measuring the company's profit rate against the average for all manufacturing and counting assets at historical cost:

Company	Company profit in ratio of manufacturing as whole	M. Commission's comment
Proctor & Gamble	3·6	Very high
Kodak	3·0	High
Triplex	3·0	High
Unilever	2·0	High
Pilkington	1·7 (excluding float glass)	Went beyond reference goods, and approved overall
Courtaulds	1·5	Fairly high given a period of unfavourable markets

(12) It is notoriously difficult – as witness the experience with the Robinson-Patman Act in the US – to identify, *ex ante*, objectionable behaviour, or to prescribe in advance by statute what constitutes objectionable behaviour. Satisfactory rules against discrimination are likely to be found only after much more experience. Satisfactory enforcement of the rules may mean relying on *realized* patterns of behaviour to show, *ex post*, that damage to a specific competition rather than competition at large was intended. Effectiveness in this phase of policy fits rather better into a traditional legal approach to control rather than the current UK methods.

As Sutherland[13] points out, a company earning (as in the Flat Glass case) 1·38 times the median profit rate in 1964 was just at the bottom of the upper quarter of the profits of *The Times'* 300 largest companies.

> 'It is reasonably clear that in order to arouse adverse comment from the MC, a company must be earning profit rates on reference goods at a rate which would place it well up within the top quarter of the range for the largest companies.'

The MC has also considered whether monopoly leads to restricted output. It has generally not been convinced that there is enough evidence to make a judgement. However, it castigated a failure to meet cyclical demand in the Cellulose Fibres case, but passed over an apparent failure to meet demand for some years in the Flat Glass case. Instead, it considered the record of technical improvement and innovation; in the Flat Glass case, it felt that the innovation record outweighed a formidable array of exclusive licencing and dealership arrangements. Yet it regarded the considerable product diversification strategies of detergent firms as competitive 'ploys', not innovations to be applauded. Using innovation to stay ahead of and inhibit competition is approved, as in the Metal Container case, especially if the innovation is fairly radical. The MC implicitly ranks innovatory activity – from the trivial to the transforming – and may base its whole judgement of a company, often a critical factor in interpreting what may well be ambiguous evidence, on this. To summarize, a firm with a high market share and policies yielding substantial returns need fear little from scrutiny by MC, so long as its policies include substantial innovation and exclude attempts to inhibit, by discriminatory action, the potential growth of any one competitor.

Restrictive practices

When the Restrictive Practices Act of 1956 was passed, it was expected that a large number of agreements would survive. The expectation was confounded. To 1964, as Appendix 3 shows, ten cases only were approved. These displayed special, and in some cases (e.g. Metal Windows and Sulphuric Acid) temporary, circumstances. The chances of success now, using arguments which once seem to have impressed the Court, are dim, and would not survive

(13) A. Sutherland, *The Monopolies Commission in Action*, Cambridge University Press, 1969, p. 87.

more sophisticated rebuttal by the Registrar. For most firms, the risk of failing to pass through the public interest 'gateways' of the Act must appear too high to justify the costs. Under the Act of 1964, one case only has succeeded – medicaments. Both proprietary and ethical drugs received the Court's licence for individual manufacturer's maintenance of retail prices. Collective resale price maintenance of books is also protected under a 1956 Act decision; but these two cases will remain the sole examples. Resale price maintenance is virtually dead.

Ways to maintain agreements

There are several resources for those wishing to maintain restrictions. First, the Registrar still takes time to consider registered agreements, as was brought out by recent developments in collusive tendering. Using powers under the 1956 Act, the Registrar discovered a series of agreements for collusive tendering by electrical contractors. In July 1970, the Court concluded that several of these restrictions were against the public interest. They were: agreements on a minimum price bid; disclosure and *ex post* adjustment of bids; *ex ante* agreement on the successful bidder; and compensation by the successful to the unsuccessful. These practices were subject to the 1956 Act, but, as *The Economist* remarked, as the Registrar had only recently been able to undertake so large an investigation.[14] One can still register and hope either for exemption on grounds of economic triviality,[15] or for temporary relief while the Registrar investigates.

Second, agreements deemed to enshrine an aspect of public interest are exempt from registration. The most important of these to concern goods, and involve patents or registered designs. It is permissible to raise restrictive agreements on the exchange of patents, and to base marketing or other agreements on this – so long as the possession of patents is shown to be essential to the agreement. There is little pressure to change this position. However, there is separate administrative machinery for dealing with patents under the Patents Act of 1949. This obliges a patent holder to give reasonable terms to an intending user.

Services are also exempt from the 1956 Act; but this exemption is under scrutiny, following an MC report on Professional Services

[14]   *The Economist*, 6 February 1971.

[15]   *The DTI Journal* of 26 August 1971 noted that, since the passage of the 1968 Act, ninety agreements had been so exempted – by order of the Secretary of State.

(Oct. 1970). This report examined seven general professional restrictive practices, concluding that none could be condemned or approved outright. The professions were invited to review their activities in the light of the MC's comments and voluntarily to make adjustments. If these are not forthcoming, the Government could refer cases to the MC which would then provide guidelines for future legislation.[16] So, in the normal process of testing in the MC, a possible extension of the law was being followed. This applies also to the loop-hole in the 1964 Act, which (section 3) allows an individual manufacturer to refuse to supply where commercial damage would be done to his product by 'loss-leading' at retail.[17] The MC Report of July 1970, on Refusal to Supply, noted that refusal to supply 'in conditions which are not reasonably competitive' may damage the public interest; legislative reform may ensue. Meanwhile, recent cases have tended to restrict carefully the rights of individual manufacturers to withhold supplies.

Information agreements

The stringency of the Court's views on agreements has led to a substitute; information agreements. These must be of like effect to registrable agreements, but not clearly enough to be deemed 'to like effect' by the Court. A major current concern is thus in determining their limits. The Registrar is weighing the likely reduction of competition against the anticipated increase in efficiency from enhanced information flows. Where he thinks necessary, he then secures assurances from the parties. The outsider's impression of these informal processes is of considerable toughness in bargaining; but it is probably too early for confident predictions. Finally, firms bent on restriction can avoid recording agreements; or argue that, even if there is restriction, the parties are not truly separate; or deny that an agreement falls within the Act's definition of 'agreement to supply'. In each case, registration is avoided. These points arose in a recent case.[18] Any agreement, written or not, is in principle subject to the Acts; the Courts have carefully not limited this. In the above case, the Registrar argued that, since various (restrictive) matters

[16] The Commission was most concerned with the justification of the mainten-ance of uniform standards and the adequacy of the profession's own safeguards against abuse.

[17] There does not seem to be any case brought before the Court under section 3 of the Act.

[18] Agreement between Schweppes and others, V. Korah, *Journal of Business Law*, April 1971.

were recorded by the parties as 'agreed' or 'agreed in principle' before the agreement was rendered innocuous by writing it formally with the exempting provisions, it was registrable. The High Court rejected this. However, the Registrar might investigate further cases where negotiations ostensibly 'break down and yet the parties cease to compete in ways they did before'.

Other issues

Thus the Registrar may not infer present restriction from past intentions, but is confirmed in his monitoring; if he can obtain further evidence of a change in competitive relationships he may succeed in arguing that a registrable agreement exists. Attempts in the same case to limit registrability failed. The first was an attempt to argue that, where two companies merged a part of their interests is supplying a subsidiary of one of them, there could be no agreement between the companies. The subsidiary, being identical with its parent, could not be independent, which prevented an inference of supplying goods. The Courts decided that, in the 1968 Act, subsidiary and parent *were* 'single' persons; a registrable agreement existed for trade between them. The same case settled that an agreement existed even if it contained other terms than those concerning supply.

These examples show how registrability is being tested; what could be done by determined companies to avoid registration is now a matter of some subtlety, to be pursued with expert legal advice. However, as previously with this legislation, while the Court might make dubious decisions, if judged from an economic standpoint (it has been trenchantly critized for its few licenced agreements), it is proving relatively severe on attempts to use legal drafting to avoid the manifest intention of the 1968 Act to bring all significant restrictive agreements to the Registrar's attention. Many would argue that, given its scope, the British law of restrictive practices is one of the world's strictest pieces of legislation.

Appendix 1
Scope of the Acts relating to UK competition policy

1948 Monopolies and Restrictive Practices Act

Set up the Monopolies Commission to investigate monopolies (one-third of supply, process, or export of goods) and restrictive practices.

1956 Restrictive Trade Practices Act

(*a*) The Act prohibited agreements for the collective enforcement of resale price maintenance.

(*b*) The Act provided for the registration of all agreements in restraint of trade concerning goods. To be registrable the agreements must involve more than one party, and can refer to oral or written agreements.

(*c*) The Act established a Registrar of Restrictive Practices to maintain custody of the register of agreements, and to take cases before the Court.

(*d*) The Restrictive Trade Practices Court was to decide on the register-ability of agreements, and to determine whether registered agreements were in the public interest. The presumption was that they were against the public interest. The Court can license the agreements where they are found to have some benefit judged against seven criteria (colloquially known as the 'gateways') and where such benefits outweigh detriments to the public (see Appendix 3).

(*e*) There are certain classes of agreement that are exempt, viz. those relating to exports only, bilateral contracts of sale, conditions of employment, sole agencies, standards and patents.

(*f*) (i) Failure to register a restrictive agreement – if discovered, the agreement can be automatically declared null and void.
(ii) If the Registrar has reason to believe that a registrable agreement exists, he may give notice asking whether this is so; refusal to comply may amount to a criminal offence.
(iii) Where an agreement has been held to be contrary to the public interest, the Court has the power to order the parties not to give effect to the original agreement, and also not to make any other agreement 'to like effect'. Any breach of such a Court order may lead to contempt proceedings.

1964 Resale Prices Act

(*a*) The Act prohibits the maintenance of resale prices and those actions (such as refusal to supply) which support it.

(*b*) The Act permits refusal to supply where the supplier has reason to believe that traders are using the supplied commodity as loss-leaders, i.e. goods sold not for profit but for purposes of attraction or advertisement.

(*c*) There is no provision for exemption of classes of goods. Goods wishing to be considered for exemption have to register. Before the Court the following exemption criteria may be invoked:

(i) detriment to public through reduction in quality and variety of goods offered;

(ii) detriment from reduction in number of points of sale;

(iii) detriment through a long run increase in price;

(iv) danger to health;

(v) after sales service would no longer be provided or would be reduced;

(vi) the detriment from abandonment must exceed the detriment from retention of r.p.m. in order for the class of goods to be exempt from the general ruling.

1965 Monopolies and Mergers Act

(*a*) The scope of Commission enquiries extended to services.

(*b*) Responsible department (Board of Trade at the time of the Act) may refer to the Commission any goods or services one-third of the supply of which is controlled by one interest or agreement.

(*c*) The Commission must report on whether the condition of control of one-third of the supply prevails, and whether that condition may be expected to operate against the public interest.

(*d*) The Board of Trade was given extensive powers in the light of such an adverse decision (see Appendix 2).

(*e*) Mergers were brought within the Board's power of referral, the conditions in this case being the market share one of one-third of the supply, or the asset rule of the two companies' assets exceeding £5 m.

(*f*) In the event of an adverse decision from the Commission the Board's powers were as in (*d*) (see Appendix 2).

(*g*) Special rules applied to the merger of newspaper concerns.

1968 Restrictive Trade Practices Act

This supplements and amends the 1956 Act, as follows:

(*a*) The Board of Trade may exempt certain agreements from registration for a specified period providing that the agreement:

(i) is calculated to promote an industrial project or scheme of national importance;

(ii) has as its object to promote efficiency in trade or industry, or to create or improve production capacity therein;

(iii) itself and restrictions in it are necessary for the purposes, and that it is on balance expedient in the national interest.

(*b*) A 'competent authority' may by order approve the exemption from registration of agreements designed either to prevent or restrict price increases or secure reductions of prices, subject to certain conditions. Competent authorities include the Board of Trade (BOT), the Ministries of Agriculture, Health, Power, Works and Technology (now the Department of Trade and Industry).

(*c*) 'Information Agreements' are brought within the scope of the 1956 Act, by order of the BOT, subject to affirmative resolution by Parliament. Information agreements are defined as agreements where two or more parties give information to any persons, whether parties or not, about:

(i) prices charged, quoted, paid or to be charged for goods or processes of manufacture;

(ii) the terms or conditions surrounding the supply or acquisition of goods and similarly for:

(iii) costs, processes applied, the persons or classes of persona, or the areas or places involved.

(*d*) An additional gateway was introduced (see Appendix 3).

(*e*) Registration provisions were tightened up.

Appendix 2

Powers of the BOT (DTI) under the 1965 Monopolies and Mergers Act

It may:

1. Declare any agreement unlawful (except where covered by the 1956 – and presumably the 1968 – Act).

2. Ban certain practices, e.g. withholding goods or services, tying agreements, discrimination, giving preferred terms and deviation from listed prices.

3. Require publication of prices.

4. Regulate prices if the Commission finds that the prices charged are against the public interest.

5. Prevent the acquisition, or provide for the compulsory sale, of undertakings or assets.

6. To provide information for this, the BOT may appoint an Inspector and proceeds by making statutory instruments.

7. Prohibit merger or acquisition, require divestment or authorize with or without assurances being obtained.

Appendix 3

Criteria under the 1956 and 1968 Restrictive Practices Acts:

21. (1) For the purposes of any proceedings before the Court under the last foregoing section, a restriction accepted in pursuance of any agreement shall be deemed to be contrary to the public interest unless the Court is satisfied of any one or more of the following circumstances, that is to say –

(*a*) that the restriction is reasonably necessary, having regard to the character of the goods to which it applies, to protect the public against injury (whether to persons or to premises) in connection with the consumption, installation or use of those goods;

(*b*) that the removal of the restriction would deny to the public as purchasers, consumers or users of any goods other specific and substantial benefits or advantages enjoyed or likely to be enjoyed by them as such, whether by virtue of the restriction itself or of any arrangements or operations resulting therefrom;

(*c*) that the restriction is reasonably necessary to counteract measures taken by any one person not party to the agreement with a view to preventing or restricting competition in or in relation to the trade or business in which the persons party thereto are engaged;

(*d*) that the restriction is reasonably necessary to enable the persons party to the agreement to negotiate fair terms for the supply of goods to, or the acquisition of goods from, any one person not party thereto who controls a preponderant part of the trade or business of acquiring or supplying such goods, or for the supply of goods to any person not party to the agreement and not carrying on such a trade or business who, either alone or in combination with any other such person, controls a preponderant part of the market for such goods;

(*e*) that, having regard to the conditions actually obtaining or reasonably foreseen at the time of the application, the removal of the restriction would be likely to have a serious and persistent adverse effect on the general level of unemployment in an area, or in areas taken together, in which a substantial proportion of the trade or industry to which the agreement relates is situated;

(*f*) that, having regard to the conditions actually obtaining or reasonably foreseen at the time of the application, the removal of the restriction would be likely to cause a reduction in the volume or earnings of the export business of the United Kingdom or in relation to the whole business (including export business) of the said trade or industry; or

(*g*) that the restriction is reasonably required for purposes connected with the maintenance of any other restriction accepted by the parties, whether under the same agreement or under any other agreement between them, being a restriction which is found by the Court not to be contrary to the public interest upon grounds other than those specified in this paragraph, or has been so found in previous proceedings before the Court.

(*h*) Amendment in the 1968 Act: 'that the restriction does not directly or indirectly restrict or discourage competition to any material degree in any relevant trade or industry and is not likely to do so'

and is further satisfied (in any such case) that the restriction is not unreasonable having regard to the balance between those circumstances and any detriment to the public or to persons not parties to the agreement (being purchasers, consumers or users of goods produced or sold by such parties, or persons engaged or seeking to become engaged in the trade or business or selling such goods or of producing or selling similar goods) resulting or likely to result from the operation of the restriction.

Cases approved

1. *Water-Tube Boilers* (July 1959)
   Price and Modified Market Sharing Agreement
   Successful Gateway: Increasing Exports 21(1)(f)

2. *Bolts and Nuts* (July 1960)
   Price Agreement
   Successful Gateway: Benefiting Consumers 21(1)(b)

3. *Cement* (March 1961)
   Price Agreement
   Successful Gateway: Benefiting Consumers (21(1)(b)

4. *Magnets* (June 1962)
   Price Agreement
   Successful Gateway: Benefiting Consumers 21(1)(b)

5. *Metal Windows* (July 1962)
   Price Agreement
   Successful Gateway: Benefiting Consumers 21(1)(b)

6. *Net Book Agreement* (October 1962)
   Collective Resale Price Maintenance
   Successful Gateway: Benefiting Consumers 21(1)(b)

7. *Sulphuric Acid* (July 1963)
   Common Purchasing Agreement
   Successful Gateway: Securing Fair Terms (21(1)(d)

8. *Glazed and Floor Tiles* (January 1964)
   Price Agreement
   Successful Gateway: Benefiting Consumers 21(1)(b)

9. *Scrap Iron* (January 1964)
   Price and Common Purchasing Agreement
   Successful Gateway: Benefiting Consumers 21(1)(b)

10. *Medicaments* (June 1970)
    Resale Price Maintenance: Benefit – lower prices

The United Kingdom and EEC Trade

D. C. Hague

In this paper we look at the relationships between the British economy and that of the rest of the EEC. I begin with a brief discussion of the likely future of international monetary policy as it affects UK–EEC trade, and then concentrate on the implications of the creation of the EEC for consumers and producers of manufactured goods, and, later in the paper, of services.

International monetary policy

International liquidity

There are now two major problems in international monetary policy. First, is the total amount of international liquidity, or that available to individual regions, adequate? While there has been much disagreement about this issue, there does not appear to be a major problem now. There is no reason for believing that the growth of the EEC's external trade or of its internal economy will be seriously held back by a shortage of international liquidity, especially now that the special drawing rights of the international monetary fund provide a supplement to gold.

Exchange rates

However, as Jim Ball has explained for the UK, exchange rates between the EEC currencies do pose a problem. Contradictory tendencies have been at work for some time and it is still not easy to see how things will work out. From one side, there is pressure from those who believe that an economic community cannot be complete without a common currency. For them, the sooner exchange rates between all the EEC countries are fixed irrevocably, as a first step towards the creation of a common currency, the better.

The other side resists permanently-fixed exchange rates between EEC currencies, because this would endanger economic growth and the level of employment in some of the Ten. Many British economists and businessmen are worried by the prospect of joining an EEC with fixed exchange rates between all of its currencies. They argue that the relatively slow rise in British productivity, and the relatively rapid rise in British incomes, as compared with other EEC countries in recent years, will continue. If it does, then, with fixed exchange rates, the British balance of payments could move into a deficit for which the only cure would be a politically unacceptable degree of deflation at home. The speed with which the British balance of payments has deteriorated in the first half of 1972 gives support to this view.

Other papers have discussed the reasons for Britain's poor performance in terms of productivity and prices. The essential point here is that, whatever the causes, British export prices *have* been difficult to keep down to European levels. With no evidence that our performance will improve, many in Britain fear that the political and economic problems which would arise in Britain as a result of fixed exchange rates between the EEC currencies would be intolerable.

While at present it may seem that the UK would be the main sufferer from fixed exchange rates, this need not continue for very long. As we have seen only too clearly in the last twenty years, the relative economic performance of different countries can alter significantly over a decade or less. Putting the case against permanently fixed European exchange rates should therefore not be seen as special pleading for the UK. As time passes, the countries which would suffer from fixed exchange rates would be likely to change.

Possible solutions

There are only two ways out. Either we must *not* fix exchange rates irrevocably; or we must keep economic performance in each of the Ten roughly in line. The idea of 'harmonizing' economic policies and performance in each EEC country is in line with the whole philosophy of the EEC. A major study of the possibilities for such harmonization is being made for discussion at the 'Summit' of Heads of State of the Ten in Paris in October 1972. The problems of harmonizing the whole of economic policy within the Ten are enormous. Yet fixing exchange rates immutably before economic policies have been sufficiently 'harmonized' would be disastrous politically. One cannot imagine any country, least of all the UK, accepting fixed exchange rates before it had secured its growth rate and level of employment through 'harmonization' or in some other way. It was only in March 1972 that, for the first time, a British

Chancellor of the Exchequer stated publicly that if, in future, an over-valued currency endangered economic growth the foreign exchange rate would somehow be reduced. I find it inconceivable that so soon after this pledge, which promises to break the stranglehold that for twenty years the balance of payments and the exchange rate have exerted on UK economic growth, we should abandon even the relatively infrequent changes of exchange-rate parity under the present international monetary system for a completely inflexible system. Unless our balance of payments is adequately protected in some other way compatible with full employment and growth, I do not believe that the UK will accept the arrangements currently being discussed. The floating of the £ sterling in June 1972, even if only temporarily, suggests that this is correct.

I believe that European firms can plan to export to, or set up subsidiaries in, the UK confident that, however the international monetary system develops and whatever the speed at which European monetary union is brought about, the level of activity in the UK will no longer be held down significantly by the exchange rate or the balance of payments.

The prospects for EEC – UK trade

Trade creation and trade diversion

The EEC is a Customs union – an area of industrial free trade surrounded by a common external tariff. In looking at the effects on industrial trade from the enlargement of the community, the standard economic method distinguishes trade creation and trade diversion.

Trade creation is the building up of new trade and its distinguishing characteristic is that it is two-way. Not only will the elimination of tariffs help Britain to export to the EEC; at the same time, it will help the Six to export to Britain and the other new members. The enlargement of the EEC will also cause trade diversion; countries within the EEC will reduce imports from suppliers outside the EEC and use British products instead. At the same time, British importers will buy less from third countries and will import from the EEC instead. There is here no counter-balancing effect within the EEC. Each country was already importing these goods in any case. The question is simply whether Britain and other EEC countries will import from within the enlarged EEC rather than from outside. The losses are borne by countries outside the EEC. Thus, from the point of view of the British balance of payments, the question is whether the gains from diversion are, or are not, reinforced by the effects of trade creation. Individual industries may gain even if the net effect, on the aggregate, is zero or negative. Trade diversion could well be significant. Only 7 per cent of the EEC's exports of manufactures, towards the end of the 1960s, went to the UK and only 18 per cent of British exports went to the EEC. (Because of the favourable balance of trade in manufactured goods in all these countries, the proportion of *total* imports coming from the UK and the EEC respectively was significantly bigger.)

Calculations of the net effect on the UK (or indeed any other EEC country) of the extension of the Community are very difficult to make. Not least, the effects of the 'Kennedy Round' of tariff reductions confuse the calculations. Similarly, it is not clear how UK sales to Commonwealth countries will be affected by the loss of British preferences there. Britain is likely to lose some markets in Commonwealth countries, but many argue that British exports to overseas sterling area countries have been falling so rapidly recently that none will remain by 1978. However, at the same time, Britain will gain access to the ex-French African territories and to several Mediterranean countries through preferential arrangements which the EEC has with them.

After looking at all these factors, Professor Williamson of Warwick University concluded that the net effect on the UK balance of payments would be about £100 m. per annum, a small figure compared with the UK's prospective contributions to the common European agricultural policy and to the European budget. Indeed, it also looks small when compared with the benefits to the balance of payments that Britain now hopes for from the discovery of gas and oil in the North Sea.

Specialization

As Professor Williamson argues, evidence suggests already that one result of the creation of the EEC has been to increase intra-EEC trade for particular categories of product. For example, with, say, electrical goods, one finds that particular EEC countries have increased both exports and imports of such goods since the creation of the Common Market. At first sight this looks a little odd. However, if one looks more deeply, one discovers that the reason for it is increased specialization. Individual countries have exported more of those electrical goods which they can apparently make more efficiently; at the same time, they have imported more electrical goods which other countries make more efficiently. Traditional economic theory shows that international trade is based on specialization, but it argues far too much in terms of homogeneous commodities like wool, wine or cloth. With most modern business, products are *not* homogeneous; specialization can occur just as well *within* each broad category of product as between them. Joining the enlarged community is likely to enable Britain to specialize more effectively. Similarly, it will allow European producers who enter the British market to specialize more profitably themselves.

It is also important to recognize that specialization need not be specialization in production. It is clear that one of the benefits that a bigger market gives is that it allows more firms to concentrate on supplying a small number of customers and concentrating on doing this efficiently. Even in a market of the size of the UK, firms argue that the total number of customers is too small for it to be safe for them to concentrate on supplying a small number of very large customers. The dangers that the firm faces if one or two are lost are too great. However, experience by British firms in Europe suggests that the EEC market is big enough to allow firms to concentrate on smaller numbers of big customers than in the UK. If one big customer is lost, there are enough other big ones to turn to instead.

The results of specialisation

Like Professor Williamson, I would argue that too much economic discussion has ignored a major factor linked to specialization. Professor Kaldor, in particular, has argued that major economies in manufacturing production have been achieved during the rapid economic growth of most European countries since the War. One can identify three reasons for them.

Economies of scale and of 'learning'

First, there are 'ordinary' economies of scale. An enlarged market allows a firm to produce at lower cost. Second, and linked with this, there are economies of 'learning'. The traditional argument for 'ordinary' economies of scale is that cost per unit is lower the larger is the output of any commodity during a given time period, say a year. It is now also argued that cost per unit will be lower the bigger is the *aggregate* output of any commodity which has been produced since that product was first made by the firm. This phenomenon has long been recognized in the aircraft industry. As more aircraft of a particular type are built those in the firm 'learn' how to build them more quickly and cheaply. The phenomenon should probably be looked at more broadly. Indeed, the Boston Consulting Group in the USA has emphasized the need for firms to base their pricing strategies on economies of 'learning'.

The argument is simple. Where the economies of 'learning' are important, a strategy which aims at a low price will yield a greater market share. A greater market share will mean bigger economies from 'learning'; the firm gains a permanent (and possibly growing) advantage over its competitor(s), whose continually smaller market shares – though their total output is also accumulating – mean that they suffer from a persistent cost disadvantage. Third, technological advances can be made in a large market. In many manufacturing industries since the Second World War, economies of scale have not only made possible lower prices with given techniques; they have also made it more attractive to develop and to apply improved technologies, in part at least, because they allow R & D expenditure to be spread over bigger outputs.

It is arguable that the UK will gain more benefit from these factors after she joins the enlarged community than did firms in the original Six. For Britain has been deprived of some of these benefits over the past fifteen years, partly because she has often had an over-valued currency. The new market to which Britain will have access is larger than the British market so that economies may still be reaped. However, this leaves the important question whether, especially during the first few years of the EEC membership, British firms should expand their sales in the EEC by increased exports from Britain or by establishing subsidiaries on the Continent. This is a question to which we shall return. Obviously, the converse of it holds for firms in the existing EEC.

So far we have seen that the enlargement of the EEC is unlikely to lead to a significant change in the balance of industrial trade between Britain and the Six, though some of the Six will gain or lose more than others. At the same time, this increased trade could well be accompanied by a lower level of costs and prices in real terms. There will be benefits both for Britain and the Six because the bigger market will allow economies of scale and learning, and the benefits of technological advance to be reaped *without* monopoly. In 1957, the International Economic Association discussed *The Economic Consequences of the Size of Nations*. The conclusion of this impressive array of economists fifteen years ago was, as Austin Robinson put it, 'that most of the major industrial economies of scale could be achieved by a relatively high-income nation of 50 million; that nations of 10-15 million were probably too small to get all the technical economies available; that the industrial economies of scale beyond a size of 50 million were mainly those that derived from a change in the character of competition and specialisation'.[1]

While the conference emphasized the benefits of market size and scale, it did not believe that countries like Britain, with a population of about 50 m., were likely to suffer from having too small a market, except perhaps for some extremely expensive products like aircraft. It appears that the benefits of a change in the *character* of specialization and competition is likely to be a most important result of the accession of Britain to the EEC.

The effects of entry on particular industries

We now turn to the important problem, both for the economist observing the British economy and for the European businessman deciding which sectors of British industry to enter. This is to try to identify those sectors of industry which are likely to gain rather than lose from EEC membership.

Few British firms have taken in the full implications of joining the EEC. Senior managers in some of the biggest British firms seem to believe that joining the EEC will be as big a 'non-event' as the decimalization of the UK's currency was. I profoundly disagree with them. They have not taken sufficient account of the likelihood that, once Britain joins, firms from other parts of the EEC will set up, or acquire, subsidiaries in the UK. Neither have they fully realized what effects the increased specialization and faster technical progress already mentioned are going to have on the degree and kind of competition in British industry, quite apart from the increased competition in the UK from firms based in the EEC.

The background

While such work must be largely crystal-gazing, something has been done, especially by Han and Liesner, in a monograph on *Britain and*

_____

[1] *The Economic Consequences of the Size of Nations*, Edited by E. A. G. Robinson, London (Macmillan), 1960, p. xviii.

the Common Market.[2] Han and Liesner emphasize the orders of magnitude with which we are involved. As we have seen, both the UK and EEC, send relatively small proportions of their total exports of manufactures to each other. Looking more closely, we discover, as indeed one would expect, that the UK has been more successful in exporting to some EEC countries than to others. For example, British exports of manufactured goods represent almost 30 per cent of total imports of manufactured goods into the Benelux countries. But goods coming from the UK represent only about 15 per cent of West German imports of manufactured goods, and a little over 20 per cent of those of France and Italy.

There is an extremely important point here. If the UK is already successful in exporting to a particular market, this suggests that consumers in that market have a preference for British goods and/or that British manufacturers have a cost or marketing advantage. However, the fact that Britain already has a big share of exports to a particular national market means that the scope for increasing exports to that market may well be more restricted than in other markets, where the UK has so far been less successful. It is true that things work both ways. For example, in a market where Britain has been successful in the past there may well be a 'learning' effect, helping British manufacturers to be more successful in the future. Similarly, there is the possibility of 'building on strength' by using the knowledge acquired about customers, thoroughly tested marketing methods, and so on. However, there is clearly a limit to the proportion of a national market that any other country's exporters can hope to obtain. My instinct would be that where, as with Benelux, British exporters already hold 30 per cent of the market the possibilities for expansion must be limited.

Consequently, the fact that the UK has obtained such a large share of the Benelux market probably means that the scope for further expansion of exports to Benelux countries is correspondingly restricted. Unless British exporters anticipate an above-average growth of demand in the Benelux countries, they will probably be well-advised to concentrate on seeking new markets in West Germany, France and Italy rather than in Holland and Belgium. The same must be true of EEC exports to Britain. While those firms and countries which have been successful in obtaining modest market

[2]　*Britain and the Common Market: the effect of entry on the pattern of manufacturing production*, S. S. Han and H. H. Liesner, University of Cambridge, Department of Applied Economics, Occasional paper no. 27, Cambridge University Press, 1971.

shares can hope for expansion, those with very large market shares already can probably hope for little more success.

So far as tariffs are concerned, these appear commonly to be 5 per cent higher in Britain than in the EEC. Indeed, at the end of the 1960s, 33 per cent of British manufactured goods had tariff rates of 20 per cent or more. In the EEC, only 10 per cent did. While there are some products, like tractors, some ferrous and non-ferrous metals and cotton yarn, where tariffs in the UK are generally lower than those in the EEC, other product groups are broadly favoured by British tariffs. One example is chemicals. Broadly, the frequency distributions of rates of tariff seem to be similar in Britain and in the EEC, though Britain's average is a little higher. However, it does not seem to be true that British tariffs are usually highest for goods where British industry is least competitive.

An empirical study

The study by Han and Liesner gives some idea of the likely effects of the removal of tariffs from the British economy. It looks at the effect of entry on British industry, assuming that joining the EEC opens EEC markets to British firms and British markets to European firms.

First, we must remember that no industry in Britain is likely to have a significant competitive advantage (or indeed weakness) in every field. Each industry has its strong and weak sectors. A firm is likely to be successful after EEC entry in two circumstances: if it is in a part of its industry which is in a strong competitive position internationally; or, failing that, if it is one of the most efficient producers in even a weak industry. With those provisos, we can summarize Han and Liesner's study.

Chemicals

In chemicals, they think that more of the industry is likely to perform rather poorly in the EEC than to perform well. They can see considerable benefits for British producers in paints, dyes and pharmaceuticals. They expect fertilizers to perform rather badly, as well as basic chemicals, which are currently protected by a rather high tariff.

Textiles

In textiles, they see the promising and unpromising sectors as about

MM

equal, each covering about 25 – 30 per cent of the industry. They suggest that British performance may be better at the earlier rather than the later stages of production. For example, they expect yarn producers to be more successful than weavers or knitters. However, many British managers in the textile industry disagree with this.

Ferrous and non-ferrous metals

In ferrous and non-ferrous metals, while there are some fields, like steel rods and alloys, where British performance is expected to be rather poor, the iron and steel industry is thought likely to compete well with Europe over a wide range of products. The non-ferrous metals producers seem more likely to perform well than badly.

Mechanical engineering

In mechanical engineering, Han and Liesner expect more of the industry to do badly than to do well. In their view, the promising parts of the industry include aircraft engines (!) as well as internal combustion engines generally, pumps and mechanical-handling equipment. They predict that Britain will perform rather badly in producing industrial equipment, especially that for the textile, paper and printing industries. This prediction is not very surprising. It confirms a good deal of evidence that Britain has been losing ground in these industries, and indeed in the machine tool industry as well, in recent years. Moreover, despite stagnating industrial investment in Britain, imports of machinery of various kinds appear to have been rising steadily in recent months.

Electrical engineering

The prospects for the electrical engineering industry are seen as mixed, with the good and bad parts of the industry about equal. The better parts seem to be concerned with industrial goods, for example, control and telecommunication apparatus and electrical equipment for vehicles. The poorer parts include those making television and radio sets, electric lamps, valves, etc. The future for British producers of consumer goods in the electrical industry do not appear too bright.

Transport

One of the brightest sectors of all, on these predictions, is transport equipment. Here, British producers of lorries and trucks are expected to perform well, but producers of motor cars and motor cycles are expected to be less successful. Again, the authors predict that British performance will be more satisfactory in making engines and components for vehicles rather than in assembling them – except for lorries.

Miscellaneous products

Finally, Han and Liesner look at a wide range of miscellaneous products. They see good prospects for British photographic equipment (but *not* film) and for sporting goods. On the other hand, they are not optimistic over the future for UK producers of optical devices, watches, clocks, ciné cameras and projectors.

A summary

While remembering that one should not expect the whole of any industry to do uniformly well or uniformly badly, it seems likely that industries where, on balance, things are likely to go against Britain once she joins the EEC are chemicals, mechanical engineering, textiles, optics, watches and clocks. British performance may be good in iron and steel, non-ferrous metals, and transport equipment. However, one of the most promising fields may well be components – especially for motor vehicles.

In other words, if this analysis is correct, it appears that British firms are likely to be more competitive in the production of basic materials, and components than in finished goods. Similarly, the study suggests that Britain will be more successful in producing industrial than domestic products. Perhaps this is not surprising. Certainly many, inside and outside British industry, suggest that we are better at engineering than at marketing, and that insufficient attention has been paid to marketing methods in the UK.

Some conclusions

This suggests possibilities for development within the EEC. Should some European firms either set up or purchase British firms where local skills in engineering can be supplemented by European skills in marketing? Should British firms be seeking ways in which they can link their own engineering abilities with European abilities in marketing? Again, should European businesses be looking for opportunities in Britain to take advantage of the apparent British weakness in marketing, including design? And will British technical and engineering excellence be sufficiently great to make it difficult for European firms to compete with British technology, except in the areas like industrial machinery in general, and machine tools in particular, where Britain appears relatively uncompetitive?

It is important not to overdo this argument. As we insisted earlier in a slightly different context, there is no business field in which the British are wholly bad or wholly good. This is as true of marketing as of anything else. The *best* British marketing is very good indeed. Nor does it follow that British marketing, if it *is* bad, will remain bad. Nevertheless, the conclusions emerging from the study by Han and Liesner are ones which I would have suggested from my own observations of British industry and from teaching its managers.

Towards a company strategy

Perhaps I may now set out a few tentative rules which apply equally to British and European firms.

What markets to tackle

Let us suppose that a British producer is considering exporting to the EEC and that a European producer is considering exporting to the UK. First, the firm has to choose the markets where it is most likely to be successful. In the case of Britain, this probably means her moving into markets where she has not already been so successful that there is little prospect of increasing Britain's market share further. While we have seen that, up to a point, Britain should capitalize on its strengths, this probably means that she should concentrate on expanding sales in West Germany, France and Italy, rather than in Benelux countries. Of course, this implies that European firms should expect the keenest British competition in those countries and industries where British competitive strength is greatest, but the biggest expansion in British exports is still likely to come in those countries where Britain's market share is currently rather small.

Looking from outside the UK, European firms should discover those markets in Britain where their own penetration has not yet been very great, and where the British competitive position seems to be rather weak. This means more than just identifying particular products where the British are unlikely to compete very successfully. It also means identifying functional activities, I have suggested marketing and design, where British performance is likely to be rather bad. For example, there seems to be considerable scope for Italian producers of consumer durables of all kinds to expand their sales in the UK. Within this field, Italian prospects are probably brighter for those products, like gas cookers, where the Italians have so far captured little of the British market, than it is with shoes or washing machines, where Italian producers have already captured a good deal of it.

How to specialize

Second, the implication of this paper is that in almost every industry there will be areas where British and European producers can establish strong market positions by specialisation. Intra-EEC trade based on specialization is likely to be very important. Care needs to be taken both in identifying those countries where it will pay to set up plants to specialize in the production of particular products, and in working out where to produce a range of products to sell in one country in a single plant and where to produce one product in each of a number of individual countries, distributing a single product from each centre throughout the European market.

Location

Finally, we turn to the question of where to produce. We must now distinguish explicitly between the activities of exporting to the UK goods produced within the EEC and establishing plants within the UK to produce for the British market. On *a priori* grounds, one might expect that the main initial effect of the creation of the enlarged EEC, would be an increase in trade between the Six and Britain. One would expect producers both in Britain and in the Six simply to increase their exports from their existing, nationally-based plants to any market where tariffs had been removed. However, it is likely that the creation of the EEC will lead to a good deal of British investment in Europe and much European investment in Britain, for two reasons.

First, with the enlargement of the community, a producer from any of the Ten who sets up a plant in any of the member countries will do so to produce for the 'home' market. Any firm of any nationality investing in another EEC country will feel that it is taking fewer risks in doing so than it would have done before the Community was enlarged. The second reason seems to be much more important. There do seem to be forces leading firms to set up organizations to carry out at least some of their activities, perhaps assembling or marketing, within the countries where markets are sought. Why is this?

A seminar organized in March 1972 by the Centre for Business Research, closely associated with the Manchester Business School, showed that a cross-section of British industrialists believed that it was important to locate a plant close to each major market. Two reasons suggested for this were the need to reduce delivery time, and, second, the inter-dependence of distance, travel time and the cost of warehousing. Most important seemed to be the belief that only close to a market could one obtain an accurate 'feel' for it and get an adequate feedback of information. It is not possible to assess these points here. However, many British firms are currently asking themselves seriously whether EEC markets can be served from the UK or whether European subsidiaries should be established. This suggests that European firms which have not already done so should also be considering seriously whether to establish plants in Britain, either to produce a range of products for the British market or to specialize in making one product in Britain for the whole of Europe.

How industrial structure may develop

Some facts

In a paper on 'The Location of International Firms in an Enlarged E.E.C.', not yet published, Professor John Dunning of Reading University points out that the sales of goods produced by subsidiaries of American manufacturing firms located in the EEC rose by 140 per cent between 1962 and 1969. This is much faster than the increase in manufactured exports from the USA to the EEC in the same period. They rose by 90 per cent. Second, over the same period, the manufacturing output of subsidiaries of American firms operating in the UK rose by 80 per cent as compared with the much larger increase (150 per cent) in manufactured exports from the USA to the UK. Here, perhaps in part because of the removal of restrictions on imports into Britain from the USA, there was a smaller tendency for the expansion of output in subsidiaries.

Professor Dunning also explained that investment by UK firms in the EEC rose by 169 per cent over the period 1962 – 69, while the value of total UK exports to the EEC rose by only 76 per cent, less than half as much. There has apparently been a tendency already for UK firms to increase investment in the EEC rather than export to the EEC. Indeed, Professor Dunning gives figures to show that the factors leading British firms to move closer to their overseas markets were stronger in the case of the EEC than in other parts of the world. These are, presumably, the kinds of factor mentioned earlier, especially proximity to the market and the possibility of thereby obtaining a true understanding of it.

For all the reasons set out above, it would not be surprising if British investment in the EEC increases much faster than British exports to the EEC during the period immediately after the UK enters the EEC. As these figures suggest, since the formation of the EEC, American investment in the EEC has grown faster than American investment in the UK. American firms, too, appear to be attracted by the larger, faster-growing market of the EEC, despite the fact that there are fewer language difficulties in setting up subsidiaries in Britain and the fact that British labour is probably cheaper, even allowing for differences in productivity, than European labour.

Possible developments

This brings one back to whether the creation of the EEC – with the accompanying changes in markets, incomes and technology – will lead to a significant change in the location of European industrial activity. A study of the way industrial location has developed in Europe emphasizes the importance that sources of energy have had in determining the pattern of industrial location. In the days of coal, industry was concentrated on or near coalfields in Britain, Belgium, Northern France and Western Germany. Areas without coal, like the southern parts of France, Spain, Italy and Greece, lacked industrial development. Now that the dominance of coal is passing, the sources and costs of transport of oil, gas, etc. are likely to be important influences on industrial location.

Until the discovery of substantial oil and gas deposits in the North Sea, there was a tendency for industry to move gradually southwards. On the one hand, oil from North Africa and the Middle East could be transported more cheaply to southern Italy and southern France than to Northern Europe. On the other hand, supplies of cheap industrial labour in these areas meant that firms could, as the USA has done in South Korea and Formosa, establish production units in areas of cheap labour. With increasing levels of income in northern Europe, this process could well continue. If it does, it will mean the development of increasingly important industrial areas in the Rhone valley, around Marseilles and the new

Europort at Foss, in Southern Italy and perhaps in Greece. Instead of importing workers from the south, firms in northern Europe (especially Germany) may establish plants to employ labour where it lives.

At the same time, many experts look towards an increasing concentration of industrial activity in the broad area between Dunkirk, the Ruhr and Paris with an extension southwards, probably confined largely to a relatively narrow band extending through the Rhone valley to Marseilles.

Even the discovery of oil and gas in the North Sea may not counter this development. There is no great difficulty in transporting oil (by ship or by pipeline) to any point around the North Sea. To this extent, the advent of North Sea oil may simply reinforce existing locational forces, concentrating development in the Dunkirk – Ruhr region, with oil brought ashore at Antwerp, Rotterdam and Dunkirk. The questionmark is over the position of Britain. One possibility is that there will be simply an extension of the industrialized zone westwards from the developing area between the Ruhr and Dunkirk. However, transportation between the UK and Europe is, at least marginally, more inconvenient. The Channel Tunnel remains a dream, so that, unless air transport is widely used, conventional routes may become crowded. And at least some British businessmen argue that they would be unhappy about putting too much emphasis on exporting from Britain so long as goods have to be handled (twice) by dockers, whether British or European.

Possible problems for Britain

Indeed, one of the fears already voiced is that Britain may become the 'Ulster of Europe' or, at least, 'the West Virginia of the European Federation'. Market forces certainly tend to work slowly, but they work inexorably. Could it be that those who express these fears sense that fundamental forces underlying industrial location are beginning to pull activity away from Britain into the Low Countries, and will do so increasingly in the future? If so, membership of the enlarged Community should not be seen simply as a way of obtaining employment for Britons who still live in Britain. Perhaps it will provide a way of allowing the whole European labour force, including the British, to move to the most satisfactory locations, wherever in the Ten these are, either inside or outside Britain. There may be some reduction in the population of Great Britain and a movement of British labour into Europe.

This may appear discouraging to European firms considering whether to establish plants in the UK. But we have seen that the UK offers a large enough market to provide the economies of scale required by most manufacturing operations. In particular, if economies of scale depend on spreading research and development costs over a large market, these benefits are open to a plant in Britain which either sells its product in both the UK and EEC or manufactures the same product in the UK as is already being manufactured elsewhere in the EEC. While there may be doubt about the future rate of growth of the output of British manufacturing firms in the UK, any absolute or relative decline could well be offset by a rise in the output of *European* firms manufacturing in the UK.

Moreover, an important reason for optimism, in line with some points made earlier, is the suggestion that in the longer run those actually engaged in production will be located further and further to the south, leaving the more northerly areas of Europe to deal with problems of company planning, finance, administration and above all, the creation of 'systems'. It could be that British industry will *not* move into Europe. If so, it may well be because Britain will move increasingly into the activities of planning, the development of 'systems' and other work at the head offices of multi-national corporations. This would offset the disadvantages which Britain suffers from its lack of easy land communication with Europe. Ideas and information do not need the same kind of transport system as physical products. Equally, it may be that firms based in France, Germany, the Netherlands and Belgium, will be affected in much the same way. Production may be in under-developed parts of Europe, or indeed in North Africa or Asia. Marketing (as we saw on page 206) may need close contact with the consumer; but other activities may be carried out in northern Europe and the UK. Indeed, one may have an increasing number of British firms whose products are 'systems'.

This is looking very much into the future and into an area of great uncertainty. One cannot give definite predictions about the way industrial location will alter under the impact of the development of the EEC and such events as the discovery of North Sea oil. We simply do not know what will happen. However, those concerned with the location of their firms' activities will need to take all possibilities and uncertainties into account. While Britain's entry into the EEC will remove some uncertainties, new sources of energy and the growing international mobility of firms, partly a result of

Britain's entry, seem bound to alter the international pattern of industrial location. We cannot yet be certain how that pattern will develop; what does seem likely is that it will change significantly over the next ten or twenty years.

Postscripts
and discussions

Postscript and discussion   Paper 2
Marketing in the United Kingdom
Kenneth Simmonds and Philip Law

Postscript by Kenneth Simmonds

Since the paper was written there has been a consumer-led boom starting with decimalization and economic relaxation and this is now converting itself into a capital goods boom. The North Sea expenditures are building up just as the consumer boom seems to be subsiding a little. For the first time for years, heavy capital-good firms have experienced a reduction in their marketing problems. This is a remarkable change. Heavy industry is now the 'get up and go' part of the economy.

Without spectacular growth in consumer expenditure, the aim of many consumer firms is to squeeze extra profit out of a declining market, and this requires a much more constrained and controlled managerial approach. For new products they are seeking areas where switches in consumer expenditure are taking place, or can be persuaded to take place. For example, the leisure and hobbies sector is growing rapidly. Money that might have been spent on, say, cinema-going is now being transferred to, say, boating.

One outstanding feature of the United Kingdom marketing scene is the heavy advertising expenditure as compared with other Common Market countries. Heavy magazine and newspaper reading has been a particularly British characteristic. The figures for television viewing, however, are now rather frightening. The average British viewer watches television sixteen hours a week, and the figure is still increasing. With limited channels and condensed viewing hours the result is greater viewing of television advertisements than anywhere else in the world.

The development of hypermarkets and of out-of-town shopping centres is still hampered by difficulties in getting planning permission. Moreover, economists will no doubt continue to find strong arguments against them, pointing particularly to the social costs of closing down the shops in the town centre. Nevertheless people have cars and do like out-of-town shopping centres, and these developments will eventually go forward, though ten to fifteen years behind what is happening on the Continent. One or two large sites have already been developed by Woolco and by Carrefour, but so far these are in out-of-the-way places.

Radio advertising is also about to break on us. I do not believe that there will be much switching of advertising from television to radio, nor from local Press to local radio. I expect an addition to advertising expenditure, much as in the USA. I even expect an increase in local Press advertising, as local competition between the supermarkets and other larger stores increases. They are likely to turn to the local news media to put across their weekly price and 'specials' messages.

Marketing skills and understanding in the UK are extending rapidly now. There has been a remarkable change in the last ten years. When I talked to British businessmen a decade ago, I found them very offhand about marketing. There were long discussions about how to define marketing. The heritage of economics suggested that all one had to do was to apply sound economic thinking. However, there has been a profound and rapid *social* change. People no longer ask what marketing is. It is no longer *de rigueur* for businessmen to claim that they do not understand it and to imply that it is probably not worth understanding. Marketing is now acceptable and businessmen want to be 'with it' in discussing the subject. The teaching of marketing at the undergraduate level is building up and the activity has come to be seen as an acceptable field for the young to enter.

The tendency to see marketing as an organizational grouping in the firm, covering market research, advertising, distribution, etc., is dying. There is less active discussion on where to *put* marketing. It is better understood that marketing is largely a matter of the way in which decisions are reached, that the whole firm must begin its discussion of the way it should proceed from the market place. The UK has gone further in this than the other Common Market countries. Continental firms coming into the UK will find at least as good an acceptance of the 'marketing concept' as anywhere else. British firms moving into the Continent, on the other hand, will find it difficult to recruit people with this view of marketing and may have to look to specialists for at least ten years.

While these ideas have gained wider acceptance in the UK, many firms have failed to make them stick. In many cases, the task of introducing management through marketing into the biggest British firms fell to American consultants. A standard report by an American consultant would call for centralizing strategy, i.e. new markets and acquisitions, at head office, and for decentralizing tactics into product divisions and, when this had been pushed as far as possible, for the appointment of product managers responsible for smaller segments of business. This organizational structure would then be backed up with five-year plans with annual reviews, and annual operating plans with monthly reviews. Where such a policy failed it was usually the result of a failure to adopt a marketing way of thinking at the top. Top managers have not asked: 'What are you going to do and why?', and then required a market-based answer. The preparation of plans has mainly fallen into the hands of financially oriented managers. With chartered accountants asking the questions, there is a concentration on costs and not on marketing rationale. Only one person can force such an approach through – the man at the top. If the right questions are not asked there, one will have no pressure to force justification of what has been done down to the next level in management. So, while many managers in firms where a marketing approach did not catch on may understand the marketing approach fully, they could do little when the main line function did not adopt it.

Discussion

In his first reply, Professor Simmonds said that heavy industry was where growth was taking place, partly because of North Sea oil and the planned increases in investment in the steel industry. With expenditure on heavy capital products increasing, as it had not for a long time, there was new excitement in marketing there.

Asked about standardizing promotion in the EEC, Professor Simmonds said that one could not generalize. One could ask a motorist to 'put a tiger in your tank' in all countries and one could have a 'man on the spot' in every city. However, with branded products such as food and detergents, if one held country managements responsible for performance, one had to allow advertising on a country-by-country basis. In each country, the manager might choose a different image for the product. Where one was aiming one's advertising at a cross-national segment, as in a bank dealing with international businessmen who read *Time* and *Fortune*, however, one could standardize across national boundaries.

Professor Simmonds was asked whether in British 'new towns', like Peterlee, it was possible to approach decisions on out-of-town shopping centres by using a systems approach. Did not welfare arguments lead one to integrated systems? Professor Simmonds replied that he believed that, despite the social costs of leaving old town centres, entrepreneurs would go ahead. There would be increasingly bigger shopping precincts because these were where customers would go. A total system approach incorporating outside values could delay development, but would not do so permanently because the new out-of-town shopping centres *were* wanted. This was an issue rather like that of television advertising where, at some times, the social welfare approach had tried to restrict television advertising, television broadcasting hours, etc.

Asked whether he felt that in future businesses should be made to pay the social costs incurred by their investments, Professor Simmonds foresaw a big expenditure on cost/benefit studies in this area. However, he thought that the result could be rather like the studies for the third London airport. People would pick the numbers they wanted and make their own choices. Numbers would be put on various aspects of the problem, but then the argument would begin.

A questioner suggested that housewives would be driven from the High Street because they could not park and because there was a declining amount of public transport. However, they would not patronize the hypermarket because they liked it but because there was no alternative. Professor Simmonds said that this reminded him of an interview on television. A woman was asked what she thought of the Common Market. She said she did not like it because of all the sexy music and because she was made to buy what she did not want. If one had lived outside the UK and become used to these large markets, one found it almost an entertainment for an evening. He did not agree that anyone would be forced to enter hypermarkets against their wishes. People liked them when they got there. In addition it was easier for the big markets to deal with problems like car parking. There had been a noticeable increase in the size of the High Street chain stores in recent years and they would continue to get bigger, but they could never be as big as the hypermarkets.

A speaker from the floor recalled that Professor Simmonds said that the British had good technical marketing specialists as well as good retailers, but were behind Europe in hypermarkets because of planning problems. The speaker wondered whether continental retailers would come here, and/or whether British retailers would go to the EEC, backed by British marketing specialists.

Professor Simmonds thought that European retailers coming to

Britain would be hit by planning problems so that it would be easier for British retailers to go into the Common Market. He did not think that the relative qualities of marketing specialists were very relevant here. The problem was not the 'boffin' but whether the strengths of 'the City' would be available to help British retailers in buying continental chains. There had been some resistance to take-overs in some European countries recently, and it was increasingly difficult to exploit take-overs to the full. As a general rule of thumb he thought that British firms would develop retailing on the Continent and that continental firms would develop manufacturing activity in Britain.

The difficulty with British boffins was that one could not really use much of their speciality outside Britain. What mattered was the quality of management 'in the front line'. Once a manager had succeeded in one environment he could repeat what he had done in another. As for market researchers, British firms would be able to buy what they needed in the EEC. There were fewer figures to use in market research there, but one should not take a man from the British culture to do market research in Europe. Perhaps firms would first use some transnationals. British firms operating in Europe might 'piggy-back' on America, using business school graduates from the USA who were Europeans. But the real success did not lie in market research. What one needed were broad, bold strokes in marketing.

It was suggested to Professor Simmonds that he had implied that marketing was almost overdeveloped in the UK in general. This might be true even in the capital-goods industry. Perhaps, if a capital-goods firm obtained a big market share, then a lot of its marketing activity would be negated because of financial and other constraints. How good, then, was marketing?

Professor Simmonds said he had been referring to professional aspects like figure-pushing. He thought that market research skills in the UK were ahead of management skills. In the capital goods industry, one found pockets of advanced analysis but it was only recently that the marketing concept had got through to management of many capital goods firms. Yet, once established, it had been spreading rapidly in firms like GEC, British Steel and Tube Investments. As for constraints through finance, he did not think that this was a problem. Entrepreneurship might once have been a problem, but perhaps not now. He did have a distinct impression, though, that British managers were tired of British labour problems. They tended to be giving preference to opportunities where labour problems would be minimized. Finally, in the North Sea, America had a know-how lead but this would be quickly reduced.

It was suggested by a participant that the concentration of population in the South-East made it an attractive area to penetrate. How did this link up with the problem of development areas? Would not continental firms prefer to operate in the 'soft-under-belly' of South-East England and should not some protection be devised?

Professor Simmonds replied that he wondered whether one should ask such questions. He knew that the 'law of the jungle' operated on most international issues. But were we really to protect the UK market, even while entering the EEC? Or should we say that we would encourage everyone to 'go places', whatever their nationality? The London market was very competitive, and firms not as experienced as UK firms in using the media might find it hard to break into the market. Conversely UK firms that had done well by selling in the South-East, and in using television advertising, had an advantage over European firms. Continental firms might do better *outside* the South-East, particularly in machine tools, for example. The UK firms appeared to be better on the 'soft stuff'. However, why should one worry?

A questioner from the floor wondered whether the development of the hypermarket might not help European firms to move even into consumer goods industries in the UK. A hypermarket could sell several brands of each product, for example, consumer durables.

Professor Simmonds emphasised that consumer durables needed advertising too. He thought that British firms would keep their market shares, perhaps by putting a UK brand mark on goods from the Continent. He did not see hypermarket firms from Europe selling their own goods in the UK. However, firms like Carrefour bought up large lots and that could cause havoc with other UK retailers. It would certainly cause problems for the city centre, not-so-large department stores.

Professor Simmonds was asked as to why British motor vehicles were losing their share of the UK market. In reply, he pointed out that in the motor car industry the employment pattern had for many years divided primarily into the three streams of production, accounting and commercial. In production and engineering and in accounting, moreover, practical training was seen as better than 'ivory tower' experience in a university. For those who moved into commercial, sales and marketing activities, however, there was almost no training beyond public school. The British motor vehicle industry had been like this for a long time. It had only really changed during the last half dozen years, though not all the changes had worked well. Apparently contributing to the recent fall in market share, British Leyland had finally tidied up its distributor system by discarding some of its distributors at just the time when Volvo and the Japanese were moving in and were happy to take up their services.

A questioner suggested that with cars, design and delivery dates were important. People chose to import cars rather than buy them from British firms. The British motor industry was also affected by British economic policies. It was *more* than a question of distributors.

Professor Simmonds said that he would look behind all these aspects to find the real explanation in the industry's management. Foreign firms in the UK, after all, confronted the same economic climate. Perhaps one could add to the stereotype of manager that Professor Morris had put forward in his paper. In the motor industry, it seemed that the 'get up and go' type of manager had been absent. The manager of the motor firm had been the stereotype for a subculture. He certainly did not say to himself: '*I* will perform.' It was significant that the top level of a firm like British Leyland had been largely grafted on in recent years.

Asked about the likelihood of further growth of private labels in food, Professor Simmonds said that if one read the literature one became confused. In some areas, private-label trading had been squeezed as, for example, Heinz had extended its market share at the expense of private labels. Yet the increasing power of the super-market meant that it could 'push through' a private brand if it wished. Similarly, Marks and Spencer could create their own brand and quickly have the largest share in the country. While one should not generalize, perhaps supermarkets would not go as far as they could.

Professor Simmonds thought that market performance was not just a question of quality, as was suggested by one questioner. The quality of any goods was very subjective. With baked beans, for example, there was a good deal of advertising which had been shown to be effective. He thought that even for cars more than simply quality issues were involved in relative performance.

A speaker from the floor pointed to the difficulty of measuring the quality of a motor car, when no one could try all models during a life cycle. Another participant pointed out that in a recent study of several successful cars it had been found that, in terms of quality, the Jaguar came out worst but still had high owner-acceptability. The same speaker asked for clarification on a general issue. He had come to the Conference convinced that British retailing was good and that this would help European or Japanese firms to obtain a large market share quickly in the UK. Was this not really true?

Professor Simmonds agreed, adding that retailing was generally more developed in the UK not least because population was less geographically spread and the media more developed. But he thought British firms were better at handling pull-through advertisement and this would give them an advantage in Britain and other EEC countries over firms from other countries which were less good at using the media.

Asked whether one reason why manufactured imports into the UK seemed to be rising rather rapidly was that British design was bad, Professor Simmonds replied that he did not think so. It was certainly possible for the market for consumer durables to be segmented in such a way as to make room for a larger range of products than the British were already producing. This was true, for example, of cars. However, these gaps in the product range were not filled by British firms and he wondered why. If foreign firms were able to fill those gaps, then, in one sense, the British could fill them too. The explanation for poor performance lay more in attitudes of managers than in the product itself.

For example, one could look at the experience of the Mini in the USA. The Mini was not a *bad* design and had appealed in many ways in as many markets. In the American market the Mini had built up a significant share before the Japanese moved in. However, British Motor Corporation had seemed to stand still on developing its distribution, servicing, repair and parts services to the extent that the market demanded. It was a problem of management attitudes.

To a suggestion that in many fields the British did have design skills, Professor Simmonds suggested that design was a cultural element. British designers' skills were conditioned by what they and their British market considered good design. They had skills, but perhaps only within the British culture. He did not himself like many British designs. He thought a good cross-culture design was possible and if one's national design did not fit into this, one's goods sold badly. Perhaps this had been true at various times with British textiles, clothing and furniture. It was ironic that the name of the designer of the Mini was Issigonis.

The prospects for
the UK economy

R. J. Ball

Postscript presented by Terry Burns

Professor Ball's paper emphasized the important problems of inflation and the balance of payments and the extent to which they were potential constraints on the United Kingdom growth rate. In the period since it was written, unemployment has fallen by 200,000; the £ has been floated; a statutory incomes policy has been introduced, and a balance of payments surplus of about £1,000 m. has disappeared. The months since the paper was written have certainly been eventful and yet most of the predictions made in it have stood the test of time, although there has not been the falling-off in the rate of inflation that Professor Ball hoped for.

The fact that the rate of economic growth in the UK was around 2 per cent did not matter in the period 1900–50, because Britain kept a leading place in the world. Since 1950 growth in the UK has been more rapid, but in the EEC countries it has been more rapid still. The result is that, though in absolute terms British performance has been good compared with what happened in the past in the UK, Britain is falling relatively farther and farther behind.

Several factors are important. For example, the percentage of GNP which Britain invests is low, though it has increased considerably in the past twenty-five years – from around 11 per cent to about 18 per cent. However, this is a lower percentage than in the rest of the EEC. Similarly, Britain has been short of labour compared with the rest of the EEC, where all countries have been able to take labour from agriculture without reducing agricultural output. There is also a feeling that the British tax system does not help economic development. Similarly, the fact that Britain was the first country to industrialize means that there is resistance to change. However, economists do badly at explaining differences in rates of growth between countries. They can list the factors involved but there is still an absence of a coherent theory.

From the point of view of the UK there are some hopeful signs that the underlying rate of increase in output is rising, if not dramatically. In the early 1950s, the rate of growth of productive capacity (of productivity) was about $2\frac{1}{2}$ per cent. That rate then moved up to 3 per cent and is now probably within the range $3\frac{1}{4}$–$3\frac{1}{2}$ per cent. A major question is whether this process will continue. Even if there is continuing progress here, the relative position may not improve much, as growth in the EEC is likely to continue to be above this.

On the other side, demand management kept the rate of growth of output below that of productive potential in the latter part of the 1960s. Initially, this was in order to protect the exchange rate. After devaluation it was in order to shift resources from consumption, in the hope that they would be taken up by exporting, but then not allowing them to be used when the extra exports failed to fill the gap entirely. Recently there has been a change. With tax cuts, the country is now experiencing 5 per cent growth and the number of wholly unemployed has fallen to 660,000 – a reduction from 4 to 3 per cent of the labour force. Output is expected to continue to grow at $4\frac{1}{2}$–5 per cent through 1973, and Professor Ball and I agree with the Treasury that unemployment will fall rapidly throughout 1973. Our view is that it could fall below 400,000 in early 1974. This will represent about 2 per cent unemployment which many people see as the minimum acceptable level. Indeed, there is considerable talk of overheating and recently *The Times* called for a deflationary budget. The consequences of 2 per cent unemployment are by no means certain, but we can expect further upward pressure on wages and that any shortfall in domestic production will be filled by imports. There will undoubtedly be problems in both these fields in 1973 and it is probably unsafe to allow unemployment to fall below 400,000. The implication is that by the end of 1973 we may have to cut back the rate of growth to $3\frac{1}{2}$ per cent.

I feel that it was correct not to deflate at this point. Forecasting is still very uncertain and it could be that growth may yet fall short of 5 per cent. There is still time in the autumn to take action and then perhaps there will be a need for a touch on the economic brake. Even so we can still look forward to $5\frac{1}{2}$ per cent growth in 1973, $4\frac{1}{2}$ per cent in 1974 and $3\frac{1}{2}$ per cent in 1975. This is the fastest and most sustained expansion for a long time. One merely hopes that it will continue, without inflation or the balance of payments over-whelming it.

Unfortunately, in recent years the inflation rate in the UK has been higher than in other industrial countries. During the years 1960–69, our performance was not too bad. Prices increased by $3\frac{1}{2}$ per cent per annum as compared with an average of 3 per cent in other industrialized countries. Inflation has been much more rapid since 1969, and this has been true throughout the world. However, British prices have increased by about $7\frac{1}{2}$ per cent per annum, compared with about 5 per cent in the other industrialized countries. So the gap has widened as worldwide inflation has become more rapid.

Since the war a wide variety of diagnoses have been offered to account for the rate of inflation in the UK. Economists argue a great deal about the effect of monetary restrictions and not least over how far a reduction in the money supply will affect the rate of inflation. The difficulty is that no one is sure what effect such a policy would have on unemployment and growth. What most would agree is that the price to be paid in terms of unemployment and falling growth would be too high.

In the 1960s, too, there was over-employment with too much pressure on the labour market. It used to be thought that increasing unemployment to around $2\frac{1}{2}$ per cent would reduce the rate of increase in wages. More recently, this idea has lost credibility, because we have experienced both high unemployment and rapid inflation. There does seem to have been a short-run relationship between unemployment and the rate of growth of prices before 1966. However, it is a complicated one and perhaps not the same in the long run.

There have also been problems over organized labour. Here there are two views. First, there are those who argue that the unions and Government should get together. Second, there are those who would try to reduce the monopoly power of unions.

Professor Ball and I would argue that a major problem arises when the full benefit of a large increase in productivity is paid out to any group in increased wages. The implication is that inevitably similar awards are claimed by employees in low productivity-growth service industries which inevitably tends to raise service prices, hence partly offsetting the effect of the higher money incomes. Workers in industries where productivity is growing faster than average must be prepared to take less than their own increase in productivity. So far we have not been able to devise arrangements to achieve this. The only relief has therefore been through inflation and this is inevitable without an accord between organized labour and the government, with explicit arrangements with regard to income distribution.

In recent years, we also believe that inflation has been stimulated by 'income frustration'. First, consumption was held down to benefit the balance of payments directly via lower imports; later, it was held down to make the 'hole' to be filled by exports. People became frustrated because real consumption was rising by only about 1 per cent per annum and they took matters into their own hands. However one may disapprove of this, one can see that it made sense to the individual citizen.

Yet all countries have suffered from the same phenomenon of accelerated inflation since 1969. In the UK, it seems to have resulted from 'income frustration'; in the USA it has been attributed to falling unemployment; in France it appears to have stemmed from the troubles of 1968. Yet, while one may doubt whether one should put too much emphasis on national explanations, it is not clear why there should have been an international transmission mechanism at work during this period.

When this paper was written, Professor Ball was hopeful about inflation but these hopes have not been fulfilled. The floating of the £ in June 1972 led to increased import prices and so to an increase in the cost of living within the UK. At the same time there were pessimistic feelings about such things as the effect of the introduction of VAT. Expectations of an increased rate of inflation grew and earnings regained their momentum until by October 1972 they were about 15 per cent higher than a year earlier. Inflation had obviously got out of hand. It was extremely unfortunate for the Government that, at precisely that moment, the terms of trade were moving against the UK by more than at any time since the Korean war. World prices were rising rapidly, and the exchange rate had been falling, so that the Government was trying to introduce an incomes policy at the worst possible time. The outlook was uncertain but it is clear that one could not have left matters to the CBI and the TUC. As I have already outlined, the problem is essentially one of income distribution, and it therefore follows that we need an overall view which only the Government can provide.

It has been suggested, at times, that it might be easier to alleviate inflation rather than to fight it. In the past, governments in the UK have not attempted to alleviate the suffering from inflation immediately; this is no doubt in part because of a fear that there would then be less of an incentive to maintain inflation at tolerable levels. However, now that we have *got* rapid inflation, perhaps we should try to learn to live with it a little more easily and to link more incomes to the cost of living.

There was a record surplus on the balance of payments in 1971 because of devaluation, the high rate of growth of world trade and domestic stagnation. However, Professor Ball's paper explained that the balance of payments was probably not in equilibrium even at the time when the paper was written; if unemployment had been pushed down to about $2\frac{1}{2}$ per cent, there would have been a deficit. In 1972 there was little increase in exports and the terms of trade moved rapidly against the UK. The floating pound increased import prices, and import volume increased rapidly in line with the rising rate of economic growth. The balance of payments surplus in 1972 was only about £60 m. and imports are still increasing rapidly, while the terms of trade continue to move against us.

Unfortunately, the long-run problem looks equally serious. If output increases at $3\frac{1}{2}$ per cent, it appears that the volume of imports will increase at 7 per cent. (The income elasticity of demand for imports seems now to be about 2.) So exports will need to increase at 7 per cent per annum to keep the balance of payments in equilibrium: 2–3 per cent faster than the average of recent years. Perhaps to assume that exports might increase at 5 per cent per annum would be considered optimistic. However, it follows that unless there is an improvement in the terms of trade, one can look to a gap between imports and exports of about 1–2 per cent per annum. This will increase the balance of payments deficit by about £300 m. each year.

In the short run, the only possible remedies are deflation, devaluation or import restrictions. The first two would lead to big problems in the present situation because of income frustration and increasing import prices. Import controls are not possible within the EEC. The long-run problem is no easier than the short-run one and would be complicated even further if we yielded to the desire of many in the Common Market to bring about monetary union by 1980. It has already been complicated by the recent decision to float jointly many European currencies.

If, in order to obtain $3\frac{1}{2}$ per cent growth, the sterling exchange rate has to fall continuously by perhaps 2 per cent per annum, then it is obviously not possible to peg the pound. A fixed exchange rate would be possible only if other EEC countries made transfers to offset our negative balance of payments. Fixed exchange rates would be extremely bad for British growth, as we would eventually return to the experience of the late 1960s when output fell below productive potential.

If there is such an annual depreciation in the exchange rate, then, as outlined earlier, perhaps from 1973 to 1976 growth will be more rapid than ever before. There is unlikely to be an economic miracle, but an outstanding performance all the same. Growth prospects are therefore good, provided that the exchange rate is not fixed. Yet at the very time when the balance of payments was deteriorating, in late 1972 and early 1973, there was strong pressure from within the EEC to fix the sterling exchange rate.

Discussion

Asked how the Government could bring about a reduction in the rate of growth from 5 to $3\frac{1}{2}$ per cent, and how this could be reconciled with the continuing problem of unemployment, Mr Burns said that two issues were linked. There were now many people who wanted a reduction in Government expenditure. Its increase was partly a lagged result of the attempt to reduce unemployment over the past two years. Unfortunately there would be similar lags if we attempted to reduce Government expenditure and this also would probably be insufficient in the short run. There was, therefore, currently pressure for deflation (March 1973), but the tools available were limited, given the incomes policy. Some increase in taxation would be necessary, however, and interest rates were likely to remain high for at least eighteen months. He did not see how it could be otherwise.

In answer to questions about the balance of payments deficit, Mr Burns said that the deficit in 1973 would be substantial. His figure of £300 m. was the deterioration in the balance of payments in each year, assuming a fixed exchange rate and no worsening in the terms of trade. In 1973, this would give the UK a deficit of perhaps £400–600 m. partly because of a rise in imports of perhaps 10 per cent. This figure also assumed that exports would increase by more than the long-run trend would allow. Estimates that others had published, of a balance of payments deficit of £1,000 m., assumed 5 per cent growth in the UK, a slower increase in exports, and further deterioration in the terms of trade.

Asked whether the deterioration in the balance of payments of £300 m. per annum was simply in the balance of trade and ignored the British contribution to the EEC, Mr Burns replied that this was true. However, the contribution of £500–600 m. to the EEC would represent a once-for-all worsening in the balance of payments, though of course the contribution would have to be paid annually. He also pointed out that the deterioration of £300 m. in the balance of payments was at 1973 prices.

Mr Burns reminded his audience that a 1 per cent deficit on the balance of payments represented a bigger and bigger absolute number as time went on, with economic growth and with inflation. One was tempted to think of total British exports still being £5,000 m., which was what they were ten years ago. Now, they were £10,000 m. There was a danger that the import position of the UK would become worse with membership of the EEC. Before 1967 the elasticity of demand for imports had perhaps been 1·5, so that if the GNP in Britain grew at 2 per cent per annum imports rose by 3 per cent per annum. With increasingly free trade the income elasticity of demand for imports had risen to about 2. The reductions in tariffs resulting from membership of the EEC were almost certain to lead to a further increase in imports.

To a suggestion by a participant that the moral was that it would be foolish to fix the sterling exchange rate, Mr Burns said that he saw no possibility at all of a fixed sterling exchange rate unless there was a reduction in the rate of growth in the UK, and with it an increase in unemployment.

Another participant questioned Mr Burns about the international aspect of inflation, wondering whether Mr Burns had under-emphasized the problems of income frustration. For example, in France this appeared to have led to the unrest of 1968 and, perhaps it had operated, though differently, in Germany. There might have been a similar situation in Italy after 1969. If so, there was a growing similarity in the inflationary problems of the West.

Mr Burns replied that to say this was simply to argue over names. It was true that there had *been* a shift from profits to wages and salaries during the period in all countries. However, while in the UK income frustration arose from the fact that the rate of growth was below the long-run trend, elsewhere there had been much more rapid rates of growth and any frustration was not due to recent adverse movements. If one took the view that there was income frustration in these other countries as well, then the implication was that even a faster rate of economic growth would not help Britain to solve the problems of inflation. Mr Burns argued that *every* Government was likely to interfere in the bargaining process eventually, so the problem was one of income distribution.

Another participant suggested that the whole UK economy had been 'toned up' by unemployment. If, by the year end, Mr Burns was suggesting that we should be short of manpower, it was important to change the climate. Should not the business schools be taking steps to point out that labour would soon be short again and to urge the necessity of doing something? At the same time, could Mr Burns say how much, on average, sterling would have to be devalued up to 1980?

Mr Burns replied that there was increasing awareness of the danger of labour shortage. Indeed, this was why there was argument over whether the British Government should deflate now or later. The case for doing something quickly was that British Governments always seemed to act too late. He would urge the Government to wait, because forecasting was so hazardous and there was still a possibility that unemployment might not fall as rapidly as outlined earlier. However, he did not see much hope of avoiding a labour shortage in the short-run. Over the past two years many firms had reduced their labour forces without reducing their output. However, a major problem was why, if there was still surplus labour in industry, unemployment has fallen so far. Economists had been assuming that the increase in labour productivity achieved by industry in recent years would be permanent, but there were now doubts about this. Certainly the fall in unemployment was not consistent with an increase in the trend rate of growth of productivity of between $3\frac{1}{2}$ to 4 per cent. As for exchange rates, he would expect a 3 per cent per annum deterioration in the sterling exchange rate with the Deutschmark up to 1980. Similarly, he would expect the pound to be worth $2 in 1980.

It was suggested by a questioner that there *was* evidence for recent increases in productivity and that the fall in unemployment had been deliberately created by workers accepting cuts in overtime and by pressure from some trade unions, for example in the gas industry, for delay in making men redundant. Mr Burns replied that, with an incomes policy, one would imagine that workers would be asking for an increase in amounts of overtime. Moreover, other statistics did suggest that there was a shortage of labour.

There was a suggestion from one participant that it was not too difficult to live with inflation. Brazil had a fantastic rate of inflation. It was true that the country was not yet industrialized but it was in the process of becoming industrialized, with a fall in rate of inflation. One could say that the Brazilian Government had used gimmicks, but they did seem to work. He wondered whether Brazil was a freak, or whether one could learn from its experience. Mr Burns said that one could certainly live with more rapid inflation. Problems arose from a *change* in the rate of inflation rather than from its level. However, it might be easier to get down from abnormal rates of inflation like that in Brazil rather than the British rate. He emphasized that inflation was a problem of income distribution and that the Government had to get to grips with this problem. He also re-emphasized that where productivity increased rapidly one could not give away the whole of the increase in productivity in wage increases.

A participant wondered whether, if world-wide inflation was associated with an increasing share of the national income going to wages, trade unions in various countries would collaborate with Governments. If not, fully fixed exchange rates should make it possible to keep trade union activities under control. Mr Burns said that where, in the late 1960s and early 1970s, there had been a shift in the share of GNP going to wages, there had been a rise in the share going to profit in 1971. The difficulty over fixed exchange rates was that the Government could not adequately control the rate of inflation. In the long run, with the kind of society we had, how could the Government legislate to reduce inflation? Moreover, he had argued that even if inflation in the UK were no more rapid than in other countries, there would still be a balance of payments problem because our income elasticity of demand for imports was so high. Our recent export performance was very good by historical standards because of the increase in world trade and the floating of the pound. Yet, there was *still* an increasing gap between exports and imports.

A member of the Conference said that when inflation became more rapid in the early 1970s, his firm had consulted colleagues in Argentina. Apart from the big problem over finding finance for investment, Argentina had been forced to devalue twice a year. If the UK learned to live with inflation, this would not be acceptable if other countries did not. Mr Burns said that he was thinking of 5 per cent inflation. With such a rate he thought that if the pound could be consistently devalued, and the sufferers from inflation protected, there would be no real problem. It was true that there was a difficulty if inflation was more rapid than in the countries that were one's trading partners. But it was also true that the pound could be allowed to depreciate; he wanted to remind his audience that since 1948 the sterling exchange rate had fallen on average by about 2 per cent per annum.

A questioner wondered whether Mr Burns thought that invisible exports would make a bigger contribution to British exports in the future. The surplus on invisibles had increased and Britain had a comparative advantage here. Mr Burns said that while he hesitated to give an answer, he thought one should not bank on such a surplus. Certainly it was not likely to be big enough to alter the balance of payments. Another questioner wondered if we were in danger of reacting too quickly to what would be unusual events in 1972 both with regard to imports and unemployment. Mr Burns agreed that some of the increase in imports was the once-for-all result of renewed expansion in the UK. However, this major change in British demand for imports had certainly not taken place during the preceding twelve months. It had perhaps begun in 1965, though the surcharge on imports had concealed things. It had certainly begun by 1967. This was therefore not a problem of the last few months but of at least five years. In 1972, because of renewed expansion, the apparent income elasticity of demand for imports was likely to be above 2. In terms of the balance of payments, he did not think he was reacting too much. The paper written for the Conference was nearly a year old and had pointed out that even then the balance of payments would not have been in equilibrium had there been full employment.

On productivity, there had perhaps been too much optimism recently, but the true position was not known, as we still had inadequate estimates of recent output movements. However, the fact was that, on any figure, there would be a shortage of labour by the end of 1974. He had originally hoped that we might reach the end of 1974 before unemployment fell to 400,000. It was now clear that this would not be possible, but there was only a slight change in timing. It was true that, as expansion continued, the labour force might increase too, but if one looked at vacancies as well as unemployment, one found unemployment falling farther than one would expect. Mr Burns thought it worth pointing out that in the past British income elasticity of demand for imports had always been less than in the EEC. What had now happened was that we had moved to the EEC level.

Asked whether it would not be possible to raise British productivity to the levels achieved in other countries, Mr Burns said that the underlying rate of productivity increase was rising; but without more information about why this was happening it was far safer to assume a continuance of past trends. To increase the rate of growth of productivity from $3\frac{1}{2}$ per cent to, say, 4 per cent per annum would require a big change in habits and values. Yet the rate of growth of productivity in the EEC was $4\frac{1}{2}$ per cent per annum. Even to close the gap in growth rates would mean a one-third increase in the rate of productivity increase; to close the gap in productivity levels would require an even more outstanding performance.

Professor Hague pointed out that this kind of discussion had taken place before, in the early years of the NEDC, and especially in 1963. Since optimism over the possibility of increasing productivity had been misplaced at that time, it seemed safer to assume that it would be misplaced now, unless there was concrete evidence to the contrary. In particular, if one based one's economic planning on the assumption of too high a rate of increase in productivity, one was likely to try to expand the economy too rapidly, with all the consequences for the internal economy and the balance of payments which would follow.

Mr Burns pointed out that even if the rate of growth of productivity in the UK could be raised to 4 per cent per annum by 1980, which would be a major achievement in the light of past history, there would still be a gap between the British and European rates of increase. He agreed with Professor Hague that the attempts in the 1960s to plan on the assumption of an increased rate of growth, based on false hopes about productivity increase, had led to many of the problems of the Labour administration. In the short run, there would be difficulties over both labour supply and productivity and we had to accept that there were underlying problems of attitude and motivation which would not be easily or quickly changed.

Industrial Relations
in the UK

Tom Lupton

Postscript

The newcomer to industrial relations in the UK is struck by its
confusion. The more one learns about the system the more
confusion one finds. I shall not deal with the problem in its international context because I would argue that joining the EEC will
have little influence on relationships between employers and trade
unions in the short run. There will certainly be growing contact with
the rest of Europe but this will not be significant in the period we
are considering. Let us look at Fig. 4.1. The idea that there is an
industrial relations 'system' is perhaps a strong statement, but there
are certainly national negotiations on such things as basic rates,
holidays, etc. These are negotiated in smoke-filled rooms in London.

Then at company and plant level there is consideration of more
detailed matters, such as pay structures. Again, at the departmental
level, there is a great deal of negotiation over nitty-gritty matters
such as performance standards. This kind of negotiation creates
some of the problems we shall discuss.

There are arrangements to feed back the results of these
negotiations through the levels to the top. This feedback loop seems
to cause a lot of our problems. Perhaps many of these problems arise
from the fact that those who drafted the Industrial Relations Act
had not seen the importance of this feedback loop.

Another feature of the system is the various types of union, as
shown in Fig. 4.2. One set of distinctions, now considered old-
fashioned, distinguishes between the craft, the general and the
industrial union. A new classification distinguishes the 'open' and
the 'closed' union. For example, a university researcher studying
industrial problems could enter an open union but not a closed one.
There is also a new crop of administrative and technical unions – the
Clive Jenkins syndrome. A union like the National Association of

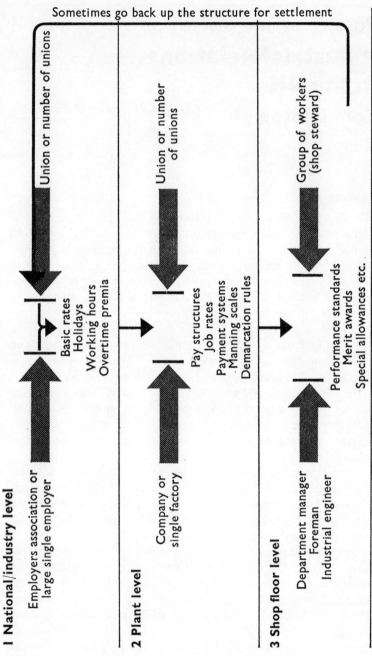

Sometimes go back up the structure for settlement

Union or number of unions

Union or number of unions

Group of workers (shop steward)

1 National/industry level

Basic rates
Holidays
Working hours
Overtime premia

Employers association or large single employer

2 Plant level

Pay structures
Job rates
Payment systems
Manning scales
Demarcation rules

Company or single factory

3 Shop floor level

Performance standards
Merit awards
Special allowances etc.

Department manager
Foreman
Industrial engineer

FIG. 4.1

Type of union	Examples
1 (Open) Craft unions	Engineering and Foundry Workers
	Electrical Trade Union
2 (Open) General unions	Transport and General Workers
	General and Municipal Workers.
	Union of Shop, Distributive and Allied Workers
3 (Open) Clerical, admin and technical unions	Association of Supervisory, Technical and Managerial Staffs
	National Union of Local Government Officers
4 (Closed) Clerical, admin and technical unions	Association of University Teachers
	Civil Service Clerical Association
5 (Closed) Industrial unions	National Union of Mineworkers
	National Union of Railwaymen
	British Iron and Steel and Kindred Trades Association

1 British unions display a variety of forms
2 Many companies and plants bargain with groups/federations of unions
- from 1 2 3 and also 5
FIG. 4.2

Local Government Officers (NALGO) is now more open and secretaries in institutions like the Manchester Business School can join it. Again, an industrial union is closed to its own industry.

So in most plants one has a number of unions with different forms, reasons for existence, etc. Negotiations are therefore complex, and some unions will not negotiate together with others. This often puzzles, for example, the management of a subsidiary of an American firm. In one case in which I was concerned, negotiations could only be carried out by putting the two unions in different rooms and having a messenger travelling between the two.

Let us now look at Fig. 4.3. The lowest level of most unions is the branch. This is usually located in the plant or some other geographical area. The shop steward is the representative for the members. One then has district and regional committees, often made up of lay members, but with full-time officers who will negotiate at the regional level and also intervene, if necessary, in plant level negotiations. The national officers are attached to the executive committee and will bargain for the whole industry.

We can see here the special character of British unions. It is not only that the union members can control the policy of the union and its execution. There is also a deep rooted ideology that this is the right arrangement. The result is that even powerful leaders of unions *say* constantly that their members run the union.

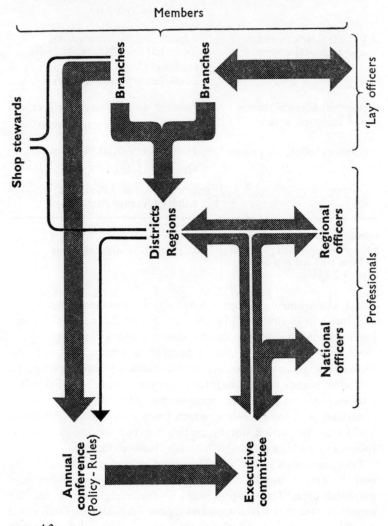

FIG. 4.3

While the detail varies at the national level, one usually has 'professional' employees of the union – certainly in the sense of paid employees but *not* always in the sense of highly trained persons using professional skills to carry out the rules and the ethics of the profession. In most unions, certainly at the shopfloor, the key man is the lay officer (branch officer or shop steward). The personnel officer sees the convener of shop stewards as the key man in the union.

The TUC is frequently misunderstood and Fig. 4.4 helps us to see why. People say, in respect of some major issue, why does the TUC do nothing when 80 per cent of unions belong to it? The reason is that the TUC has no power. It is simply an annual meeting of its members. These represent the various sectors of the economy so that the TUC General Council is simply a collection of interest groups. Even the general purposes committee, which the newspapers regard as the body with power in the TUC, is equally concerned with inter-union conflict. The general secretary of the TUC will usually come up through the bureaucracy. He is the servant of the General Council and of the members, who see the bureaucracy as simply serving them. Again we have to remember the strong ideology that the unions run the TUC. In one sense, the TUC appears to be the voice of the trade union movement as a whole, but the reason is simply that there is no alternative.

On page 80 above, I provided a diagram showing the way that the Industrial Relations Act had changed the legal structure within which the trade unions operate. When I wrote, there was a good deal of talk about the importance of the Act. Now, there is very little. If one talks to negotiators, both unions and management will say that the Act now has no impact. Since the original judgments on the role of the shop steward, no other issues have come forward. Some parts of the Act, e.g. the Code of Practice, the legal rules about unfair dismissal, and so on, will continue to have an impact but, in my view, legal regulation of collective bargaining in the British context, was, and is, a non-starter.

The contract of employment is important because while bargains made at the national level may appear solely to do with cash, there is much more in the contract than employment. It covers the whole relationship between effort and reward. A successful contract of employment must meet the needs of the firm and also that of the employee. It will have to cover all major issues, including ethical problems, the structure of the task, and so on. The contract of employment is therefore a complex arrangement and official

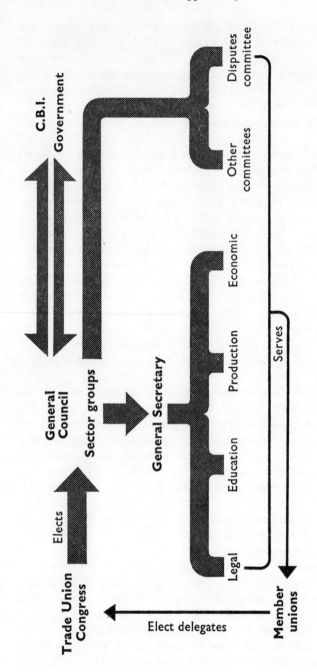

FIG. 4.4

collective bargaining at all levels covers few aspects of it.

There is no single problem concerning trade unions today. The problem one sees depends on who one is. Civil servants and politicians are concerned with such problems as the role of trade unions in inflation, or the effects of strikes on the economy. They look at the problem of controlling trade unions as very similar to that of using monetary and fiscal measures, like the rate of interest, investment grants, etc. They are looking for a new central regulator or indicator. This is obviously an important way of looking at the problem, but it is not the only one.

The Economic Department of the TUC would say that it is in business to improve the real incomes of its members in a legal and responsible way, in the context of free collective bargaining. It emphasizes the failure of government to control prices. The TUC is concerned when trade union members' wages lag behind rising prices. However, any controls must be voluntary; they must accept the views of unions; they must accept comparisons between the wages of different types of labour, relativities, etc. So, if one jacks up the wages of postmen or hospital workers, unions whose relative position has worsened will then work to restore the earlier relativities.

The view of the individual union will be that it is operating at the tactical level. There is the same aim of improving real wages, but good tactics are necessary to maximize the advantages of the union in negotiations with employers. So the union may employ, say, four levels of attack. What is achieved will then be fed back through the system to attack the whole set of arrangements at the national level. It is this kind of feedback (one of the mechanisms of wage drift) which frustrates the Civil Service and the politicians.

The employer's aim is survival, growth, etc. The employer is therefore concerned with tactics too. As we have seen, the shop steward and the worker raise most issues on the contract of employment and are therefore concerned with increasing the complex of issues. So, with a system like this, the idea of a White Paper or a speech which can by itself solve the problem of trade unionism simply does not fit the system. Nevertheless, one wants to find some kind of resolution in a situation where all the parties concerned with the problems raised by trade unionism have different objectives.

I should like to see a new move towards rapprochement at the national level. I should like to see a tripartite system of conversations and discussions between the Civil Service, the TUC and the CBI. These discussions would not be concerned with how to control incomes, or how to devise a better Industrial Relations Act; but simply with sitting down and spending a great deal of time on how to get conversations going at the tactical level. The idea would be to try to influence public opinion. One might then be able to set up satisfactory machinery.

In such an arrangement, the Government would have to be seen as a *partner*. A paper by Nettl once dealt with the issue, not of how industry influences the Civil Service, but how work on committees influences businessmen. They go and sit on committees in London. When they get there, civil servants do not become like businessmen, but the businessmen become like civil servants and can no longer run their businesses. This is obviously a caricature, but there is something in it. What is necessary is for politicians, civil servants, businessmen and trade unionists to begin to 'talk turkey' as equal partners.

I regard it as unfortunate that the Industrial Relations Act re-formed the Commission on Industrial Relations which in its original form really was tripartite. It brought together civil servants, businessmen and trade unionists, and indeed a sprinkling of young academics, who really began to learn about the system and influence public opinion by their reports. With the Industrial Relations Act most of the union people left.

Nearer the ground, I believe we need to do what Norway has done and to investigate work organisation, job design, etc. In particular, we need to get some civil servants out of London. London is simply a factory with three departments: Whitehall, the City and Westminster. The Government manages the system, but only this system of three departments. There is a wall round it, breached only at places like Euston or King's Cross. Few from within the wall ever go outside. Attempts are always feeble and secondhand. For example, there are some local advisers in the Department of Employment and Productivity who do good work. A few trained ones are in Newcastle, for example, but this should be extended at all levels in all parts of the country.

The problem of the trade unions will not be resolved by someone in Whitehall or Westminster saying that there should be a national consensus on how labour relations should go. Such an idea represents pure myth, except in a general, non-operational sense. The system is pluralist: and imposing a framework will fragment and not heal. So we must talk at all levels and see the impact of one level on another. So far we have not talked enough. One must not try to make the system of industrial relations an instrument of economic management.

Discussion

Professor Lupton was asked why he had not said more about trade union relationships with the EEC. He replied that he found that if he studied French trade unions, strikes, etc., he had a better picture of industrial relations in France, but that this understanding threw no light whatever on trade unions in the UK. Structures, cultures, habits and ideologies were different. Professor Lupton took the view that perhaps we could take ideas from other countries, but not the whole apparatus from any other country. While it was true that more trade union officials from the UK visited the EEC than ten years ago, that kind of contact did not have much effect. Professor Lupton also thought that each kind of trade unionist was good only in his own culture. A British trade unionist would not be very effective in France.

Another questioner suggested that a recent agreement between the National Union of Mineworkers and the German Mineworkers Union could have a catastrophic effect on Europe, and not simply on the UK. Professor Lupton replied that such agreements were not new. There had been an international union of transport workers since the 1890s, and much to-ing and fro-ing between countries. So far this agreement had worked only at the level of exchanging notes. He was not too disturbed when a new agreement, couched in nineteen-century language – signed in blood, etc. – was made, and he did not see it as significant. Suppose that the National Union of Mineworkers were to call a one day strike: he doubted very much whether the Germans would join it. These were two separate movements and without much firmer organizational links between them he saw little for anyone to worry about. What should be done in the here-and-now was very important and could indeed affect Common Market countries too. He thought that trade unionists in the rest of Europe would learn from rather than teach the UK.

Asked about the increasing role of the worker director, Professor Lupton replied that he did not think this would have much impact. It was a good idea because it satisfied the workers' desire to be in on decisions, but cut little ice on real day-to-day issues. He thought there was more to learn from work restructuring in firms like Volvo and Saab. The worker director was likely to become too separated from the shop floor. Introducing management into unions would be a good idea in some cases, but not all. For example, with the tendency to centralization in British Steel, there was likely to be a call for representation where the decisions were made. So far, this had not happened because of the traditions of the shop floor.

A questioner suggested that Professor Lupton was wrong in suggesting tripartite negotiation between equals. They could hardly be described as equals when one party, the Government, could alter the rules. Professor Lupton insisted that *all* had 'big sticks'. If the Government said 'let us talk at different levels', then, if the Government brought in its 'big stick', the unions would do the same. It was a question of the legitimacy of big sticks. The kind of discussion he had envisaged represented the *only* way to get to a position where all parties left their sticks in the hall for *this* exercise. Unfortunately, the Government usually called in the trade unions when a scheme had already been formulated without their help.

Professor Morris said that Professor Lupton had represented the unions as accounting for a large percentage of society, standing for democracy, participation, etc., which forced him to see Government as negative. However, the Government did respond to pressures. Could one not allow that Government *did* represent society as a whole? Professor Lupton replied that he had explained how matters would look from his vantage point. He thought that Professor Morris's view of the Government's role was perfectly legitimate and followed from democratic ideas. However, when one looked for levers, if there was no sensitivity in what one was manipulating this would lead to disaster. Those who looked at any system from the top downwards must not see it in too simple a way. Governments lurched from one expedient to another. A lot of their difficulties were part of the syndrome and perhaps if a move towards discussions were not made soon there would be too much polarisation in the UK for *any* resolution of the problem to be possible.

Professor Lupton was asked whether the UK would fall behind other countries because of strikes, etc. Perhaps tougher legislation even than the Industrial Relations Act would have to be brought in. He replied that any attempt to push even the existing Act as far as possible would polarize opinion and lead to an increase in strikes. However, he still approved of the Code of Practice in the Act. As for the effects of strikes, these were hard to measure. Some strikes were perhaps even cathartic and brought benefit. There were also theories that strikes had a seasonal pattern, and some organizations made use of strikes to sell off their stocks. In these cases strikes did not have much effect. Perhaps British managers were beginning to *accept* strikes as a fact of life. If that happened, it would be difficult to see what effect they had. There would be a state of abdication and despair, but this had not happened yet. However, even if strikes were disadvantageous, central control over them would not help.

A speaker from the floor suggested that there was a real possibility of confrontation between Government and unions followed by an election. If the Conservative Government was returned to power, then perhaps the only way to improve the situation would be to impose authoritarian controls on the trade unions. Professor Lupton said the trade unions would accept this as necessary if it impinged on everybody equally, but *not* if it only applied to the unions. It was always hard to control prices and therefore hard to introduce the kind of prices and incomes legislation that the present government had brought in. This led back to where we began – to trying to get agreement through lengthy discussions. Similarly, while it was probably true that social security payments underpinned strikes, a change in legislation for this reason would be dangerous.

In reply to a final question, Professor Lupton said that the cooling-off ballot could be useful but that on the whole union members would support the executive. The reason was that executives did not usually move unless they were sure that they had the support of their members.

In conclusion, Professor Lupton said that to get talks going would need magnanimous action by the Government. If the Government had a line to be toed the talks would not work, because all would take their 'sticks' in. The talks had to be about what the problem was, and not to discuss a cut and dried pay and prices policy.

Management in Britain
John Morris

Postscript

In my paper I started with stereotypes and tried to improve on them. The stereotype of the 'British manager' is that he represents good material, but is outmoded, insular, conventional and concerned with the quality of the product rather than meeting the needs of the market. I do not aim to demolish this stereotype, but my paper tried to set it in perspective by a rapid historical survey. Since I am not an historian, perhaps I have fallen into several traps, but I think the paper provides food for thought.

My theme is that one can look at two 'ends' of a rather complicated spectrum. At one end, there is the resourceful manager. He uses energy to bring change into the economy, nowadays dealing with the problems of pollution, security of employment, and so on. The entrepreneur is one type of resourceful manager. At the other end of the spectrum, the conventional manager looks to personal experience, to what has happened in the past. He uses the lessons of history to point to the dangers of change. During an interval in the conference, Professor Rose suggested that we should make two important changes to improve the performance of the British economy. First, we should abolish all titles of rank, including that of professor. Second, we should end the teaching of history because it represents a constraint rather than an opportunity. I did not agree with either of these propositions, but I sympathized with his underlying irritation with rigidity and traditionalism.

During the industrial revolution, Britain 'pulled out all the stops' on resourcefulness. It used dispossessed peasants, for example, to bring about economic development through the Empire and international growth. The British were very resourceful through this period but, first, the revolution used a vast amount of social and technical energy; second, it led to the development of institutions that prevented a major breakthrough. So, for seventy to a hundred years, there was a slow rate of growth, with the resourceful able to work only in the few 'spaces' left by the conventional. If this is true, then the British may win the admiration of the world for their quality of life, but what has happened is a depressing symbol of the price one can pay for this.

During two wars the British have been extremely resourceful and the question is how, in peace, they can find a creative blend of the resourceful and the conventional. One needs a dynamic balance, and if the emphasis is put on *balance* this is because of the experience of the first industrial revolution. This has not been so frightening as in Ireland, but it has left a very strong impression.

There is no need to update my paper because I used a 'broad-brush' approach and nothing has happened to suggest that the paper is less relevant than when I wrote it. I have tried to sketch the importance of resourcefulness not just in the economic/technical field but in the social field as well. We have developed new social forms, for example, educational institutions and voluntary and fraternal institutions. The resourceful have also created an array of political institutions to fit the individual citizen into central decision taking. The UK is very rich in infra-structure linking the individual to the centre. In his session, Professor Lupton asked not for an empty talking shop but for an on-going consultation. The reason for this is that if consultation leads to a decision, there is a great deal of understanding of it and of commitment to it.

So resourcefulness is concerned with how institutions can bring about evolutionary change. Political and social order is jut one variable in a model. But I see so many threats to social order, even in the family or the club, that I sometimes wonder how a society of several million can possess stability at all. *Any* social order is an achievement, and it is extremely difficult to get social institutions to return to order after a major change. Social systems appear to be strikingly disorderly.

I should now like to put my argument in slightly different terms. Resourcefulness is useful in a 'dramatic' period. There is no routine solution, because we are concerned with unfamiliar activities. Conventional people will adapt to routine. One therefore has three social forms: drama, ritual and routine. Ritual balances the conventional and the resourceful and links the creative aspects of resourcefulness and drama with order in the form of routines. One has to distinguish development methods which add to system effectiveness from those which lead to breakdowns. The alternation of development and breakdown provides drama. Routine breaks down when the environment changes rapidly. I have put this in a diagram (see Fig. 5.1).

Routine is necessary to keep things going, because it is necessary to continue to do new things. There is also the problem of coping with failure, often called 'trouble-shooting'. One also needs a

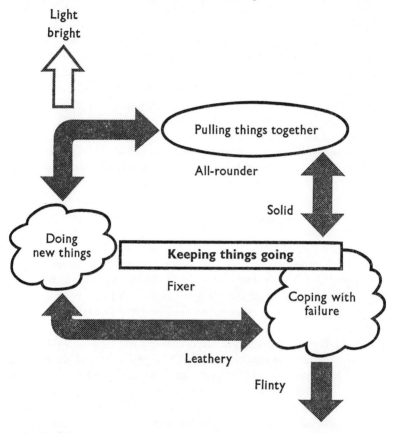

A sketch of the relationship between types of managerial task and 'styles' of management

FIG. 5.1

mechanism to pull things together and to account for what has been done. At the same time, one has the conventional, working in the middle – keeping things going. However, the resourceful are needed in doing new things and in coping with failure. Most conflict arises where people are doing new things. Here I would distinguish those people I would describe as the 'light' and 'bright' who bring about innovation. The British system has a rich apparatus for denigrating the innovatory. We describe them as airy fairy, Cloud nine, Utopian, and academic. Even among academics, this last word is a term of abuse! So why is Britain so rich in these people? The answer is partly because it is an open system. The innovator can be recruited from different social classes, and not least from immigrants. Studies show that the light and bright are often first and second generation immigrants. Such people can see things 'as they are' and can use social skills. The bright can translate the ideas of the light into success; they are the entrepreneurs.

In most organizations, too, one finds the solid, nailed to the earth with their own brass tacks. We are not very approving of them in the UK either, but we put value on ritual stability. In our public life, we see any threat to the existing way of doing things as dangerous. The fixers are often Celts rather than Anglo-Saxons.

If all the new possibilities thought of by the 'light' overlap with the field of activity of the 'bright' then there are new problems. The job of the fixers is to work with the bright managers of the organization as a way of achieving continuing growth, in saleable products and not just ideas.

Perhaps one of the reasons why Japan has been so successful is that while growth is stressed, it has a very integrated social system (though this is beginning to crack a little under the continued load of rapid growth). In some ways Britain appears to be more like Japan than like France or Germany. What is involved is that in Japan all four roles work quickly and smoothly together, while in the UK one often finds wasteful confrontations between the light and the solid, because we seem to have an insufficient supply of the bright and the fixers. But there are encouraging signs in the UK of a new generation of 'bright fixers' emerging, particularly from the business schools. Institutions like the IRC, the Prices and Incomes Board and the Industrial Relations Agencies have also been developing confident and able managers who can take on coordinating roles.

It should not be forgotten that firms also contain the leathery and the flinty. These are the company doctors and the company executioners (the latter sometimes called 'hatchet men' or the Mafia). In this sense the entrepreneur is the opposite to the undertaker! We now have a new generation of undertakers. Their critics would say that they set fire to companies (through asset stripping) and look for a phoenix to emerge in the form of new opportunities. All too often they find only ashes. In most organisations, the flinty are regarded with great suspicion, and are kept outside in specialized agencies.

In my paper I suggested that perhaps joining the EEC would

represent the equivalent of a war in pulling the resourceful and the conventional elements in management together. I can now restate this issue slightly by saying that we have a particular need for 'bright leathery fixers', who are able to translate their skills in innovation and troubleshooting into the continuous development of what is really an extremely valuable and healthy set of traditions. I regard the light and the flinty as much more marginal to our needs. I am particularly concerned about the danger of a wartime sense of emergency leading to an over-ruthless attitude to managerial and organizational effectiveness. As an example, many managers have been disposed of on the ground that this is merely 'cutting out the deadwood'. It would be better if senior managers who are responsible faced the consequences of their own actions and used a more disturbing metaphor such as 'We are deliberately shedding the blood of the unworthy and the unwanted.' Yet experience shows, even in war, that bloodletting is hardly the cure for depression. It increases the depression still further. However, I think we can end on a note of confidence. The recent upturn in the British economy suggests that we are getting rather better at responding quickly to signals from the environment (whether these are signals of threats or of opportunities). Our main need is to find more humane and effective ways of dealing with failure.

Discussion

Professor Morris was asked what should be done with redundant senior managers. Was there a training which might convert them to resourcefulness and usefulness, and was there a role for them in business schools? He said that the development of training activities in the UK represented a massive breakthrough, unique in the world. For example, there was the rapid growth of business schools, where there had been vast proliferation, which was a great achievement during a time of recession. These institutions were not simply concerned with analytical tools but with work on the social and political structure of the organization. He would be worried if there were too much emphasis on training and techniques rather than on the development of social skills. Perhaps too many resources had been put into the 'flinty' area. One had to look at the organization as built up of a complex set of human understanding and conventions.

Perhaps the 'flinty' lacked the skills required to manage the work force. In the petro-chemical industry one had to manage managers. ICI had to display great skills in managing managers, as well as in managing the work force. There was certainly no evidence that white-collar unions were easier to manage.

The problems of redundancy led to the question of bloodletting. It seemed unfortunate to Professor Morris that we were quite so wasteful with managerial self-confidence. Methods of 'instant development', such as mergers and acquisitions, still seemed to be in a very crude form and were often associated with extremely insensitive handling of the people involved. It seemed appropriate to question whether 'instant development' was a very efficient organizational device anyway. Studies of economic effectiveness of mergers often raised doubts about their ability to achieve promised results. This was almost certainly because of our relative lack of knowledge of how to secure economies of scale in matters of human organization.

In his lively book *Up the Organization* Townsend said that many mergers had been based on the idea of achieving 'synergy'. Synergy had been defined as the kinds of economies of scale that gave the equation '$2+2=5$'. But, as Townsend had caustically pointed out, in such matters '$2+2=3$'. Economics and technology might add up, but not people. The resulting struggle for power very frequently meant that merged organizations became an arena for tribal warfare. Perhaps one could even see the success of the recent film *The Godfather* (a study of the relationships of a Mafia leader) as a management training film for our times!

Some people had suggested that business schools might be suitable places of employment for redundant managers, enabling them to use their skills and experience in the education of others. But business schools had credibility problems of their own, and were usually the last places to be eager to accept people whose own credibility was in doubt. The only solution appeared to be to try to avoid making people redundant at all. An unfortunate association with the term 'resourcefulness' was with the cut and thrust approach of 'buccaneer'. We urgently needed a close link between resourcefulness and a sense of social priorities.

A questioner from the floor suggested that, given an IQ of 120 plus, most of the young could operate as the light or the bright. As their IQ faded, perhaps they became fixers. In the end, perhaps they even became solid. The questioner wondered whether that represented a realistic career development pattern. Was it now seen as socially regressive? Professor Morris replied that it could be a career pattern. It was good to have the older and wiser coping with failure, because those who had never failed were not sympathetic with those who had. We should divide the sophisticated handling of data from working with people, where one did not lose ability as one went on. However, we should not use the example of mathematicians to show that everyone became less able after the age of twenty-five. One *could* go on being bright for a long time.

People were rarely good at *only* one thing. They could change their face where this was appropriate and become allrounders. In this sense, managers could go on getting better.

Because organizations were unsympathetic, the older person was judged by his ability to handle data and use techniques. Too few British businessmen saw how the older manager could help on social and political issues. In Japan the older man was concerned with the continuity of the system. This was also true in the UK, but too many older managers let the younger and brighter push them out.

A major quality of the manager was self-confidence. If he did not have this he would not get support from his subordinates. If one destroyed this self-confidence, as redundancy did, it was hard to restore it. Professor Morris insisted that one should not call human beings 'deadwood'. If one were going to 'shed blood' one needed to be honest and explicit about it.

Another questioner asked whether the shorter working life meant that one had a longer learning period and a longer retirement period, with a shorter period of active production in between. Would one not have conflict between the smaller active population and those who were learning or retired? Was it possible to plan ways of separating the potential protagonists? Professor Morris said it was easy to see that those under the age of fifteen and over the age of sixty-five had to be inactive. However, 25 per cent of the population was under fifteen and $12\frac{1}{2}$ per cent over sixty-five. There was a growing demand for active occupation over sixty-five and the young wanted to be 'relevant', by which they meant having a productive role. One could therefore ask why people had to stop work at sixty or sixty-five. This was not required in politics, the law, medicine, etc. Perhaps what we needed to do was to find a way to let the young and the old contribute. We got absurd answers when we saw the economy as a collection of hardware. However, this was not the characteristic of a modern economy. There was now an enormous amount of software, especially in clerical and service activities. This made it easier for the young and the old to be 'useful'. So, for example, more and more higher education was concerned with projects or with sandwich courses. We also had to remember the tremendous innovation represented by the Open University.

If they saw the true problem, the social services and education could be well organized to use younger and older people. Professor Morris believed that remarkable social inventions would be made in the rest of the twentieth century. We had already invented the IRC, the NEDC, the Open University, the business schools and the mass media. It was true that Professor Simmonds had said that we spent sixteen hours a week watching television, but we had to remember that much television was educational. The Open University itself used television and a great deal was going on.

A final questioner wondered whether redundancy was related to higher demands for performance in the sense in which this was described by Michael Young. Could we learn how to handle redundancy? Professor Morris said that he should perhaps explain that Michael Young was a remarkable and gifted sociologist, who throughout his life had been concerned with documenting social realities, making critical judgments about areas of social waste and inequity, and devising means of improving the quality of life. He had been associated with the consumer movement, with the Institute of Community Studies and with the Advisory Centre for Education. He had also written a book called *The Rise of the Meritocracy*. He there took the view that a systematic selection of people for elite positions on the grounds of intelligence and effort would lead to a seriously lopsided society, in which the elite would become intolerably arrogant, because for the first time in history its members would *know* that they were measurably 'better' than their fellow men. The book was written in the form of a science fiction satire in which the attempt to construct a 'meritocracy' through educational testing, selective grammar schools and higher education finally led to revolution by those condemned by the system to 'bread and circuses'. The book played a part in broadening people's thinking about the selective agencies leading to the formation of the British elites. It seemed to be increasingly realized that societies, and particularly mature, complex societies like British society, could not be effectively led by those with a single set of measurable characteristics, and that the role of education in forming a social, economic or political elite was important but not overwhelming.

Redundancy was a process of rejection, the 'other side of the coin'. We should increasingly recognize that redundancy was not only an economic issue, but was linked with social values. We should be careful to avoid a lopsided 'meritocracy' in the management world. Fortunately, attitudes to redundancy already seemed to be changing. There was far more concern for individuality and a humane approach to the problem. Many agencies were engaged in programmes for counselling and placement, as well as for financial help with re-education. The Department of Employment was soon to launch a major national programme for counselling and placement. But it would probably take five or ten years before there was a fundamental change in the handling of managerial redundancy.

Developments in the British capital market and some questions on Britain's entry into the EEC

Harold Rose

Postscript

The nature of the British capital market leads one to see its future within the Common Market with optimism, but qualified optimism; and qualifications are always more interesting to economists.

The British capital market remains unique. While it is more similar to the American than to the European capital markets, there is a big difference even from that of the United States. London possesses a range of institutions and markets that no centre outside the United States approaches, and there is in London a greater degree of international involvement than in any European centre, or even in New York. There is certainly a degree of informality in London which is found neither in New York nor on the Continent, and Government controls are less onerous in Britain than in other financial centres.

These broad characteristics of the London capital market spring from Britain's economic history. British involvement in international finance stems from its early pre-eminence in international trade. While the international position of Britain has declined, the skill of London in 'making markets' enabled London to play a leading role, even after Britain's balance of payments position had deteriorated. For example, in recent years London has been instrumental in developing the market in Eurodollars and the secondary market in Eurodollar bonds.

Even before it was known that Britain would finally join the EEC, there were movements towards financial conglomeration and a concomitant reduction in specialization. The development of the financial conglomerate is most easily seen in banking. Even before

October 1971, when direct controls over bank lending were abolished, there had been a movement by the banks into new activities such as hire purchase, factoring and leasing, but through the acquisition of subsidiaries. This was accelerated by the changes announced in October 1971. At the same time, outside banking there has been a broadening of the activities of insurance, property and other companies. One could talk of the growing development of a 'finance industry'.

As in most countries, the degree of government intervention has on the whole tended to increase, at least outside banking, and the authorities have shown an increasing interest in structural change. This trend has reduced differences between the British and overseas approach to government intervention in the financial system.

During the past year the following have been the main identifiable changes in the British capital market:

1. The difficulty of preventing an undue increase in the money supply without an unacceptable rise in interest rates has led to some retreat by the Bank of England from the policy introduced in October 1971. The banks have been asked, but in general terms, to restrain their lending for property development, for example.
2. The restrictions placed by the Bank of England on the ability of other institutions to acquire holdings in merchant banks have been considerably lightened.
3. The degree of British financial involvement in Europe has been extended still further, through acquisitions and the membership of financial consortia, especially in banking.
4. The market for personal loans has become still more integrated with the increase in bank lending on the one hand and the growth of second-mortgage and other personal loans by 'near-bank' institutions.
5. A system of computer-based pricing and dealing in shares – 'Ariel' – is being set up by large institutional investors. This should facilitate the development of any such system on a European scale; but the stockbrokers and jobbers of the London Stock Exchange have so far declined to participate. The unwillingness of members of the London Stock Exchange to take part in the system, which is primarily designed to reduce the costs of large transactions, points to a potential source of conflict between the Stock Exchange and institutional investors of wider, European significance.

When it first became clear that Britain would join the Common

Market, the reaction of the City was one of unqualified optimism about its prospects. Since then, there has been a more sober reappraisal of the problems. However, there are undoubtedly opportunities, one of which stems from the basic characteristics of the City in the form of its wide range of experience and its unique spread of financial services. This should enable London to arrange finance spanning a variety of terms which no other single centre can match.

A second opportunity flows from the pre-eminence of the London Stock Exchange. The total value of ordinary shares quoted on the London Stock Exchange equals the total value of shares in all other European Stock Exchanges added together, and the level of dealings in London is certainly greater than that in the whole of the rest of Europe.

Third, there are opportunities resulting from the existence in London of types of financial service not really found anywhere else on a similar scale. For example, there are the commodity markets and the international insurance business of London.

Among individual opportunities can be identified the following. First, the London capital market can provide a many-sided financial 'package' for large companies. Secondly, if European stock markets are to be unified, then London is the most likely candidate. Third, British property dealers are more experienced and more enterprising than those in Europe. Fourth, if there are to be more mergers as a result of joining the EEC, then British merchant banks have more experience than continental ones.

However, problems exist as the counterpart to these opportunities. First, there are many problems which will arise from the very nature of the Common Market itself and from the mechanics of movement towards the 'harmonization' of capital markets. To achieve unification of practice, the EEC tends to issue *prescriptive* legislation in a way which runs counter to the general British tradition. So far the British capital market has been relatively free from detailed government regulations, which will tend to put it at some disadvantage. For example, in banking, the imposition of a ratio between capital and deposits might make it difficult for some of the smaller British banks to thrive. So might regulations about local reserves overseas. Similarly, British life insurance in particular is currently free from the controls which look like being imposed in the EEC, for example, on the rules for calculating premiums and on the selection of investments. In commodity markets, too, the common external tariff and restrictions on, say, dealing in metals might make life difficult for the lead and zinc markets of London.

There may also be problems concerning size. If the development of the EEC really does provide a stimulus to the growth of multi-national companies with large financial requirements, the question arises whether the merchant banks will be big enough to deal with the commitments which may be required. British merchant banks have the necessary expertise, but are perhaps not large enough to provide funds themselves on a sufficient scale if this proves necessary.

It may be worth looking at some of the detailed institutional problems that lie ahead. First, if one looks at the advantages which the size of the London Stock Exchange gives it and asks whether London will really be the European centre of the future, one finds distinct procedural difficulties. In the UK share registration is the rule, whereas in most continental countries bearer shares are typical. Similarly, there are difficulties with the two-weekly settlement period in London, which allows the jobber to balance his books, while in Europe dealing is primarily for 'cash'. Again, in the UK, dividends are paid after deduction of tax. This would be unwelcome to Europeans. Then there is the problem of accounting practice. While not perfect, British accounts do give a moderately true and reasonably fair view of their clients' affairs in a way that does not happen in most of Europe. All such practical differences will need to be ironed out for harmonization to take place in a manner not unfavourable to London.

There has been an increasing number of British acquisitions in Europe. For example, British firms acquired as many businesses in the Netherlands in 1972 as during the whole of the previous five years. Although British ownership of European businesses remains small, it is certainly growing, despite the reluctance of some countries, e.g. France, to allow British firms to take over firms within their own borders and despite the fact that the continental bearer share transfer system on balance makes it more difficult to make acquisitions owing to the difficulty of identifying ownership.

In general, however, one cannot take a view on how far Britain can exploit the emerging situation in Europe without a prior view of the international financial system and Britain's role in it. For example, London has been able to take advantage of American restrictions on capital movement by US firms, not least in the development of the Eurodollar market. However, one has to ask: What will be the currency system of the future? It will not be based on sterling and the role of the dollar is diminishing. While the

London Stock Exchange is still larger than all the European ones, even when they are aggregated, the volume of new foreign issues in overseas European markets is growing. New issues both in France and in Germany appear to be greater than in London, and even Italy is rapidly catching up. If the future European currency is to be either a multi-currency or a European currency of account, one wonders what role this will leave for sterling. How can the UK increase its share of world money market activities unless the pound becomes a much stronger currency in the long run? In the last resort, London's opportunities depend on the free movement of capital in and out of the UK. How open a financial system London can offer will ultimately depend on the balance of payments position of Britain.

Discussion

It was suggested that it might not be important if merchant banks did lack 'financial muscle'. Merchants banks could act as brokers, putting together a package and farming it out. If Professor Rose was saying that the British merchant banks *as a whole* were not big enough to do this, it was an interesting comment. Professor Rose took the view that if there were to be a standard new issue practice for Europe based on the British system of underwriting, then the merchant banks were big enough. However, if new issues needed the direct support of their sponsor, then individual merchant banks were too small to do this. He doubted whether any single merchant bank could provide adequately for a large multi-national company. The merchant banks could arrange for the provision of the necessary money through underwriting or consortium facilities; but the question was whether the large 'comprehensive' German banks, for example, would be in a stronger position to undertake the task themselves.

Professor Rose was then asked whether the 1972 monetary reform, with its changes in the liquidity rules, had contributed to raising the rate of interest. He said he thought the changes made it harder to control the money supply. The argument put forward by the Government and the Bank of England was that flexibility in rates of interest would do the job of earlier methods involving more direct restriction of advances. He had already expressed the view that the new policy would have to involve greater fluctuations in the rate of interest than the government or the public might tolerate. However, it was true that, *if* an incomes policy were to work, then 'competition and credit control' could work satisfactorily through open market operations. Otherwise, the authorities would lose control of the supply of money if they were not prepared to see still higher interest rates than in early 1973.

Commenting that Professor Rose had said that German banks were closely linked with industry, a speaker from the floor asked whether he would like more banking participation in British industry. Professor Rose replied that in Germany, especially, the deposit banks were investment banks, as indeed they were in Japan. They were long-run lenders and investors and behaved rather like conglomerate industrial managers. There was a familiar argument in favour of British banks going the same way. Indeed, there was some government support for this, but the Bank of England would probably be worried about the viability of such a system in the event of a recession. The involvement of the banks in industrial investment increased their potential insolvency in depression: to see this one could look at what had happened in American banks with their large involvement in both industry and agriculture, and at German banks with their investment in industry, in the 1930s. The Bank of England argued that such involvement was neither desirable nor necessary on any large scale. If the merchant banks could do the new issue job, then the clearing banks would not need to become too close to industry, and Professor Rose would prefer them not to be as close as was the case in Germany and Japan, if only to preserve a competitive environment.

It was suggested that one reason why German banks had greater influence in German industry was that their direct investments in industry allowed them to intervene in management. The questioner wondered whether Professor Rose saw a similar role for institutional investors in the UK. Professor Rose replied that many people did look to the institutions to take a more active role in company meetings, and on boards of Directors. The Bank of England, for example, had convened a working party of financial institutions for this purpose. The closer involvement of institutional investors might, however, run counter to attempts to control insider trading. But the attempt to do something on these lines was certainly an example of the new interventionist attitude of the Bank of England and of the positive role that it wanted the financial institutions to play.

It was suggested by another questioner that one difference between France, Germany and Britain was that in Britain each firm aimed at a given return on capital employed or turnover, and that each assumed that its competitors in other countries behaved in the same way. However, there was a different ownership structure in Europe and it appeared that the rate of profit there was lower. Perhaps those who provided capital in Europe were prepared to accept a lower rate of profit from it but then obtained hidden subsidies, perhaps from government. Professor Rose agreed that perhaps bank officials did not put so much emphasis on the rate of profit as did shareholders or financial analysts, provided, of course, that the investment survived. Perhaps this was in the nature of banking, which was concerned more with short-term liquidity than with long-run profitability. However, if this was true, one could not also say that the involvement of banks spurred managerial efficiency. Nor did Professor Rose think that continental banks took a longer view than British institutional investors as a whole. Insurance companies and pension funds took a very long view. In addition, individual shareholders in the UK appeared to hold shares for an average of about ten years, contrary to the opinion that personal holders were mainly short-term speculators. However, Professor Rose did agree with a suggestion that perhaps the recent increase in the number of mergers had led the market to take a more short-run view.

A participant from Japan suggested that the close relationship between banking and industry in Japan was not deliberately created by the government or anyone else. It was a result of historical developments in industry and in international trade. Japanese industry always had too few funds to bring in technological improvements which it saw as necessary. The banks therefore had to help. In reply, Professor Rose emphasized that the British system had not developed in that direction because of its well-developed stock exchange, a relatively early creation. He also suggested that the important problem in the UK was not whether British businesses aimed at the wrong rates of return on turnover or capital. It was why they did not achieve the rates they aimed at.

Postscript and discussion   Paper 8
Government/business relations in the UK
Grigor McClelland

Postscript

The paper on Government/business relations is divided into four
parts: a review of the field under the title 'a mixed economy', and a
discussion of each of three modes of action by business, concerned
respectively with prediction, adaptation and influence. Taking each
part in turn, this postscript will be concerned, first, to add any
comments that appear necessary to update the material from the
spring of 1972 to the spring of 1973, and secondly to add a European
dimension to the argument – to consider explicitly what difference
is made by the UK's membership of the EEC.

A mixed economy

Since the paper was written, there has occurred a sharp shift in
government policy which could be described in traditional terms as
one away from *laissez-faire* and towards detailed intervention. But
it is 'symbiosis' with a difference. Far from marking closer relationships between government and business, it results from the breakdown of triangular talks between the government and the two sides
of industry. The breakdown occurred in the Government/trade
union side of the triangle rather than the Government/employer
side. But that makes no odds: the result is to subject employers, in
the context of a statutory prices and incomes policy, to more
detailed direction than they have experienced since the end of
rationing in 1950.

It is, of course, highly paradoxical that this should be imposed by
a Conservative Government, above all one that came to office with a
stronger belief in the efficacy of the untrammelled free enterprise
system than had been held by any of its postwar predecessors.
Nevertheless, the current approach to the problem of prices and

incomes, and in particular the readiness to embrace a statutory policy, is itself coloured by the Conservative philosophy of arm's-length relationships. Legislation provides new statutory constraints within which businesses must still pursue their own ends in competition with each other. The shape of the ring has changed but it is still Government's role to hold it and the role of firms to compete within it. 'Stroking of the ears' is out.

It is difficult, however, to see this extreme situation lasting. There are not only profound technical difficulties primarily concerned with distortion away from economic optima as relative costs change for technological and other reasons; there are also difficulties in terms of the social fabric, of the patterns of cooperation between men and institutions.

Anyone looking at the prices and pay codes sees how much discretion is given to the Price and Pay Boards, and it is significant that the Chairman of each is a man with experience in consultation between government and business, as well as direction by government of business. The Chairman of the Price Commission has worked both in central government and in private industry and was one of the earliest members of the principal interface institution – the NEDC. The Chairman of the Pay Board is a senior civil servant but has twice worked outside the civil service, latterly as Director-General of the NEDC, and played a major part in bringing the 1972 tripartite talks as near to success as they came.

This is not to say that the Government can only act through a concordat, any more than it can act only through regulation. Both modes are needed. The two can be graphically illustrated by two seating plans. In the Restrictive Practices Court, the five members of the Court sit in a row, high above the rest of the participants. Below them the two contestant parties, that of the Registrar of Restrictive Trading Agreements and that of the business Respondents, sit on opposite sides of the court. The procedures have the formality of a stately minuet or a medieval tourney, the centrepiece being provided by the examination-in-chief, cross-examination and re-examination of a succession of witnesses called first by one side and then by the other. The culmination is the announcement, normally after an adjournment, of the Court's decision. Here is the arm's-length relationship. The sharpest possible contrast is provided by the regular monthly meetings of the NEDC, at which the participants engage in free and frank discussion under highly informal chairmanship, and, significantly, sit at a round table, a tradition in British government which goes back, one might observe, to the days of King Arthur. There is the attempt at symbiosis. Both modes have existed together and must continue to do so.

A critical view might be that the law operates through a mechanism that is fair but cumbersome, while the mechanisms of consultation are simple but ineffective. This does not perhaps hold out a very hopeful prospect but it spotlights weaknesses in each mode which reinforce the view that government should not rely wholly on either.

What are the implications for Government/business relationships of Britain joining the EEC? British business now has to look at both Brussels and Whitehall. UK membership of the EEC means that the Commission in Brussels is often now the 'Government' itself. An important factor here is that because of national tensions and loyalties the Commission has to be objective and fair. The result is clear, detailed, and enforcable legislation with obvious principles, and in the EEC the main principle is the enforcement of competition. Take, for example, the question of non-tariff barriers as they affect the motor industry. Through these the import of heavy vehicles into Italy is almost totally prevented. The Commission hopes to eliminate such barriers, but to do so means an immense array of regulations.

What of the Government in Whitehall? The British Government and British industry have common interests vis-à-vis the rest of Europe, and though they have separate representation in Brussels this is already resulting in drawing them closer together. While, therefore, business faces a primarily arm's-length relationship with the Government at Brussels, its relationship with Whitehall becomes over the same issues more symbiotic.

Prediction

A number of recent events illustrate points made in the paper. The pragmatic reversion to earlier measures, or a passable imitation of them, has continued with the new consumer emphasis on the top-level structure of the Department of Trade and Industry, and the establishment of the Price Commission and Pay Board a couple of years after the demise of the Prices and Incomes Board. The growth of public feeling on profits from the North Sea has helped to influence Government action, and the placing of Mr Peter Walker at the Department of Trade and Industry has certainly affected its actions. The next general election is already in some ways casting its shadow before.

The most important effect of the European dimension is to increase the difficulty of prediction. Trying to predict what will happen in the EEC means predicting international agreement or disagreement. There are nine partners negotiating, each with its own purposes, pressures, constraints, perceptions and tactics. Information is hard to obtain because the parties in negotiation keep their cards close to their chests. Nor is there anything like an isolated decision, because those who are negotiating realize that if they give way on one issue then others will give way on a different issue, and vice versa. Discussions between representatives of Governments sometimes seem inexplicable until one finds that, for example, the Ruritanians are opposing the Suchmen in negotiations on one issue because the Suchmen had opposed the Ruritanians on some other issue.

Though much work has been done in business schools and elsewhere on group decisions and on the relationship of such decisions to the interests and strategies of members of the group, this work is not yet of much help in predicting this kind of decision. However, there are some parallels with the domestic situation analysed in the paper. The division of portfolios in the Commission, for example, is perhaps as significant for prediction as anything else.

Frequently in European organizations one reaches deadlock. The question then is, what is the result of the deadlock? The unanimity rule favours the status quo. There are also certain domestic political imperatives. For example, Britain joined the EEC despite the burden of the agricultural policy, partly on the arguments (*a*) that we would have a better chance to influence it from the inside than as a matter of entry negotiations, and (*b*) that the burden it imposes on us strengthens the case for a strong regional industrial support policy. The British Government may therefore be expected to be particularly assiduous in trying to bring home the bacon in at least one of these two ways.

Adaptation

This section of the paper includes a discussion of the paramountcy or otherwise of shareholder interests and, in that context, of the CBI's 'voluntary restraint' policy of 1971-72. The issue has been subsequently highlighted by the enforced departure from the CBI of its Economic Director, Mr Bracewell-Milnes. The difference of opinion seems to have revolved around the proper role of the CBI in relation to the interests of its members. Should it submit advice to the Chancellor which if taken would, in the short run and other things being equal, increase their net-of-tax profits? The converse view, which prevailed, is that the CBI is an estate of the realm with an obligation to have regard to the general prosperity and growth of the British economy, within which context alone can its members prosper.

Another current trend is the increasing effectiveness of public opinion. The pressure on Distillers over the thalidomide compensation issue and the more recent concern in the UK over wages paid to black workers in British firms operating in South Africa are significant examples. Business must not simply seize economic opportunities, but do its public relations work well too. And PR also means predicting and adapting, not just influencing.

Europe will bring Britain increased individual opportunities but also more competition and will therefore put a higher premium on quick-footedness. An unanswered question is whether any individuals, organizations or groups in Britain will develop a European loyalty. For example, there has been a lot of discussion recently of water pollution in the Rhine. This could lead to a supra-national public opinion in the riparian countries. And something similar might happen later for the English Channel, where pollution already crosses from one side to the other.

Influencing

When one says that business can influence the civil service one is not implying bribery, because the British civil service is still more incorruptible than perhaps any other. However, the Poulson case reveals some problems, especially in local government. Perhaps British public administration does not have a 100 per cent record; but if the figure is 98 per cent that is still very good. The danger of the Poulson case is that it may mean that the central Civil Service will return more than ever to its in-bred seclusion, a cure which would be almost as bad as the disease.

Britain's entry into the EEC immensely complicates the task of business in seeking to influence government action. The Government in Whitehall becomes one channel through which the Commission in Brussels may be reached. How it will respond to representations from a particular pressure group representing a sectional interest in Britain depends on how in its view the line proposed would affect the British national interest, directly and indirectly. Trans-national sectional membership associations have also developed, such as UNICE, which make representations direct to the organs of the Communities. British business interests need to, and do, work through these as well as on their own government. Given limited resources to devote to lobbying, an estimate is necessary as to where they will be most effective; in cases where a small minority interest within the UK is a more substantial interest in other EEC member countries, the trans-national group is likely to be the more rewarding channel.

Discussion

In reply to a question, Professor McClelland took the view that some of the EDCs set up by the NEDC did achieve good results. Those concerned with the EDC for the Distributive Trades felt that it had achieved a good deal – probably partly as a result of the structure and nature of the sector. The distributive trades were fragmented and there was no other satisfactory forum for a dialogue between government and the industry. So, for example, the EDC had been able to get modifications to the way that SET had applied to part-time workers. It had also been able to promote and publicize good practice. Finally, it had managed to bring about a merger between trade associations; as a result, the retail consortium had been brought into the tripartite talks to give a retail view. The role of EDCs in national economic planning, however, was not valuable in industries with a few large companies, especially where the lead time for investment was long. Because the EDCs were closely involved with particular industries, they had in some cases done more effective and realistic work in this field than Whitehall sponsoring departments.

Another questioner said that in its current exercise in economic forecasting the NEDC was assuming two alternative rates of growth on GNP – $3\frac{1}{2}$ per cent and 5 per cent. Yet prices policy, as set out in the recent Green Paper, must damp down the recovery in investment, and hence the growth rate. The DTI agreed with this, yet the Treasury continued to assume the same growth rate, which made the whole exercise unrealistic.

Professor McClelland replied that while it was not easy to do such an exercise it could throw light on problems of the individual industry and so was not wholly wasted. It brought in a lot of current factors unknown to Government which could not be deduced from past history. One had to look ahead in an iterative fashion. One was simply doing at national level what the individual firm had to do. Moreover, investment was determined not simply by existing profit margins and financial resources but also by expectations as to market growth. Confidence was as necessary as finance. Phase 2 would clearly squeeze profits but it might reduce prices sufficiently to sustain growth. The questioner agreed that such an exercise was not a waste of time, since he believed that it would show a need for relaxation in Phase 3.

Another questioner suggested that it was unfortunate if major firms spent time sitting on Government committees, but then a different Government department could come along and impose an incompatible policy. What was the relationship between the Treasury and the NEDC? Professor McClelland replied that it was not at all easy to know what happened. One problem in the past was that the Board of Trade had been seen as obsessed with obeying international trade agreements. The Treasury had the stigma of being more concerned with the balance of payments than with growth. So, the NEDC and later the DEA had been set up to give counterbalancing views to the Treasury. Though financed by H.M. Government, the professionals in the NED office working outside the Treasury were able to report to the NED Council and perhaps to the public. The general anti-planning philosophy of the Conservative Government in 1970 had led it to soft-pedal NEDC forecasting work. However, the NEDC had continued to play an important role, for example, in initiating the 'four wise men' exercise.

Professor Hague said that the education of the Treasury might be a long process but business should be ready to spend time on it. The worrying thing was the way that the civil service recently seemed to have become less rather than more open. At the end of the 1960s it seemed to be agreed by everyone that more openness in government was both desirable and possible. However, perhaps because of the Fulton report, and especially the unfortunate first chapter which gratuitously offended almost every civil servant, we were faced with a less rather than a more open system. One way in which one could see how things were moving was the way the Civil Service College was operating. There had been hopes that if business schools like London and Manchester would take civil servants on their courses for businessmen, the Civil Service College would take businessmen on their courses for civil servants. Instead, the Civil Service had increasingly withdrawn members from business school courses and one could see little sign of businessmen being taken into the Civil Service College. This seemed to be a very clear example of the way the civil service was becoming more and more inward looking.

A questioner asked how entry to the EEC would cause industry to view its internal problems differently. If one put the EEC on top of the present system, how much more effective must business be? Perhaps British business was too intellectual and concerned with the long run, and not sufficiently concerned with the short-run actions needed to make short-run objectives come true. Professor McClelland replied that the idea of 'Great Britain Limited' put forward by Lord Robens seemed to envisage a symbiotic approach, but one could also point to the 'economic miracle' in Germany working through an arms-length government policy. The Manchester Business School had recently circulated to influential businessmen a paper by Mr B. R. Cant entitled 'Britain's economic problems in international historical perspective'; the paper showed a profound understanding of the differences between Britain and other countries going back to the seventeenth century, and had to a remarkable extent been given careful study by senior people in Government and business.

A Japanese participant asked about the reference on page 162 to Government appeals to business. It would be interesting to know exactly what happened in the UK to compare this with the orientation of public administration in Japan. Professor McClelland said the sort of appeal varied at any particular time and indeed over time. Similarly, companies varied in their response. However, it seemed that the more monopolistic a firm was the more sensitive it was. Since there appeared to be a trend towards that kind of business in this country perhaps there would also be an increase in responsiveness. A problem with the UK was that, unlike Japan, we were not currently experiencing great success, we had not hit on any formula for success, and were therefore likely to continue to change policy.

A speaker from the floor rejected the earlier suggestion that the Treasury had intervened to impose the $3\frac{1}{2}$ and 5 per cent growth rates on which the current exercise by the NEDC was based. He thought it more likely that the 5 per cent growth rate had been chosen because the trade union members of the NEDC had been pressing for the even higher rate of 6 per cent. A $3\frac{1}{2}$ per cent rate was itself purely illustrative. But it did enable one to ask what would be the demand for particular goods if growth were at that rate, what capacity would be required and what shortages would be likely. This would lead on to the question, raised by the earlier speaker, of whether the finance would be there. Restraints on profits, resulting from Phases 2 and 3, now had to be introduced. The new external environment would be included in such a forecasting exercise.

A questioner returned to the question of 'Great Britain Limited'. The Government was increasingly involved with business, and Ministers and civil servants had little information about it. Was a democratic government capable of handling such involvement in business life? Professor McClelland replied that ours was a complex industrial society in which it was inevitable that Government decisions intimately affected industry. How could one see that the necessary facts got into the decision-takers' heads? Perhaps one solution would be a wide range of different sorts of training and career patterns for civil servants. The job of the Government machine was to provide analyses of the problems to be solved. Ministers were there to provide a political dimension. The fallacy in the 'Great Britain Limited' idea was that the politics could be taken out of what were essentially political decisions.

Competition policy in the UK

Michael Beesley

Postscript

The possible Competition Commission foreshadowed in the paper
has not been created, but we have instead a Fair Trading Bill of 123
clauses. While this is only a Bill, it has passed its second reading and
is therefore likely to become an Act with little amendment. I should

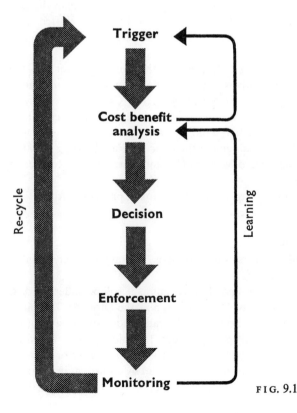

FIG. 9.1

like to look at this through the model implied in my paper, which I used to contrast the two systems of control for competition policy, the DTI/MC system and that of the RTPC.

Fig. 9.1 shows a task flow which someone must trigger. There follows a cost/benefit analysis, comparing what has been found with what is thought desirable; a decision about what to do; and a process of enforcement and then of monitoring the effectiveness of action. The process may be recycled as a result of monitoring. There is also a feedback process, with learning taking place, in particular to improve the cost/benefit analysis and trigger phases.

Each part of the task flow may be performed by the same administration, or not. The main point about the Restrictive Trade Practices Court system was that most of the functions are carried on within one body. This was not so for DTI/MC system. For example, the Monopolies Commission carried out the cost/benefit analysis but the DTI had to enforce it. I argued in the paper that different parts of the system were more or less well done. The RTPC was stronger on enforcement because, being a court of law, the 'majesty of the law' is behind it. I also noted that the work load has lately shifted from the RTPC to the DTI/MC, as the Court has largely gone through its case work.

With the Fair Trading Bill, a new institution will be set up – the Consumer Protection Advisory Committee, giving protection against misleading trading. This is a new idea, the Conservative Party's answer to criticism when it abolished the Consumer Council. There is now to be an Office of Fair Trading with a Director General (DG). One now has also to distinguish: the Office of Fair Trading with the DG; the Monopolies and Mergers Commission; and the Restrictive Trade Practices Court.

In the context of my paper we have to look at provisions for:
1. Monopoly (high concentration)
2. Mergers
3. Restrictive practices.
(Monopoly and Mergers are split here, because they are treated separately in the Bill.)

I follow through each task flow system as it will be under the Act. The trigger mechanism for Monopoly is now the Director General of Fair Trading, as well as Secretary of Trade and Industry and other Ministers who had this power under the old system. Potential monopoly is now defined as a situation where a quarter or more of the market is served by one firm, rather than by a third, as in the past. The Bill also now covers complex monopolies, where two or three firms together take a quarter of the market, or in other words a situation which economists call a 'close oligopoly'. The cost/benefit analysis now includes exports in the relevant market, and may now look at individual parts of the UK. This raises more acutely than before the question of what *is* a market for the purpose of assessing monopoly affects. The nationalized industries are also brought within the scope of the monopoly provisions, something which has been sought for a long time.

The Director General of Fair Trading can directly trigger action and can also seek information on which to advise Ministers that they should refer cases to the Monopolies and Mergers Commission. In such a case, the Secretary of State can negotiate for assurances about future conduct rather than referring the case to the Commission. However, if it is referred, the Commission will, as before, do its own cost/benefit analyses. The Commission must then judge each case in the light of a number of elements. I was unkind about these in my paper and I still feel that my criticisms are valid.

If the Commission feels that something should be done, there will often be negotiated assurances of good conduct. However, the DTI still has its old powers to control prices, etc. The negotiation for terms of assurances will undoubtedly continue. The new DG will be very important in these but the process and those of enforcement and monitoring are relatively unchanged and there is little on feedback. So the latter parts of the control mechanism are still rudimentary. However, the DG's staff can gather free-ranging information on what is going on and over time may build a basis for more effective action.

On mergers there has been little change. The DG is not involved, and the trigger is still the DTI. However, the DG *can* be required to monitor a merger *if* required.

The Restrictive Trade Practices Court is still there, but now the DG takes over the role of Registrar. Here, apart from a new trigger in the form of the new, wide-ranging DG and his staff, there are changes in scope. The RTPC can now look at restraints on trade through designs and patents. We shall have to wait to see what happens, but in the past the Court has been very severe in upholding competition. The Court can also now look at commercial services. The suggestion that it should extend its activities even to the professions has been rejected and the line, for example, seems to be drawn to include estate agents, who appear to be subject, whereas surveyors are not. It seems unfortunate that the more dignified professions are exempt! Insurance is presumably not exempt, an interesting extension of RTPC's scope in view of what Professor Rose has said. The result is that the RTPC has a big new field to consider.

These are the facts, but this Bill is notable because it extends the scope of the activities of the DTI/MC and the RTPC. It is traditional for our competition policy to extend gradually. The control of restrictive practices began in a very tentative way and was extended in 1964 and 1968. Now, after careful debate, its scope is extended again to commercial services and patents. The Monopolies Commission's power is further extended, for example, by the 25 per cent rule. There is also an increase in the power of investigation by the Commission, which is now able to report on restrictive labour practices, although these are at present only powers to report, with no specific provision for consequent action. This does mean that the activities of labour monopolies will be open to public discussion, if not yet to action. But the tradition of tentative beginnings and later action may well be repeated.

It is not clear how much more *effective* the new system will be. One does have the new DG to pull together the trigger process, but the system is still rather fragmented. Nor is it clear what the role of the DTI will now be, though it certainly appears to have discretion in the way it implements the new legislation. Nor are there any explicit rules about mergers, while the abuse of monopoly is still to be dealt with by 'assurances' rather than legal measures.

Obviously, what matters most is attitudes. They are likely to be much the same as my paper suggested. Ours remains perhaps the toughest law in the world on restrictive practices. As I said, monopoly is not seen as bad *per se*; the Monopolies Commission apparently welcomes innovatory companies in particular, even if they are highly profitable ones. Its reports since my paper seem to be even less critical of high profits than earlier ones. For example, one can compare the report on detergents with that on breakfast cereals, when the activities of Kelloggs appear to be approved, despite their high profits. Yet with detergents, the Monopolies Commission made very sweeping recommendations for change. Thus there appears to be growing tolerance of high profits if these are of value to consumers as well as, perhaps, a greater tolerance of what in the past have been seen as wasteful sales promotion expenditures.

Discussion

In response to a question, Professor Beesley explained that the

Monopolies Commission could only *report* on the activities of nationalized industries. Action thereafter was up to the sponsoring ministers. In the short run, the nationalized industries would be permitted to operate as before, but it was less certain how things would proceed as time went on. The main change was that there was any probe *at all*. We had to remember that resale price maintenance had been investigated by the Monopolies Commission and killed by the Restrictive Practices Court. It was true that bringing the nationalized industries into the scope of the Commission's activities was only a small step, but it might lead to further measures in the future, and publicity had been shown to be very important. While publicity could go in two directions, it was hard to resist the idea that more light being thrown on the nationalized industries would be valuable.

Another questioner said Professor Beesley seemed to regard the enforcement of findings on monopolies as weak. This view was reinforced if one remembered that the report on resale price maintenance had been an unusual one. Professor Beesley pointed out that cartels had been harshly treated by the 1956 Act. The new Bill proposed that the Commission should now move on to the nationalized industries. The process was a continuing one, though on unions and the nationalized industries we might be faced with a 'long-haul' of perhaps twenty years.

Another questioner referred to the harmonization of anti-monopoly laws in the EEC. There was not much point in making our own rules very different from those of the rest of Europe. The last Labour Government appeared to be ready to fight the views of the EEC Commission on mergers and the Conservative policy outlined in the Bill appeared to be very much a 'little England' one, with the UK having its own rules.

Professor Beesley replied that in international trading it would be necessary for all countries in the EEC to have the same rules on international trade. However, all countries were allowed their own rules at home. This situation would persist, at least for some time.

Another participant to the conference pointed out that in Europe the EEC's law was the superior one. So, for example, German courts could be overruled by the European Court. Professor Beesley replied that this was a matter of choice, not of sovereignty. For example, cost/benefit analysis carried out by the Monopolies Commission or the RTPC could take Europe into account. However, the Court was concerned with what the public interest was and did not have to be influenced by what happened in the EEC. The new Bill certainly suggested that the British Government wanted to go on with its own rules.

As for merger cases involving the conditions for research, like Glaxo, it was not true that one would necessarily get a better result if one had independent research activities.

However, at the moment it seemed that immediately there appeared to be any possibility that the Monopolies Commission might act over a merger, the bidder was likely to withdraw. Firms felt that dealing with any reference would be time-consuming and that the judgment was likely to be adverse. But, there was the alternative view that mergers would not be carefully enough considered if an institution like the Commission did not look at them; there was the view that mergers should 'stand up'. There was also the possibility that any suggestion of a reference to the Commission might lead to a counter bid. Yet, if the bid were not made very quickly the strategy would be undermined. One also wondered how good a merger would be if it was thought up in two or three days.

From this point of view, any mechanism that put a merger into 'cold storage', so that it could be considered slowly, was a good thing. It must also be remembered that while no one merged in order to 'gouge' the consumer, over a period a monopolist might be forced to do so if other, looked for, economies and advantages did not occur. If one obtained monopoly powers, was there not a danger that one would use them? There certainly seemed to be ground for objecting to rapid mergers, and a good argument for delaying them. The difficulty was holding conditions on the Stock Exchange constant. If a merger was postponed, there might be a general fall in share values and such a favourable situation might not recur again. However, it had to be remembered that the fact that there were such arguments meant that more than one line of logic was acceptable and it was very hard to balance these.

To a suggestion that, if the Monopolies Commission were to study the steel industry, it would simply be taking over the role of the Steel Users' Council, Professor Beesley argued that the Commission would do rather more than this. The Consumer Council was bound to represent particular interests and therefore to be biased. The Monopolies Commission had to look for particular benefits from a general point of view. While agreeing that it was a similar animal, he thought that the Commission was more efficient, and one had to remember that the Commission did allow those coming before it legal representation. There was therefore a possibility of some formal conflict of views.

The United Kingdom and EEC trade

D. C. Hague

Postscript

I feel bound to admit to considerable relief that the prediction in my paper about the sterling exchange rate proved correct. There have been two significant international monetary crises since I wrote the paper. During the second, in early March 1973, a decision to align sterling, at a fixed exchange rate, to the jointly-floating European currencies seemed more than possible. We appeared to be prepared to do so at roughly the rate to which sterling had floated downwards since June 1972, provided that we were promised some support by other EEC countries. However, there was no question whatever that, whether the UK joined it or not, the 'joint European float' would move the European exchange rate upwards relatively to the currencies of the rest of the world taken together. During the first part of March 1973 I therefore became very apprehensive about the accuracy of my assertion (p. 195) that the UK would not return to a system which was either completely inflexible or, worse still, allowed flexibility in the sterling exchange rate, but upwards only.

Even before this, in September and October 1972, I feared that the floating of sterling would soon end. As explained on p. 193 there are many, especially in Europe, who argue that the plan for European Monetary Union, which aims at a common European currency not later than 1980, must soon begin to be implemented. Indeed, in the autumn of 1972 the UK was technically committed to fix the parity of sterling relatively to those of the remaining European currencies before joining the EEC on 1 January 1973. Clearly this was an important reason why the British Government decided that it must introduce a prices and incomes policy, preferably a voluntary one but if need be a statutory one, in November 1972. In other words, if there is any one person whom we ultimately have to thank for our statutory prices and incomes policy it is not Campbell Adamson or even Edward Heath, but Georges Pompidou.

Unfortunately, the prices and incomes policy was introduced at a particularly bad moment, with import prices rising sharply, partly as a result of the downward floating of the pound and partly because the prices of many imported commodities were rising quite independently of the change in the value of sterling. Of course, the more the statutory policy is able to reduce the rate of price increase in the UK relatively to that in other countries, the more possible it will be to peg the sterling exchange rate again. However, until it is clear that the British economy is strong enough to stand it, I expect sterling to continue to 'float'. As I said on p. 195, I think that all to whom it matters can safely assume that the level of economic activity in the UK will no longer be deliberately held down in order to protect the exchange rate.

Moreover, I believe that *British* firms planning to invest in the EEC can assume for the foreseeable future that exchange rate changes are likely to make their overseas investments more rather than less profitable. As for British exports, I think that the likelihood that sterling will continue to float is important. As Professor McClelland noted, Germany and Japan, two countries with very different economic systems, have both experienced rapid economic growth in the postwar period. I believe that the important thing they had in common for much of that period was underdevalued currencies and that this was an important reason for their postwar economic success. Abandoning a fixed exchange rate has removed an important obstacle for the UK, and one which has held back economic growth during much of the period since 1960.

As for the effect on UK trade of joining the EEC, I do not wish to amend anything that I said on pp. 195–204, although I should like to add something. I have recently been pondering on the figures given in the table below.

TABLE 10.1   *UK exports and imports as percentages of the GDP at 1963 prices*

Year	Imports	Exports
1963	21	21
1964	23	21
1965	23	22
1966	23	21
1967	24	22
1968	25	24
1969	25	26
1970	26	27
1971	27	28

These figures show a substantial increase in both exports *and* imports as percentages of gross domestic product over the period since 1963. Between 1960 and 1963 a little over 20 per cent of GDP was both exported and imported. With rapid growth in the British economy in 1963 and 1964, the percentage of imports to GDP increased sharply in 1964 to 23 per cent, the figure at which it remained until 1967, the year of devaluation. Even after devaluation, the percentage of imports to GDP continued to rise, reaching 27 per cent in 1971. While devaluation and slow economic growth within the UK meant that the percentage of GDP exported was able to rise somewhat faster than the percentage imported after 1968, over the whole period the process has been an 'import-led' one. There have been all the consequences for 'income-frustration' and for the size of the 'hole' discussed by Terry Burns.

Moreover, there is something else that no one has yet mentioned. The fact that the rate of growth of GNP was held down for balance of payments reasons helps to explain why there is so much competition for resources in the UK at present. If the rate of growth GNP since 1965 had been only 1 per cent per annum greater than it has been, this would have given us, in 1973, something like £4,000 m. of extra resources to use each year for public or private purposes. And, of course, each extra 1 per cent by which one believes that concern for the balance of payments held down the rate of growth of GNP represents a further £4,000 m. unavailable for use within the British economy. We can imagine the extra freedom that the Ministers responsible for, say, Education, Health and the Social Services would have had with so many extra resources available. Moreover, not only would we have that much extra GNP in 1973. We would also have had increasing amounts of GNP available in each year after 1965.

The figures in Table 10.1 call for one or two further comments. First, there is no reason to suppose that the process whereby increasing percentages of GDP were both exported and imported is about to come to an end. It must have resulted, at least in part, from the kind of trade liberalization that joining the EEC will bring about in the next five years. We must expect the process to continue. This means that foreign trade will become increasingly important to the UK. The worrying question is whether the process can continue only if there is a progressive deterioration in the sterling exchange rate. For each downward movement worsens the terms of trade. It improves the balance of payments (if it does so at all) only by forcing us to export a greater volume of goods and services to bring in a given volume of imports. So, the more the terms of trade have to move against us in order to enable us to increase export volume by the necessary amount, the greater the deduction from the standard of living within the UK. Joining the EEC seems likely to be more clearly favourable for the volume of overseas trade than for the standard of living of the UK.

However, businessmen have to operate at the level of the firm and industry, not of that of the economy. What suggestions can I give to British firms intending to extend their operations in Continental Europe and to European firms intending to extend their operations in Britain?

First, I hold by my suggestion that it is wrong to suppose that the result of joining the EEC will simply be that British firms remain within Britain and increase their exports to the rest of Europe, while firms in the rest of Europe remain there and increase their exports to the UK. For reasons I give in the paper, I expect a good deal of investment by British firms in the other eight member states of the EEC and by firms from those eight countries within the UK. However, I see the process as a somewhat gradual one.

Nevertheless, if they have not already done so, I believe that all firms, whether from Britain or from the rest of the EEC, should decide quickly on their strategy for the enlarged EEC. They will have to decide which markets to concentrate their attention on: which markets to specialize in. I explained in the paper that there seems to be little point in British firms aiming at any significant expansion of sales in those EEC countries where their products are already selling very well. It is markets where there are good opportunities, but ones which have not yet been fully grasped, that are most attractive. This is why I believe that British firms should pay greater attention to the possibility of selling more in Germany, Italy and France than to that of exporting more to the Benelux countries.

Second, there are a number of other issues to be considered, all to do with specialization. For example, how should the firm organize itself in the new situation? Should it specialize on the production of some products, or on the carrying out of some processes of production, in individual countries? Or should it make its whole product range in each country? How should firms specialize between customers? Some firms argue that a bigger market reduces the risks in concentrating on supplying a limited number of customers. Following the well-known 80/20 rule, a firm might wish to concentrate on doing business with only the biggest 20 per cent of potential customers. Before joining the EEC, a British firm may have felt that it was dangerous to specialize in this way. If it lost one big customer there would be only the small number of firms in the British home market from which to seek a replacement. Within Europe, the firm could more safely aim at supplying the same *proportion* of potential customers (or even the same absolute number) because if one large customer were lost it would then be easier to find a replacement within the whole 'home market' in the EEC than it was within the UK.

As I explained in my paper, I believe that there are important reasons why British firms are likely to transfer at least some of their activities to Continental Europe and vice versa. First, now that Britain is in the EEC the factors set out on p. 206 mean that it will pay the firm to establish some of its activities near to its important markets within the EEC. This reduces time delays and provides information about, and an understanding of, the attitudes and behaviour of customers in relevant markets. As I also explained in the paper, non-British firms should be considering, for similar reasons, whether to transfer some of their activities to the UK.

However, all firms considering such a move should remember that many of the British firms which have been most successful in establishing themselves in the Six have been very cautious in doing so. Their experience suggests that the best first step is to employ an agent to sell the firm's products in those EEC countries where investment is contemplated. The aim would be to discover which products would best sell there, without at this stage committing the firm to a large investment in Europe. Even when sales by the agent reach a level where it is clear that the establishment of a production and/or selling unit is worthwhile, those firms which have been most successful in operating within the Six argue that the best course is to take over an existing firm in the country in question. They argue thus because they say that only nationals of that country have a sufficient understanding of its buying habits, culture and the legal and financial framework within which its business operates. There seems to be a consensus among British firms that to operate successfully within the EEC it is essential, at least initially but perhaps in the longer term, for any overseas subsidiary to be operated by nationals of the country in which that subsidiary is located. This suggests that British firms which have not yet begun to operate subsidiaries within the rest of the EEC should first appoint an agent with a view to later taking over an existing EEC firm. This being so, the 'Great Britain Ltd' we spoke of in the discussion of Professor McClelland's paper may turn out to be 'Great Britain (Overseas Holdings) Ltd'.

The final topic in my paper was the way that long-run influences are likely to change the geographical pattern of industrial location, and the general pattern of business activity, in Britain and the EEC over the next ten to thirty years.

I do not want to add very much to my paper here, except to say that all the evidence suggests that the immediate effects of joining the EEC and of discovering North Sea gas and oil are likely, at best, to pull British industry towards the eastern side of the country. At worst, they may pull even more of British industry towards the South-East.

However, I feel more confident even than I did when I wrote the paper that over the next two or three decades the UK will move increasingly into two main areas. First, I expect a growing percentage of the labour force to be engaged, at the centre, in the planning, financial and marketing activities of firms whose manufacturing plants are increasingly in less developed countries. This would simply mean that we should be emulating, say, American electronics firms whose assembly processes are carried out in South Korea, Formosa, etc., while the central activities are carried out within the USA. In Europe, I believe that we shall see an end to the system whereby German industry, in particular, imports labour from southern and south-eastern Europe as and when it is needed. I think that industry in northern Europe will increasingly establish plants to carry out manufacturing activities in places like Spain, southern Italy, Greece or North Africa.[1]

Second, I expect an increasing percentage of the British labour force to be occupied in service industries.[2] Those who gloomily predict that, if the sterling exchange rate continues to float downwards, Britons will find it more and more difficult to take their holidays abroad rarely seem to accept the obverse of this argument. This is that those from countries with appreciating currencies will find it increasingly cheap to take their holidays in the UK. Instead of bolstering Upper Clyde Ship Builders, we should perhaps be converting Scottish shipbuilders into hoteliers and waiters. More seriously, we should be encouraging an increasing percentage of those leaving schools, colleges and universities to realize that future

[1]   While I am amending the final manuscript I notice that Norman McRae, in a fascinating survey article in *The Economist* for 28 April 1973, takes much the same line. In particular, he suggests that the next European plant for producing motor cars may be a multi-national venture established, say, in Tunisia or in one of the Communist countries of eastern Europe.

[2]   This view also is taken by Norman McRae, who in the survey article quoted suggests a number of fields into which he believes British business will move or where its existing activities will grow.

openings in growth industries are likely to lie increasingly in the service sector.

There is no doubt that the whole pattern of economic activity in the UK will alter radically during the rest of the century. This will be brought about partly by the development of the EEC. It will also depend on more fundamental factors, such as changes in the location, growth rates and characteristics of markets, and of the supply conditions for raw materials and other productive factors. I wonder whether we are preparing adequately to meet these changes.

Discussion

A questioner asked whether, in the light of his concluding comments, Professor Hague would argue that the UK should be moving towards subsidizing services, like hotels, rather than giving grants to manufacturing business. Professor Hague replied that there was a good deal to be said for such an argument. While perhaps one should not be subsidizing capital expenditure in the service sector, or indeed anywhere else, he had put the case for training an increasing proportion of the next generation of school and college leavers to work in service industries.

When asked if his argument suggested that overseas companies should avoid setting up manufacturing subsidiaries in the UK altogether, Professor Hague replied that he would not go so far. There would clearly be an *absolute* increase in the output of British manufacturing industry, even if manufacturing did not grow as rapidly as the service sector. Similarly, while the percentage of the labour force occupied in manufacturing might fall, this would be because it was becoming increasingly capital-intensive. There was every reason for overseas firms to set up (or to take over) manufacturing businesses in the UK, many of which would become increasingly capital-intensive as time went on. There was certainly scope for new firms outside the UK to move into British manufacturing as well as into the UK service sector.

Asked when he thought that there would be complete freedom of movement of capital between EEC countries, Professor Hague said that he could not see this before 1985 at the earliest.

A participant from a firm with an EEC division emphasized that, when any firm decided to move beyond selling through agents in the EEC by acquiring a subsidiary, it was important to allow nationals of the country in question to plan the development of that subsidiary's new products so that these would fit national characteristics. In his own firm, there were very few British nationals working permanently in overseas subsidiaries, though there were more on secondment. This was true, even though the language used in the European division was English.

Another participant emphasized that there were many ways in which a firm could specialize and, indeed, that it was most unlikely that the *whole* firm would specialize on one product or on one production method. However, he agreed that there were considerable advantages in getting 'close' to the market, not least in being able to adapt products so that they were acceptable to particular markets.

To a questioner who pointed to the amounts of some products, like steel, that were cross-hauled, Professor Hague noted that cross-hauling was likely to be the result of specialization. Of course, it could also result from a decision not to put one's firm wholly at the mercy of one's supplier. In these circumstances, one would expect ships in the English Channel or lorries on a motorway to be carrying the same product in opposite directions. This could happen only if it was worth while, either because of the increased economies of scale that specialization gave, or because the benefits from not being tied to one supplier were worth 'paying for' in increased transport costs.

Index